STRONGER
THAN YOU
THINK

STRONGER
THAN YOU
THINK

The 10 Blind Spots That
Undermine Your Relationship...
and How to See Past Them

Gary W. Lewandowski Jr., PhD

Little, Brown Spark
New York   Boston   London

Little, Brown Spark
Hachette Book Group
1290 Avenue of the Americas, New York, NY 10104
littlebrownspark.com

First Edition: February 2021

Little, Brown Spark is an imprint of Little, Brown and Company, a division of Hachette Book Group, Inc. The Little, Brown Spark name and logo are trademarks of Hachette Book Group, Inc.

The publisher is not responsible for websites (or their content) that are not owned by the publisher.

The Hachette Speakers Bureau provides a wide range of authors for speaking events. To find out more, go to hachettespeakersbureau.com or call (866) 376-6591.

Printing 1, 2020

ISBN 978-0-316-45471-1
LCCN 2020938272

LSC-C

Printed in the United States of America

When my brother and I were little, my mom told us that for as long as she could remember, she always wanted two kids. She also mentioned, somewhat jokingly, that she had dreamed of having one kid who was a musician and one who was a writer. Perhaps with this in mind, my brother wisely struck first and took up the saxophone in elementary school. Seeing that my mom had only two kids, I realized my brother had left me no choice but to write a book. This is for you, Mom.

Contents

Contents

STRONGER
THAN YOU
THINK

Introduction

Love never dies a natural death. It dies because we don't know how to replenish its source. It dies of blindness and errors.

—Anaïs Nin

E verybody deserves a great relationship. Have you found yours?

I have. But I wasn't always so sure I had. When I fell in love with my wife, I fell hard. In college, I had my eye on her for months... the girl who lived upstairs. It started the day she moved in, when I offered to help because I heard my future father-in-law struggling with her furniture through the ceiling. She politely declined, assuring me she had it under control. Fast-forward a bit, and we're in the same psychology internship course, carpooling with several other students to off-campus counseling training. During the car rides, I'd invite her to parties; again, she politely declined each invitation. For our final course project, I worked it out so that we would have to collaborate. I kept finding excuses to need her help. She was kind to the dummy from downstairs. Kind enough, in fact, to agree to a date. That night, instead of studying for the GREs I had the next morning, we talked for more than six hours, staying up until 3 a.m. I was hooked, 100 percent completely certain I was going to spend the rest of my life with this amazing woman.

Then life started to get in the way. I graduated and moved two states away to get my PhD, while she finished her last year of undergrad. After a tough year apart, she had her choice of grad schools but ultimately decided to go to mine. We moved in together and things were back on track. But it was hard. We were poor, stressed, and tired, and our relationship felt the strain. In my program, I was busy studying the science of great relationships. It became all too easy to self-diagnose relationship problems. I started to wonder: Is this the right relationship? Am I really in love? Have I found "the one"? Could I do better? Am I being too demanding? Settling for too little? It was hard to say, but fair to ask.

For me, the answer came from positive psychology and its focus on strengths instead of weaknesses. It opened my eyes to my major blind spot: I was focusing on the wrong things. Because I looked only for problems, I found them. I realized I was the problem. I needed to curb my perfectionistic all-or-nothing mentality and focus on all the things we had right as a couple. There were plenty. I wasn't seeing them because I didn't know where to look.

When doubt creeps in and starts to get the better of us, a major overhaul can feel necessary. However, the best fixes are sometimes the simplest ones. For me, it was a shift in my point of view. As computer scientist Alan Kay says, "A change in perspective is worth 80 IQ points." With a new way to look at my relationship, I felt like a genius. Instead of considering a bunch of little arguments as indicators of imminent doom, I realized they were a sign of two people who were willing to talk things through, call each other out on their BS, and push for improvement. That's what best friends do, and that's what we were then — and are now.

Before I started studying relationships, I was sure I had love all figured out. But each research paper I read made my previous insights seem shallow, ill formed, and downright silly. I've spent the last couple of decades filling in the blanks by reading hundreds (if not thousands) of studies, to gain a better understanding of relationships. Now, after twenty-plus years of reading, thinking, researching, teaching, and talking about relationships, I can confidently say that they have at least one feature in common: doubt. Frankly, it would be weird if we didn't wonder about something so important. I'm not just saying that because I had doubts, or to make you feel better. Rather, all those years have given me a unique perspective: in our relationships, we worry about the wrong things, miss many of the positive signs, and are generally harder on our relationship than it deserves.

If you're anything like I was years ago, your relationship IQ, or what you know about finding, nurturing, growing, sustaining, and leaving love, could use a booster shot. So much of your accumulated relationship wisdom probably comes from your parents, family, friends, personal experience, or even the media. You could be working from well-established facts or well-intentioned fiction, without ever realizing which is which. It's not your fault. You're not a scientist; you haven't conducted empirical studies or read countless scientific papers about what makes relationships tick. Naturally, that leaves you with lots of questions.

Make no mistake, in relationships, questions are part of the experience. The biggest ones stem from your most anxiety-provoking insecurities: Where's the relationship going? Does it have a future? Is there something better out there? Is it over? What's next? When people ask questions, they often turn to Google for answers. When Google tracked the most popular searches from 2017, questions like "How do I know when my relationship is over?"; "What does a healthy relationship look like?"; and "How do I save my relationship?" made the top ten.[1] It's clear. Lots of people have doubts about their relationship. Being 100 percent sure is 100 percent impossible.

Getting It Right

But you want to get it right. If you made a list of the most important aspects of your life, your relationship would be at the top. As David Brooks observes in the *New York Times,* "The most important decision any of us make is who we marry. Yet there are no courses on how to choose a spouse."[2] Juxtapose that with a 2017 report from Harvard University revealing that individuals in their twenties feel "unprepared for caring, lasting romantic relationships and are anxious about developing them."[3] Feeling ill equipped when making a major life decision is only going to increase the amount of uncertainty you experience as your relationship matures.

Unsettling? Definitely. That's because the stakes are high. Raise your hand if as a child you dreamed of being single when you grew up. Didn't think so. Smart choice, too, because relationships can truly be lifesaving. Does that sound hyperbolic? Let this convince you: social isolation, living alone, and loneliness all increase your chances of dying.[4] In fact, as a predictor of early death, loneliness ranks up there with smoking and obesity. As former US surgeon general Vivek Murthy suggests in a *Harvard Business Review* article, "Loneliness and weak social connections are associated with a reduction in lifespan similar to that caused by smoking 15 cigarettes a day and even greater than that associated with obesity."[5] No wonder no one wants to end up alone.

Relationships' benefits are well documented. Having a healthy relationship improves your general sense of well-being and life satisfaction, finances, mental health, and, perhaps most important, physical health and longevity. Having a happy partner is especially beneficial to your health.[6] Relationships also shape your thinking and how you look at the world. Sound lofty? In 2017, scientists from Yale University had participants look at photographs of nature and landscapes, then give their reactions.[7] Some participants did this alone, others viewed the photos with a stranger, and a third group looked with a close other. Even though everyone looked at the exact same pictures, their experiences were different. Those who looked with someone they knew and cared about enjoyed the photos more and thought the scenes looked more real.

Now, you might think, well, sure, when you're with your friend you have more to talk about while looking at a picture or can signal to each other in a way that makes it more enjoyable (insert funny remark, smirk, or eye roll here). But in this study pairs viewed photos silently, without any type of communication. Simply having a loved one right there enhanced the experience. That "partner in crime" can also make challenges feel more manageable. One study asked passersby to estimate the slant of a hill.[8] Compared to those who were alone, those who made estimates with a supportive person by their side thought the hills were less steep, especially if they had a high-quality relationship. Clearly, good relationships enhance the way we see the world, making life easier and ultimately better.

Decisions in the Face of Uncertainty

It's time to start setting yourself up for success. First step: learn to deal with uncertainty. When confronted with doubt and ambiguity, too often we put blinders on in hopes of finding bliss. When life gets tough and the pressure is on, research from 2017 shows, people prefer to keep themselves in the dark.[9] If it were possible to know when you were going to die, would you want to know? How about the cause of death—would you want to know that? If not, you're not alone. Interviews with nearly one thousand people confirm that the vast majority (85–90 percent) didn't want to know the timing or cause of their death. What about their partner's death? Tougher question, because knowing that would give them a chance to maximize their time together. More time on vacation, less on fixing up the house. Nope, nine out of ten people (89.5 percent) didn't want to know. But maybe death is just too morbid and final; maybe it's pointless to worry about something you can't control.

What about your relationship? Researchers asked: "Assume you are newly married. Would you want to know today whether your marriage will eventually end in divorce or not?" Still no; 86.5 percent wanted to remain ignorant. Too many people leave their relationship choices and outcomes to chance and then simply hope for the best.

Blissful ignorance may set you up for failure. Avoiding

potentially useful insights into your relationship makes it easier for big problems to sneak up on you. Then, when your love life starts to feel overwhelming or unsettled, it's easier to consider the extreme: ending the relationship. The French have a name for this tendency to contemplate tragic endings, *l'appel du vide,* or "the call of the void." When you feel like you're being pushed to the edge, jumping feels reasonable. Time to bail, because certainly there must be something better out there.

It's now simpler than ever to indulge that impulse to end one relationship and start another with the mere swipe of a finger. With a steady stream of available partners just a click away, technology has redefined modern relationships. Not necessarily for the better. For one, with greater access comes greater choice. A wide assortment of potential partners means there is always the nagging suspicion that there is a better partner out there. Not only has the abundance of possibilities made us way too picky; it's made us lazy. Rather than dedicating the time and effort to working things out, people casually throw relationships out to pursue other options. Modern relationships seem disposable.

Careful, though. The restless search for the next one may overlook *the* one. Everyone wants to make the right decision without being too willing to settle for less than we deserve or too quick to leave. To make better decisions, it's time to open our eyes to the blind spots that secretly undermine our relationships. But weighing our strengths and weaknesses as couples is difficult because there's a lot to consider. While lots of research predicts which relationships will succeed and which will fail, it would be helpful to know which areas are most important to think about when evaluating our relationship's fate. That research hadn't existed, until now.

It comes from Samantha Joel, a rising rock star in the relationship-science world. Sam is a motorcycle-driving Canadian professor and the principal investigator of the Relationship Decisions Lab at the University of Western Ontario.[10] In a 2018 study, along with her colleagues Geoff MacDonald and Elizabeth Page-Gould, Sam asked, What relationship issues do individuals consider when making a choice between breaking up and staying together?[11] It feels like there could be millions. To help narrow it down, researchers had participants describe what factors would be important to them when making a decision on a relationship's future.

Fifty common themes emerged, including twenty-seven reasons for staying, such as attraction, physical and emotional intimacy, improvement of self, dependence, support, hope for future improvement, fear of being alone, belief that the partner is a soul mate, and fear of uncertainty or the unknown. Participants also gave twenty-three reasons for wanting to leave, which primarily focused on many of the same themes (e.g., loss of attraction, insufficient intimacy).

To see how individuals put these reasons into practice in real-life stay-or-go decisions, the researchers conducted a follow-up study with more than two hundred individuals who were contemplating breakup or divorce. The results showed that despite having some doubts, roughly half of all participants had an above-average inclination to stay in the relationship. Makes sense. Inertia is powerful. However, those same exact people simultaneously had an above-average inclination to leave. Conflicted much? This research is important for two reasons: it shows just how common doubts are, and it helps us find blind spots in the relationship areas we think about the most. When I was picking the ten blind spots to focus on in this book, there were a lot of choices, but this research helped me select the ones that were most likely to be important.

How to Read This Book

My reliance on Sam's research to pick the ten blind spots that undermine your relationship, and how to see past them, wasn't accidental. *Stronger Than You Think: The 10 Blind Spots That Undermine Your Relationship... and How to See Past Them* is a different type of relationship book, one in which science serves as an ever-present guide. Throughout each chapter I will share an unprecedented amount of relationship science. In doing so, I will pull back the curtain on the research process so that you can better appreciate the high-quality science that my colleagues do. That said, as with scientific research in any field, it is important to recognize that one study by itself does not provide absolute proof of any phenomenon. Rather, each study represents a single step in a long line of inquiry, with each step warranting replication and further study. These steps aren't always perfectly linear, and often some are missing. Relationship scientists have done a wonderful job exploring the many facets of topics covered in this book. One of the biggest challenges for me as an academic was constantly fighting the urge to write comprehensive reviews of each research area. In the interest of space and readability, I had to be selective, and by necessity I left a lot of great research out. I hope those authors will forgive me. Much as I do when teaching or giving talks, I'll weave a narrative around the studies to tell as cohesive a story as possible. To be clear, any extrapolations I make from the data are entirely my own and not the researchers'. Shoot the messenger.

Ultimately, you should think of the research I share as pieces of evidence that provide fodder for further consideration, and another lens through which to view your own relationship. What you'll read isn't one-size-fits-all, but it should fit most. Some insights will hit home and fundamentally shift how you look at your relationship. Others may prove less revelatory. No two relationships are the same, so everyone will take something a little bit different from this book. I'll also give you a chance to answer research-like questions to better understand how concepts might apply to you and your relationship. When I do that, I'm going to give you a few questions that closely approximate the actual measures that researchers gave to people in their studies. This way we don't tip the official scales for participants in future research, while still giving you the insights into your relationship that you're looking for.

Chapters will take you on a guided tour of relationships' key friction points and the most common blind spots that plague each. In the first chapter, you'll learn how relying on faulty assumptions and bad information can lead you to find problems where they don't exist. Each subsequent chapter will focus on a blind spot that shapes how you think about love in ways that sabotage your relationship. There you'll get to peek into another person's relationship and witness the myth in action. Next, the chapter sets the record straight and reveals what relationship science has discovered about the issue. Finally, you will get actionable research-based suggestions for vanquishing the blind spot. Through this series of "reveals," you will discover areas of your relationship that deserve more attention and more credit. All of which will help you defuse unacknowledged issues and better appreciate your relationship's true value.

Stronger Than You Think is required reading for anyone in a relationship who has had doubts or is considering a transition. It is for those thinking about taking the next step and those who seek greater confidence in their relationship's current path. It is for anyone who has decided that they can't take the dating scene much longer and want to focus on finding a meaningful relationship they can grow old in. It's also for those in well-established relationships who find themselves questioning their future and considering alternatives. It is for anyone who doesn't want to have to settle in order to settle down, and for those who know what they want but don't know what they have.

I'm a relationship scientist, so people ask me all the time whether knowing so much about relationships helps my own relationship. To get the real answer, you should probably ask my wife. We've been together for more than twenty years, so that has to count for something. For me, being a relationship scientist has been immensely helpful. But probably not in the way you think. I don't quote research findings to my wife, or conduct mini-studies to test the best way to maximize our marital bliss. Instead, my understanding of the big picture is most helpful. I no longer waste emotional energy on things that don't really matter. I'm also much better at identifying all the positive signs that so many others miss. Because I see these signs, I'm more grateful for them, and my relationship benefits.

My own journey learning about relationships makes me understand that most people don't truly see their relationship for what it is. It's time to look before you leap. The stakes are too high to rely on gut instinct alone. We need a new scientific look at love, one that focuses on what's right instead of what's wrong, an approach that relies on data rather than advice, opinions, or best guesses. After all, love isn't always easy to understand. You need to be absolutely certain that you're focusing on the right things, asking the right questions, and emphasizing what is truly important.

Stronger Than You Think provides insights that will help you see your relationship more clearly, perhaps for the first time. It boosts your relationship IQ and confidence by helping you to stop focusing on the wrong parts, stop seeing problems where they don't exist, start ignoring the trivial and instead appreciating what truly matters, and learn to think more clearly about your relationship's success. By helping you see what's right with your relationship, *Stronger Than You Think* will also help you fortify areas that are a little shaky and in need of repair. The first step toward fixing a problem is to understand it. When you do, you will finally start to see what you've been missing.

Relationships are important. Time is short. Get it right.

Chapter 1

What If Everything You Know About Relationships Is Wrong?

Y ou've heard the saying that love is blind. Well, the truth is that love may also be deaf and a little dumb as well. No one wants to admit to love-induced blindness. But the fact is, it's likely you're holding on to a series of myths or fictions that leave you with relationship blind spots you never realized you had. Don't worry, you're not alone. Everyone has them. These misconceptions come in many forms: key questions you aren't asking, signals you're missing, signs you aren't seeing, qualities you're overvaluing, or indicators you're misinterpreting. Too often these blind spots cause you to overlook your relationship's hidden virtues, undervalue your partner, or create dynamics that threaten your relationship.

To varying degrees, nearly everyone has experience with romantic relationships. You, your friends, your family, and even your co-workers have this in common. This type of direct experience creates a familiarity that leads people to believe that relationships are intuitive, dependent on basic common sense. But it simply isn't true. Face it: if relationships really were based on common sense, perfect partners would be easy to find and relationship bliss would be the norm. In reality, relationships are, and often feel, perpetually complicated and difficult to decipher. Experience just isn't the same thing as expertise.

Here's the thing. What I'm about to tell you is going to sting a bit. Despite your best intentions, and without realizing it, you've likely been your relationship's own worst enemy. Talk about an awkward plot twist. My suggestion: own it. The first step is admitting there's a problem.

Don't believe me that you might unknowingly work against your relationship? Consider this. Who can best forecast your relationship's future? Obviously, it's you. Not so fast. Researchers set out to test the commonsense assumption about who's the best judge of a relationship, first by asking the most natural source of information, the person in the relationship.[1] Across two studies with more than one hundred undergraduate students, researchers asked the students about their confidence in those predictions. Here's a revelation. Researchers fact-checked their prognostications by asking each student's roommate and parents the exact same questions. Six months and one year later, the researchers followed up to see how everyone did with their predictions. As you might imagine, students were super-confident in their forecasts. After all, who knows more about your own relationship than you? Roommates and parents were less confident, and with good reason. They had less information when making their guesses.

Who was most accurate when predicting the relationship's future? Spoiler alert: it wasn't the students. Roommates were the best, followed by parents. That's right, the students were the worst. Even though they had more inside information about their own relationship, students provided the least accurate forecasts. In fact, students thought the relationship would last two to three times longer than their parents and roommates did. Taken together, the results showed that people displayed the potentially tragic combination of being supremely confident in what was the least accurate prediction about their relationship. Believing that you know your relationship better than anyone else is a myth that can blind you to outsiders' helpful insights.

How can this be? Well, you're in love. Which means you're biased. Especially in the early stages of relationships, it's easy to focus on how great everything is and become overly optimistic. We're going to have this perfect relationship forever! But that's thinking with your heart. Your friends and family think with their heads. When we're too emotional, it compromises our judgment and affects our decision-making. It's difficult to see things clearly.[2] Our feelings get in the way. But the people who surround us don't have that problem. They're not in love with our partners. Their emotions aren't involved, so they see a relationship's imperfections and appraise it more accurately. Love makes us just a little dumb.

The Limits of Self-Knowledge

One of the biggest obstacles we face when trying to see our relationship clearly is that we give ourselves a lot of credit for how much insight and self-awareness we have about our own lives. Problem is, that credit isn't warranted. A review of the self-knowledge research concludes that we don't know ourselves as well as we think we do.[3] None of this is surprising when we consider how little time we spend engaged in self-reflective thought. Despite what we see on social media, we aren't as self-absorbed, egocentric, and self-centered as you may think. We may seek attention but actually don't spend much time focusing on ourselves.[4] A couple of decades ago researchers wanted to determine just how much people thought about themselves, so they took a peek into the day-to-day lives of more than one hundred working adults. To do that, they outfitted participants with a beeper. (Note: it was the eighties, so beepers were cool.) Over the course of a week, participants received messages at random times asking them what they were doing a second ago. Of the nearly 4,700 times the researchers hit participants up on their beepers, participants reported thinking about themselves only about 8 percent of the time. Why so little? People don't find it enjoyable. In fact, when participants thought about themselves, they reported fewer positive emotions compared to when they thought about other things like food. When it comes down to it, people prefer a scoop of ice cream to a scoop of self-insight.

But that was years ago. Things are different now and, you'd hope, better. Sadly, they may be worse. A more recent survey of how American adults spend their leisure time found that over a twenty-four-hour (or 1,440-minute) period, people spent only seventeen minutes "relaxing and thinking."[5] That's only 1.18 percent of a person's day. Consider that for a moment. It seems impossibly low, but when was the last time, completely free from distractions, you sat and dedicated some time to really contemplating yourself or your relationship? With so much competing for your attention, finding time to just sit and think feels impossible. Yet there are opportunities for self-reflection during your commute, as you drink your morning coffee, in the shower, or as you drift off to sleep. But you're probably too immersed in self-imposed distractions like checking your social media feeds, catching up on celebrity gossip, or wading through political news. We're sacrificing me time for screen time.

We can blame the lack of self-reflection on being busy, but there's more to the story. What if someone forced you to have the time? Researchers from the University of Virginia and Harvard gave participants this golden opportunity: the chance to sit and simply think.[6] Researchers also gave them the option of administering electrical shocks to themselves. Weird choice, right? Especially since earlier the participants had all agreed the shocks were painful, so much so that each participant was willing to pay money to avoid them. Yet despite having the chance to peacefully contemplate whatever they wanted to—themselves, their relationship, or life—just over four out of ten participants (42.9 percent) took the electrified path less traveled. The rest decided to shock themselves instead. For them, a painful shock was preferable to being alone with their thoughts. Self-reflection can be intimidating. No wonder so many people seek out therapists, life coaches, and counselors who force reflection and aid in the journey.

Bonus Blind Spot:
The Toughest Thing to Admit

"I don't know." For the aspects of your life that really matter, confessing a lack of awareness or uncertainty, especially about yourself or your relationship, is difficult. But embracing ignorance has its benefits. Imagine a scenario where you need to take a high-stakes vocabulary test (think: SAT or GRE). You receive a list of thirty-two words that will be on the test (e.g., shameful, ignominious, pulchritudinous, allude). Next, you get a few moments to study. Time is of the essence, so optimizing your study strategy by knowing which words to study is important. To have the most success, it's better to skip words you already know and focus on the less familiar words. Doing that requires admitting you don't know some of the words (pulchritudi — what?).

When researchers gave participants this task, those who were willing to identify the words they did not know studied more efficiently and, most important, did better on a subsequent test.[7] By acknowledging and embracing where their knowledge was weak, participants ultimately reaped the benefits. Because our relationships have higher stakes than any vocab test, conceding that we don't know everything is threatening. But this research shows that identifying areas where we are less knowledgeable is helpful. Sadly, that isn't how we operate.

We need a push because, when left to our own devices, a self-guided tour through our lives may be overwhelming. But without additional insights into the self, we can't see the whole picture. We remain blind to our actual knowledge and abilities, often giving ourselves more credit than we deserve.[8] Our overconfidence is especially prevalent when other people are around.[9] Imagine you're in a room with ninety-nine other people and I give you a series of prompts. Raise your hand if you're above average in terms of your kissing ability compared to everyone else in the room. Sense of humor. Intelligence. Ability to judge others' character. Would you raise your hand for all or most of these? Likely, yes.

Here's the problem: so would everyone else. Yet, through the powers of math, we know that it is impossible for more than half to be above the room's average or midpoint. You, and pretty much everyone else in the room, are much more confident than you have a right to be. Imagine asking one hundred couples on their wedding day, "Will your marriage end in divorce?" (Note: Do not do this. Ever.) First, you might get physically assaulted, because no one (i.e., 0 percent) believes they'll get divorced, especially on their wedding day. But as we know, nearly half of them are 100 percent wrong. This bit of unrealistic optimism may seem innocent enough, but mistakes of excessive confidence are especially likely to happen in the exactly wrong cases.

For example, when we have less information about a topic, overconfidence is easy. In their award-winning paper "Unskilled and Unaware of It," Cornell psychologists David Dunning and Justin Kruger tell the story of wannabe bank robber McArthur Wheeler.[10] Mr. Wheeler might have gotten away with two Pittsburgh-area robberies if it weren't for his unfounded faith in lemon juice. Yup, you read that correctly. Lemon juice. Wheeler believed lemon juice had mythical powers to foil surveillance cameras. Aspiring rich guy McArthur Wheeler robbed two banks without any attempt to conceal his identity other than rubbing his face with lemons. Police apprehended the criminal mastermind an hour after the surveillance camera footage aired (perfectly clearly) on the evening news.

Wheeler's ignorance blinded him, but not the cameras. It turns out that when life gives you lemons, you shouldn't go and use those lemons as a cloaking device.

Wheeler's belief seems ridiculous because you know enough about how cameras and lemons work to know better. Unfortunately he knew so little about both that he could be overconfident. Psychologists have a name for this phenomenon, the Dunning-Kruger effect, or the tendency for those who are less skilled or knowledgeable to be more certain about their conclusions. You've probably seen those public service announcements on TV where a star shoots across the screen, followed by the words "The More You Know." Well, the Dunning-Kruger effect is like a meteor crashing to the ground followed by the words "The Less You Know." When we have fewer facts and less information, it's easier to see things as black or white, right or wrong, good or bad. This false sense of clarity emboldens us to feel absolutely sure of our conclusions. More data allow us to see the shades of gray, providing a more nuanced and accurate view of reality. The implication is clear. When information is incomplete, confidence comes more easily.

The Limits of Experience

For most of us, our relationship knowledge base isn't as complete as we might think. Remember, experience isn't equivalent to expertise. Because you know your own dating track record well, it's easy to believe your experiences are the norm. Sure, you've had a range of dating and relationship experiences, but you're only one person, and one person can experience only so much. It is your unique lived experience, but relying solely on that information to guide relationship decisions ignores all the wisdom you can glean from other couples. Besides, even if you have an abundance of experience, it may not qualify as the best type of information. Just because you've been in a lot of car accidents doesn't make you a better driver; in fact, it probably suggests the opposite. The same is true of having a lot of relationships. True expertise can come only from moving beyond one's own idiosyncratic background.

That's the thing. Thanks to egocentrism, we all think we're normal and assume our experiences are the standard. But we can't all be normal. Do you remember the first time you realized that others see and experience the world differently from you? I do. It was over something simple, yet it couldn't have been more shocking to me. I was in first grade and Amy, one of my classmates, mentioned the "ups truck" had been at her house. Having never heard of such a thing, and thinking she was talking about vomiting, I innocently asked, "What's that?" With all the sass a first-grade girl could muster, she turned to me and said, "You know, the opposite of downs." I managed a sheepish, "Huh?" At that moment, Amy decided I was the dumbest kid ever. She proceeded to all-too-patiently explain (you know, in that way where the explanation is so slow and deliberate that any idiot could understand it) that it was the brown truck that brought boxes to the house. At that moment it became clear to me. Amy had it wrong. She was the one who was ignorant about the world. Everyone I knew always spelled out the letters and called it the U-P-S truck. We were both relying on our own direct experiences to determine what was "right" and "normal," without considering the limitations of our experiences. (For the record, I remain convinced UPS is the right name.)

Recently, you could see the same phenomenon take place

when a picture of a dress created a debate over whether it was blue or gold, and when people argued over whether an audio clip sounded like "Yanny" or "Laurel." In each case, it's hard to fathom how others' experience could be so different from our own. To know what gives any relationship (including our own) the best chances for success, we need to draw on large-scale sets of information from hundreds of people (as scientists do). Doing so helps us know how to put the odds in our relationship's favor. For example, our best relationship so far may have been with a narcissistic and manipulative partner. But we are just one person. If research studies with sample sizes one hundred to two hundred times larger find that narcissists aren't great partners (which these studies do), which information will help you have better relationships in the future? Science wins.

But we want things to be easy, so we rely on what's simple instead of what's scientific. As computer programmers are fond of saying: garbage in, garbage out. If flawed information goes in, what comes out is unworkable or impossible to properly interpret. The same is true in your relationship. To really assess your relationship's value, you need to know what information matters. Everywhere you look there are clues, hints, subtle signs, and even blatant evidence that can reveal your relationship's value. Yet we struggle.

First, our timing usually sucks. We start worrying about evaluating our relationships way too late. Think back to when your relationship started. You were busy having fun and falling in love. Everything was great; your confidence couldn't have been higher. No one wants to risk ruining a good thing by looking for potential problems. The research suggests that maybe you should have. A classic study tracked relationships over time to see which ones succeeded and which ones failed, and if there were signs early on that foretold the relationship's outcome.[11] First, researchers looked at rewards, or all the good stuff that relationships provide (e.g., love, support, affection). Early on, relationships that eventually succeeded and relationships that failed had the same number of rewards. Which means having a rewarding relationship early on isn't unique or terribly special. But the good stuff captures all our attention. It creates a blind spot. That's a mistake.

Relationships also have costs, or negative experiences (e.g., loss of freedom and independence, conflict). Overall, for all the relationships in the study, reported costs were much lower on average than rewards. There is a lesson there: our relationship's good stuff should greatly outweigh the bad stuff. Though costs were generally low, they were higher in relationships that eventually failed compared to those that were successful. In other words, to really know how your relationship will turn out, you need to focus on costs early on. Unfortunately, costs are the exact thing we're most willing to overlook when a relationship is new. We have it completely backward.

Perhaps we're willing to look the other way on early costs because we think they'll resolve themselves or simply disappear. Things can only get better! Sorry, but those rose-colored hopes are misguided. When researchers tracked newlyweds over four years and asked them about common couple problems like dealing with in-laws, the problems that were there from the start didn't just go away over time.[12] Other research shows that couples who ended up unhappy were, from the beginning, less kind, generous, and caring toward each other and had more hesitations entering the marriage.[13] Not only did those doubts and issues continue to plague them, but they eventually contributed to the relationship's demise. Ignoring early problems doesn't resolve them; relationship issues linger.

Obviously, some problems are worse than others. If you want to know which issues are most likely to doom a relationship, who better to ask than the recently divorced? When UCLA researchers did that, the key issues divorcés mentioned were communication, not being willing to work at the relationship, and trust.[14] The surprising part was that divorcés recognized that their troubles didn't come out of nowhere. They had been there all along. Of course, hindsight is 20/20, but early on, they just didn't notice, were in denial, or didn't do anything about it. Clearly, if you don't want to get caught off guard, removing this blind spot is essential.

Now, fast-forward a bit. As your relationship progresses, you settle into a routine, life happens, and you start noticing flaws. Lots of them. Some are minor, like how your partner installs the toilet paper "wrong" or insists on clapping every time your flight lands. But some feel more substantial, like your partner's ditzy nature, how he treats servers at restaurants, how he drives, his spending habits, eating habits, messiness—the list goes on. These issues have likely been there all along, but you gave them a free pass. Not anymore. Now that the relationship's novelty has worn off and the excitement has faded, you're a much keener observer and much less tolerant. That can encourage overcorrecting and finding problems that aren't really all that problematic.

Don't Be Too Hard on Yourself

You may have assumed that people are way too easy on themselves and their relationships. But that isn't entirely true. Though positivity reigns initially, it doesn't remain that way across the entire relationship. In reality, as your relationship matures, rather than ignore issues as you did early on, you go the other way. Now you succumb to "problemicity," or the tendency to find problems where they don't exist. You create sources of conflict that aren't real. You imagine predicaments that you'll never find yourself in. You dwell on issues that are ultimately inconsequential. In other words, you're manufacturing problems that aren't real, but are really harmful.

The result: you're harder on your partner and relationship than you should be. Blame the negativity bias, which is the tendency to gravitate toward or focus on the bad or negative aspects of an experience.[15] In other words, when your relationship is going well, the positives don't register. We take them for granted. You know what captures your attention? Problems. The insensitive comments, forgotten chores, bickering, clutter, and inconveniences all stand out because they deviate from the easily overlooked peaceful and happy status quo. The tendency to notice the bad stuff is so pronounced that, according to 2018 research published in *Science,* if your relationship doesn't have any major issues, you inflate small problems into bigger ones.[16] In other words, rather than be thankful for the relative calm, we create issues where none previously existed. It's almost as if we need the drama to sustain us. Classic problemicity.

Relationships are hard enough as it is. You certainly don't need to do anything to make them more difficult. The goal should be to recognize and appreciate the good, keep small problems small, and ignore the inconsequential. Seems simple enough. But in day-to-day life it's difficult to achieve. You need to stifle overreactions and realize that in reality things are better than you think.

At this point I couldn't blame you if you were wondering, What if everything you thought you knew about your relationship was wrong? Well, it's time to get your facts straight, focus on what truly matters, and give your relationship the credit it deserves. Socrates allegedly once said that "true knowledge exists in knowing that you know nothing." When it comes to relationships, saying you know "nothing" overstates the case a bit. When I was a kid, my mom was fond of saying, "Being smart is knowing what you don't know." In life, and in relationships, that is very good advice. Mom: 1, Socrates: 0. Now it's time to tamp down your overconfidence and realize your relationship IQ could use a little work. Embrace it. Acknowledging the limits of your expertise opens you up to broadening your understanding. Perhaps Benjamin Franklin explained it best: "Being ignorant is not so much a shame, as being unwilling to learn." Time to learn.

First, please realize that the quest for relationship enlightenment is bumpy. At some point, a blind spot will pop up, and what you believe to be true will turn out to be a myth. It's bound to happen. Although everyone loves being right, every so often, when you encounter new information suggesting you might have it wrong, you'll get that pang of doubt in your gut. The key is what you do next.

The most typical reaction is a counterproductive one. It's what I call the "yeah-but." This is a commonly deployed defense mechanism meant to safeguard us from a point we don't like. Our natural inclination is to guard the status quo. When science confronts that, we fight back. We halfheartedly acknowledge an element of truth, "Yeah…," and then unleash our defense, "but…" When we use "yeah-buts," they're typically in stories about friends, someone we know, or something we once heard. They can stem from anecdotes from our own experience, alternative "facts" we believe to be true, or attacks on context ("yeah, but that's only true when..."). Let's be honest, we've all got stories to tell. The real problem is we deploy "yeah-buts" when our relationship could most benefit from science. Sticking to existing beliefs stifles opportunities for growth and encourages blind spots to take root.

Combine a tendency to put our heart before our head, a lack of reflection and self-awareness, abundant overconfidence, an egocentric overreliance on personal experience, poor timing, a propensity for finding problems where they don't exist, and a tendency to disregard evidence that contradicts our existing beliefs, and what's the result? Well, we end up with a collection of major blind spots that threaten our relationships by unnecessarily creating doubt. Time to let science shed some light on your relationship. Here's a sneak peek at the ten blind spots we'll uncover in Chapters 2 through 11:

1. Men and women aren't different, but thinking they are will create problems.
2. Looking for a "soul mate" who provides relationship perfection is a bad approach because it's unrealistic and creates instability.
3. Emphasizing your partner's hotness undermines the relationship; you'd be better off focusing on personality.
4. It's easy to focus on the wrong type of love and worry too much about sex, when in reality the amount of sex you should have is less than you think.
5. Fixer-upper partners are a bad idea, even if they say they want to change; acceptance is key.
6. Sacrificing for your relationship can backfire; being more selfish and putting *me* before *you* can help your relationship.

7. Distance in relationships is helpful; although wanting to be closer feels romantic, it's a potential sign of trouble.

8. Good communication is important, but not having disagreements may be ruining your relationship, so you need to give a "CRAPO" (*c*larify, *r*eflect feelings, *a*ttend, *p*araphrase, and ask *o*pen-ended questions).

9. Getting support from your partner is more important in good times than in bad.

10. Knowing when to call it quits is important, especially since ending the relationship won't be as bad as you think it will be.

They say that nothing worth having comes easy. For our entire lives most of us have built our relationship acumen on a compromised foundation based on flawed ways of thinking about the world. Don't beat yourself up about it. Nobody's perfect. We all believe myths that undermine our relationships and have blind spots that make the truth hard to see. We're now ready to dedicate time to thoughtful self-reflection. We're done with "yeah-buts," done with excuses. We're ready to stop being so hard on ourselves and our relationships. Instead of succumbing to problemicity and finding problems where they don't exist, we can start seeing things for what they really are. Let's start giving our relationship the credit it deserves. Over the next ten chapters we're going to delve deeper into the top ten myths that are holding back our relationships.

Chapter 2

"Men and Women Are Just Different"

*Y*ou're such a girl." *That's the last thing Nick said before he went up to bed. She hated the fact that he had said it, but Tori also knew where he was coming from. She was being overly emotional and dramatic. His crime? He didn't feel like talking, and she wouldn't let it go. Why were they so out of sync? Tori knew she was fighting a losing battle because this was just how guys were. She didn't like it, but every guy she had ever dated was this way. Heck, her father was this way. Come to think of it, Nick's was too. Guys were just wired differently. As much as she might love a partner who was more caring, kind, and talkative, that just wasn't how guys were built. Nick would counter that girls were all overly emotional, dramatic, moody, and generally high-maintenance.*

Yet Tori wanted, and felt she deserved, more. When things between them felt especially distant, she would ponder a series of what-ifs. What if I wasn't with Nick? What if another relationship was better? She couldn't help it. But Tori knew in her heart that Nick was really good to her. She couldn't blame him for being a guy, just like he couldn't change that she was just being a girl. Perhaps it was time to stop getting upset and accept what was clearly a universal truth: men and women are different.

CHECKING YOUR BLIND SPOT

Men and women differ in all areas of their lives. Not only do men and women communicate differently but they think, feel, perceive, react, respond, love, need, and appreciate differently. They almost seem to be from different planets, speaking different languages, and needing different nourishment.

—*John Gray,* Men Are from Mars, Women Are from Venus

Are Men and Women Really Different?

Yeah, no. Emphatically N-O. As relationship blind spots go, the belief that men and women are completely different is easily one of the most pervasive and damaging. It's a blind spot that artificially limits our relationship's potential. Consider a softball question. In relationships, who is more romantic: men or women? Easy, right? Women all the way. Nope, that's a myth. Men are the romantics.[1] Men are more likely to believe romantic notions such as "love conquers all" and that being in love is all that it takes to have a good relationship. Women? Realists. They have a much more pragmatic view of love. Before they fully take the plunge, women are more likely to consider sensible issues like whether their partner is on drugs, will be able to hold a job, and has a good personality.

We can see it in relationship behaviors, too. If you had to guess, who falls in love more easily, men or women? Who says "I love you" first? Easy questions with obvious answers. Participants in a research study thought so too.[2] When they responded, nearly nine out of ten (87.78 percent) thought women fell in love more easily, and three out of four (75.20 percent) believed women were the first to proclaim their love. Here's the thing. Researchers don't just take participants' word. They fact-check. To test if their assumptions were accurate, researchers asked participants how quickly they fell in love and whether they

---

How Do You Measure Up?
Romantic Beliefs

Curious about how romantic your own beliefs are? While researchers use much more in-depth ways to assess romantic beliefs, here are a few items to give you a sense of your romanticism. Indicate how much you agree with each statement using the scale provided:

1. I'm going to know the instant I meet my "true love."
    Strongly Disagree   1   2   3   4   5   Strongly Agree
2. I will have only one "true love" in my lifetime.
    Strongly Disagree   1   2   3   4   5   Strongly Agree
3. True love happens quickly, is easy, and stands the test of time.
    Strongly Disagree   1   2   3   4   5   Strongly Agree

The more you agree with each item (i.e., the higher the scores), the stronger your romantic beliefs.[3]

---

were first to say "I love you." A funny thing happens when myths get confronted with data: the myths crumble. In reality, it was the men who fell in love quicker—and by a large margin. Men were also the first to say "I love you"; men said it first 64 percent of the time. (For what it's worth, men's overly romantic approach to love may not be what's best for the relationship. More to come on that in Chapter 5.)

Men are the romantics, not women. That's a big blind spot that we didn't know existed. Mind blown. Yet that's just the tip of the iceberg. Commonsense sex differences like this often turn out not to be differences at all. For instance, we've all seen the headline: "Male and Female Brains Wired Differently." Compelling and sure to catch anyone's attention, but not accurate. It seems true because everyone can plainly see that males and females have obvious physical differences. It only makes sense that their brains would be different too. That is, unless you started actually comparing brains. To pull that off, you'd need to look at a lot of brains. That's exactly what one group of researchers did.[4] Based on their MRI analysis of more than 1,400 of them, they concluded that, structurally, there is no such thing as a "male brain" and a "female brain." But does that mean that men and women think, feel, and act the same?

To really know if the sexes are different, we can't just cherry-pick a few areas where we suspect men and women vary. Instead, we'd want to give it a fair test by comprehensively checking for differences across multiple domains—including skills/abilities, social behaviors, personality, psychopathology, and well-being—in hundreds of studies. Yet we don't want to have to read every single one of those studies. Good news! Researchers use a statistical technique called meta-analysis to combine results from all the research they can find on a topic (typically dozens, if not hundreds, of individual studies). Each meta-analysis uses information from a ton of participants, which gives researchers a lot of data-analytical power behind their conclusions. The seminal meta-analysis examining gender differences found that "males and females are alike on most—but not all—psychological variables."[5] When researchers did a follow-up review of this "gender-similarity hypothesis," they found more of the same: little or no gender differences in areas such as math and verbal skills, self-esteem, conscientiousness, leadership effectiveness, relational aggression, and attitudes about extramarital sex.[6]

If you thought meta-analyses were impressive and cool, wait until you hear about a meta-synthesis, which combines groups of meta-analyses.[7] Very meta-meta. It's one of the best ways to leverage larger pools of data and thoroughly examine a topic. A meta-synthesis on gender differences gathered more than one hundred meta-analyses. Out of the four hundred possible differences they examined, the vast majority (85 percent) were small or very small. That is, men and women are overwhelmingly similar. Welcome to Earth.

But, if there is any part of life that is bound to highlight the differences between men and women, it's in relationships. Millions upon millions of people who read *Men Are from Mars, Women Are from Venus* couldn't be mistaken about how men and women approach relationships. Could they? To see what men and women really want in relationships, a large group of University of Florida researchers conducted three studies with hundreds of participants.[8] They looked at a bunch of relationship behaviors, like spending time together, sex, relationship support, and caring. Across all the studies there was only one stable and consistent gender difference: women desired more relationship support than men. In other words, things like remembering birthdays were more important to women than to men. If men and women were truly so different, researchers should have found differences in lots of other areas as well. But they didn't.

What about the juicy stuff like sex? When researchers reviewed more than eight hundred studies and compared men and women on thirty different variables related to sex, they found more similarities than differences.[9] They discovered differences in the age of first having sex and experience with intercourse, oral sex, anal sex, and cybersex, but they were small. For sexual attitudes related to permissiveness of sex, premarital sex, extramarital sex, and masturbation, once again, there were only small differences, with men being slightly more accepting of those behaviors.

I could share even more evidence of gender similarity, but I'll stop there. There is a nearly never-ending stream of data like this, and those data are abundantly clear. It isn't that there aren't differences between men and women. There are. Yet for every difference research can identify, there's abundant similarity that tends to get overlooked. Even when there are real differences, they tend to be really small.

Some Difference Isn't the Same as Completely Different

Here it comes. The backlash, the "Yeah, but…" No one willingly harbors these blind spots or believes false information, so learning about mistakes hurts. To reconcile the uneasy feeling, it's easy to think, "These findings are garbage." Perhaps, but when a research finding agrees with an existing belief, we find it instantly believable, don't think about it too critically, and eagerly share our newfound knowledge with others. It's the case of "Yeah, but…" that we discussed in Chapter 1.

It's also likely that you've thought of examples I didn't mention where you're pretty sure there are clear-cut gender differences. You're absolutely right: those differences exist. Some of the biggest differences are physical—such as height, weight, arm size, shoulder span, and overall body shape. You won't be surprised to learn that men have the edge in physical size, and women have skinnier waists and wider hips than men. In NCAA track-and-field activities where both men and women competed, men had a clear edge in shot put, high jump, javelin throw, and long jump. Other studies find big differences in how people spend their free time.[10] Men are more likely to prefer activities such as playing golf, playing video games, and boxing, while women are more likely to prefer watching talk shows, scrapbooking, and attending to their appearance (e.g., hair styling, makeup). In addition, some of those same meta-analyses we discussed earlier found fairly big gender differences in other areas, with men scoring higher in terms of sensation seeking, the ability to think about how objects look in three-dimensional space (e.g., what would the letter Q look like upside down and backward), and physical aggression.[11]

There are some clear and legitimate differences between men and women, and those disparities are easy to see. That's the problem. Because they are easy to see, our broader beliefs about sex differences are more stubborn. However, the noticeable differences are actually the exceptions, not the rule.

You've Been Taught to See Differences

How can so many people have it wrong? It's hard to believe men and women are actually similar when so many people strongly believe the opposite. When an idea has lots of believers, we naturally think it must be correct. Yet there are many examples of widely held mistaken beliefs: "The Earth is flat." "You use only 10 percent of your brain." "Sugar makes kids hyper." Each is incorrect, but all still have a sizable number of proponents. This just shows that a lot of people can have the facts completely wrong. Pervasive mistakes are still harmful. Look around and you'll see people engaged in a wide range of unhealthy behaviors. Does that mean they're a good idea? "Everyone's doing it" wasn't a good excuse when we were teenagers, and it still isn't. But like any self-respecting teenager, we might want to blame others for our mistaken beliefs. In the case of our beliefs about sex differences, we absolutely can. We can blame our upbringing.

From birth, unbeknownst to us, we've received a crash course in emphasizing differences between boys and girls. It's actually weird when you think about it because when babies are young, it is nearly impossible to differentiate between boys and girls. Yet, we insist on doing so. Blue is for boys; pink is for girls. Seems benign, but there are consequences. A classic technique that researchers use in gender research to study perceptions takes a "Baby X" and randomly assigns the baby to get either a blue or pink blanket.[12] Because it's difficult to know if a baby is male or female from only their face, researchers then see if adults treat "Baby X" differently based not on their actual sex, but on their blanket-based beliefs of whether the baby is a boy or a girl. Even though it is always the exact same baby.

A review of more than twenty studies using the blanket test found people believed the baby exhibited different personality traits and physical qualities based solely on the blanket's color.[13] Those thought to be baby girls were viewed as more fragile and passive, while those thought to be boys were seen as bigger, sturdier, tougher, and stronger. "Boys" were encouraged to be more active and received more stimulation, while "girls" were spoken to more and received more nurturing. The fact is, girls and boys come into a world that immediately treats them differently, even based on the color of a piece of fabric. The babies never had a choice, because it wasn't ever about who they were. Instead, it had everything to do with societal expectations about gender.

As a nine-year-old kid, I played baseball for Fairless Hills Appliance. On a hot and sticky summer evening, I stepped up to the plate, ready to make something happen. Well, something happened. The pitcher wound up and, with typical nine-year-old accuracy, delivered a pitch earmarked for my helmet's ear hole. Direct hit. Now, when you're a kid and something unexpected happens, you naturally look to others to make sense of the world and to know how to react. In that stunned moment, I looked up at my coach, who also happened to be my dad. I knew what I wanted to do. I was ready to cry, big-time. My dad had other ideas. His expression showed concern, but his response was full of tough love: "Not here, not now." Okay, then. I stifled my tears and whimpered my way to first base.

My father's message was clear: I had to be tough and not show weakness. Man up. If I had been a girl, would my dad have reacted the same way? To be honest, knowing him, he might have. But as someone who has coached a variety of girls' sports for more than half a decade, I can assure you girls' parents tend to be much more protective and treat injuries, especially anything to the face or head area, with a much softer touch. You see it outside of sports as well. Little girls get spa-day birthday parties with their friends, to focus on relaxation and appearance. There just isn't any parallel for boys. Girls get pampered; boys don't. If you've grown up this way, it's easy to assume this is the only way, or the right way. In fact, a common reaction to questions about upbringing is "I turned out okay." True, but it's fair to wonder if a better way might have led you to turn out better than okay.

Potential alternate life paths can be hard to recognize because we may have never experienced the world any other way. Classic stupid-smart question: "Do fish know they're wet?" Though impossible to know for sure, the answer is "Probably not." That's because fish live their entire lives in water. It is the only existence they have ever known, and ever will know. The same is true about gendered beliefs you might hold. Stereotypes and oversimplifications are everywhere. Your beliefs have been formed over many years and in many contexts—from the moment you entered kindergarten and the teacher innocently said, "Good morning, boys and girls," to the last time you had to use a public restroom or fill out a form. The world groups, categorizes, and enforces distinctions between men's and women's experiences.

Society is partly to blame, but we play a role as well. If we believe there are differences and go looking for them, we're probably going to find them. Psychologists call this a confirmation bias.[14] If we think women are worse drivers than men, anytime we see someone do something dumb on the road, we'll immediately look to see if it is a woman. If it is, *success!* Proof that we are right. If it is a male driver, it is an exception to the rule, or we reframe it into further evidence of our belief that men are reckless and impulsive. Maybe we're not trying that hard to find proof of men's and women's differing planetary origins. But if we hold a preconceived belief, we're more likely to remember the hits, or the times that something backs us up. At the same time, we tend to forget the misses. By repeating this process throughout our lives, we'll have created an impressive database of examples that support our existing belief. All without ever realizing that we've been using a biased process.

Not Just a Harmless Belief

Remember, a faulty premise will lead to a faulty conclusion. Garbage in, garbage out. If we've been led to believe men and women are so completely different, any sexist beliefs we hold will seem natural, normal, and acceptable. Those beliefs have consequences. They make us and our relationships vulnerable. When we start down the rabbit hole of buying into gender differences, our relationships can end up in a world of trouble. Take, for example, a key claim from *Men Are from Mars, Women Are from Venus:* men have a distinct "intimacy cycle" that functions like a rubber band.[15] Also known as "the Rubber Band Theory," the basic claim is that men fill up on intimacy, then need to withdraw and spend time away before they bounce back for an intimacy refill. First, the theory that men uniquely need solitude is incorrect. All humans seek connection at times and independence at other times. Connection isn't a uniquely female impulse. Isolation isn't a uniquely male impulse. What drives those tendencies has a lot more to do with factors such as personality and previous life experiences. The notion that men need their space normalizes and excuses a behavior that is potentially problematic for harmonious relationships. Research on couples communication shows that isolating oneself and refusing to discuss issues, otherwise known as stonewalling, is one of the worst possible things to do.[16] That is, unless you're trying to end the relationship.

Bonus Blind Spot:
A Belief in Gender Differences
Attracts the Wrong Type of Partner

Your gender stereotypes may set you up for relationship failure by drawing you to problematic partners. There are a lot of ways to attract potential relationship partners. These courtship strategies can be as simple as walking up to someone, saying "hi," and introducing yourself. However, for some, picking up a partner is like a game in which you can use tricks, or what researchers would call "assertive mating strategies."[17] These can involve purposefully manipulative tactics like insulting, teasing, paying backhanded compliments, or isolating the "target" from friends. Ick. Yet these strategies wouldn't exist unless they worked. Who falls for this? According to two studies of more than one thousand participants, men and women who held sexist attitudes (e.g., agreeing with statements like "Women should be cherished and protected by men" and "A good woman should be set on a pedestal by her man") were more likely to use or respond favorably to assertive strategies. In particular, in both studies, women who held more sexist beliefs were more susceptible to finding assertive approaches appealing. In addition, men from the national sample who held sexist beliefs about women attempting to usurp men's power (e.g., "Women seek to gain power by getting control over men") were more likely to use assertive strategies. Taken together, these findings show that holding stereotypical gender beliefs makes women more vulnerable to manipulative courtship strategies and encourages men to use them more.

The myth of male and female differences also corrodes our relationships in more subtle ways by shaping our decision-making. First, too much faith in inescapable differences encourages a sort of tyranny of low expectations. Sounds menacing, and it is. Gendered beliefs are rarely flattering. Case in point: "Women are overly emotional." "Men are awful communicators." If this is our starting point for what we anticipate from our partner, what are the chances that our relationship reaches its fullest potential? Low. Just like our expectations. When we anticipate that our partner will exhibit undesirable qualities, our tolerance for bad behavior increases. We're more permissive. We would never buy a phone that we thought wasn't going to work well; expecting the worst in our relationships makes even less sense.

When we expect the worst, we get the worst. And getting the worst means that a lot of our partner's characteristics annoy us. We push. We prod. We nag. All in hopes of molding and shaping our partner a bit more to our liking, so they are a little less abrasive. Of course, our partner could make things easier by trying to improve and change. But our partner has a great excuse: they can't help it. Not only do we buy that excuse, but we're the major driving force for making it viable. Deep down we think men and women are fundamentally different, which makes change nearly impossible. And if we believe that all men are the same and all women are the same, and the man or woman in our life isn't being the best partner, it's not even worth changing partners. The next one would just be more of the same. We're stuck.

Having low standards, not expecting improvement, and feeling like we're trapped are problems. Each of these holds our relationship back because each inhibits relationship quality.

Worse, each is self-imposed and may seem innocent because it is so ubiquitous. So much so that you may not have recognized the issue until now.

It's simple: differences create distance. When you bust the myth of male and female differences, the distance between you and your partner will begin to fade. Instead of being adversaries, you're teammates. Trade in your archrival for an ally.

HOW TO SEE YOUR RELATIONSHIP MORE CLEARLY

> We love the tangible, the confirmation, the palpable, the real, the visible, the concrete, the known, the seen, the vivid, the visual.
>
> —*Nassim Taleb*, The Black Swan

It's true, we like to take the easy route and not get caught up in the nuance or complexities. When trying to understand others, it's simpler to think in terms of men and women than to take into account all the traits and qualities that make a person who they are. We have a natural bias toward efficiency because we're cognitive misers who conserve mental energy by seeking simplicity and minimizing mental effort.[18] Differences are easy to spot, so we do. There's no denying that men and women look different, vary in their physical capabilities, and have distinct hobbies. But these facts are largely inconsequential for relationships and they bypass any deeper consideration of what makes a person tick. Who's got time for that? Well, anyone who really wants to get it right.

Think in Terms of Continuums, Not Categories

To see past a blind spot, we must look beyond basic gender differences. The first step is to take the time to seek out and celebrate the abundant similarities inherent in every relationship. Relish the common ground. Make an effort to notice, and appreciate, all the ways you and your partner are similar, for example, in your age, where you're from, or your ethnicity, socioeconomic status, family values, religious beliefs, upbringing, schooling, political beliefs, thoughts on marriage, interests, personality traits, and favorite TV shows, movies, music, and sports teams, to name a few. Similarities are hiding in plain sight.

We also need to stop cutting corners and put in the effort to think more deeply. We need to realize that we often use superficial indicators like gender to shape our impressions of others. It isn't as helpful as we think. Rather, we're just falling back on generalizations that overshadow individuality. Worse, delineating groups automatically creates a "me versus you, us versus them" mentality. To break this habit, we must stop reacting in terms of basic either-or distinctions. Instead of reflexively deciding someone is either an introvert or an extrovert, we need to focus on where a person falls along a continuum. We all fall somewhere in between the extremes. It's a key life lesson: black-and-white thinking is always wrong. Everything is a shade of gray. True enlightenment about how our partner thinks, feels, and behaves comes from seeing past their gender and appreciating their intricacies.

When we do, we should know that the research is on our side. A study of thirteen thousand individuals looked at more than one hundred characteristics on a wide range of variables, including many that directly impact relationships like intimacy, masculinity-femininity, sexual attitudes and behaviors, mate preferences, empathy, and interdependence. The researchers wanted to see whether there were sex differences in the variables or if men and women merely fell on a shared spectrum. Which ones tended to fall on a continuum? Every. Single. One. The researchers said it best: "Contrary to the assertions of pop psychology titles like *Men Are from Mars, Women Are from Venus* and *The Rules,* it is untrue that men and women think about their relationships in qualitatively different ways." When we're ready to ditch oversimplified categories, we can embrace the next big insight: to truly understand our partner, we need to think more like a psychologist. To do that we need to shed our reliance on stark demographic categories in favor of richer information sources, such as our partner's mood, personality, skills, abilities, motivation, characteristics, and behaviors.

Fill in the blanks: "In relationships, _____ care more about sex, while _____ care more about love." It's tempting to think, "Men are definitely sex crazed, while women care about love." But we need to think deeper. Allow me to introduce you to sociosexuality.[19] It's a psychological variable centered on how much a person views sex, love, and commitment as interconnected. At one end of the continuum are individuals who are "unrestricted." For them, love and sex are distinct. They differentiate the experiences and are able to have sex with minimal emotional closeness or commitment to the other person. On the opposite end are the "restricted." For them, love and sex are intertwined and inextricably linked so that it would be difficult to experience one without the other. However, unrestricted and restricted are just the two ends of the spectrum.

How Do You Measure Up?
Sociosexuality

Curious whether you're more restricted or unrestricted in your sociosexuality? Consider these items, inspired by the original scale researchers used.[20] To what extent do you agree with the following statements?

1. I could have sex with someone and not be in love with them.
   Strongly Disagree 1 2 3 4 5 6 7 Strongly Agree
2. In order to really enjoy sex, it needs to happen in a long-term loving relationship.
   Strongly Disagree 1 2 3 4 5 6 7 Strongly Agree

If you agree with the first item more than the second, you're more unrestricted. However, if your score on the second was higher than on the first, you're more restricted. If they're equal, you're right in the middle.[21]

That means that most people, both men and women, fall somewhere in between. To be sure, there are men who are predominantly unrestricted. But there are also plenty of unrestricted women, as well as highly restricted men. A person's sex doesn't dictate their sociosexuality, and vice versa.

Ultimately, a person's sociosexuality tells us a lot more about their behavior than knowing if they're a guy or a girl. Their sociosexuality relates to their interest in casual sex, sex with multiple partners, and a propensity to cheat. According to a 2018 study, sociosexuality can even help identify who uses Tinder to cheat on their partner.[22] "Typical guy move, right?"

Wrong. Now that we're thinking in terms of psychological variables, the study results won't be a surprise. Men and women with unrestricted sociosexuality, who consider love and sex distinct, were more likely to use Tinder to cheat. In other words, who a person is psychologically, not their gender, influences their relationship behaviors.

Share the Power

When trying to pin down other psychological variables that influence relationships, there are plenty to choose from, but power is perhaps the most revealing of all. Power is the ability for one person to exert influence over how another person thinks, feels, and behaves. Many alleged male-female differences are actually the result of power imbalances that favor men. One meta-analysis focused on societal gender differences confirms this.[23] In societies that are more egalitarian, with greater nationwide gender equality, gender differences are smaller—in other words, men and women are more similar. But in societies that favor either men or women (most typically men), the sexes are a lot less similar. That's power at the societal level, but you can also see the impact of power within the relationship, starting from the very beginning.

When it comes to choosing a relationship partner, you might assume that women are pickier. They often are.[24] But that is in the context of traditional dating scenarios where men need to take the initiative and approach women. The problem is that this situation has very clear power dynamics. In fact, it's one of the rare instances where women have all the power. In this context, men must work up the courage to introduce themselves and risk rejection; women simply need to accept or reject. When you have the power, you're going to make sure you get what's best for you. When you don't have the power, you have to take what the powerful are willing to give.

Researchers became curious about this dynamic and wanted to flip the dating script.[25] They tested what I call the "Sadie Hawkins effect," or what happens when women have the opportunity to invert social convention by assuming the role of relationship initiator. To do this, the researchers had more than three hundred undergraduates participate in a speed-dating event, where participants had a series of quick meet-and-greets with potential partners. In half of those meetings, participants followed the standard script, where men circulated and approached women, who each stayed in one place. For the other half, the men stayed in one place while the women circulated around the room, Sadie Hawkins style. In both kinds of meetings, regardless of whether they were male or female, those who remained stationary and had people approach them were pickier. Those who moved around the room and repeatedly made the approach were less picky. Ultimately, a person's pickiness was more about their power in the situation and less about being male or female.

Because power exerts so much influence, it's important to get a handle on our relationship's power dynamics. First, figure out who wields more power by applying the "principle of least interest."[26] In this context, "least interest" indicates who needs or cares about the relationship less. Key signs of lower relationship need include exerting more influence on their partner and relationship, making more decisions, winning more arguments, and generally controlling the relationship. Importantly, the person with less interest has more power. This imbalance of power traditionally favors men.

How Do You Measure Up?
Your Relationship's Power Dynamics

In your relationship, does one of you have the upper hand? Or do you and your partner share the power? Circle the best answer for each of the following questions:

1. Who makes most of the decisions?   Me   My Partner
2. Who has the most influence over the relationship's future?   Me   My Partner
3. Which person has the views that carry the most weight?   Me   My Partner
4. Which person gets their way most often?   Me   My Partner
5. Who is more persuasive?   Me   My Partner
6. Which person is less emotionally involved in the relationship?   Me   My Partner
7. Who could find a new partner more easily if the relationship ended?   Me   My Partner

For each item, the person you circled has more power. If you add up all the items, you can get a sense of your relationship's power dynamic. Note that this is merely a snapshot based solely on your opinion. When researchers assess power, they collect information from both partners and then compare the results to determine relative power levels.

Power imbalances have consequences. To see how power differentials masquerade as gender differences, consider a person's ability to decipher another's unspoken signals. There's pretty consistent evidence that women are better than men at reading a partner's nonverbal cues, like facial expressions, gestures, and body language. Why? Deciphering nonverbal signals isn't easy, so perhaps women try harder. If men typically have more power in the relationship, it means they can get by on less effort. Men may not necessarily be worse at reading subtle signals; they may just not bother.

To see if guys had a true skill deficit or simply weren't bothering to pay attention to others, in one study, researchers had male and female participants work on a series of word puzzles while seated across from another male or female participant.[27] During the task, half the participants were told the puzzle task was a competition with the winner getting five dollars; the other half just thought they had to complete a puzzle. Afterward, the researchers asked everyone what their partner looked like (e.g., facial features, clothing). Importantly, participants didn't know the researchers were going to ask this ahead of time; therefore, they would have had to take the time to notice during the task.

The results indicated that without incentive, women were much better at giving details about the other person. However, once there was prize money and glory on the line, men closed the gap and were better at describing their partner. The prize money gave men an incentive to pay attention. In other words, paying attention to others isn't necessarily a hardwired male-female difference. Instead, it depends on a person's willingness to put in the effort. When you have more power (as men often do), taking the time to consider others isn't a priority. That said, men can do it but need a reason to care. That's an important conclusion because our partner can't change their gender, but we can work on our relationship's power dynamics.

Regardless of which partner is "winning" the power struggle, it is important to realize that an imbalance of power isn't good for anyone and threatens your relationship. The ideal situation is one in which partners share power equally, with a balance in decision-making, control, and influence. Keeping a strict equality in all areas is less important than having a fair overall balance, so if one person really wants to dominate in car care while the other wants to be the interior-decorating czar, that's fine. The good news is that power dynamics are malleable.

This gives us something absolutely crucial: hope. Change is possible. Gender isn't destiny. Using purely gender-based explanations locks in our partner's behaviors. If we think guys aren't very thoughtful, assuming our male partner will always be a guy, there is very little room for improvement. You'll be perpetually stuck with an inconsiderate male partner. However, if instead we focus on thoughtfulness, there is a path for improvement. Our partner making himself less of a guy is a tough ask, but with a bit of effort and practice anyone can work on being more thoughtful. Ultimately, believing the myth that men and women are different is an excuse. It's a way to absolve both partners of responsibility for their actions. "It's not me, I'm just a dude. This is how we are." This type of "boys will be boys" and "she's such a girly girl" mentality holds our relationships back. It's past time to realize that we have more control over our beliefs.

RELATIONSHIP RECAP

- Men are the real romantics in relationships.
- The scientific evidence overwhelmingly shows that men and women are from the same planet.
- Your beliefs about men and women can attract you to the wrong people and undermine your relationship by lowering your standards, discouraging you from looking for a better partner, and discouraging your partner from improving.
- Want a better explanation for male and female differences in love and sex? Look no further than sociosexuality.
- You keep blaming gender differences. The real culprit is your relationship's balance of power (an imbalance that favors men).
- According to the Sadie Hawkins effect, when dating roles are reversed, women act just like men, and vice versa.

Chapter 3

"True Love Should Be Perfect and Effortless"

appy Anniversary." At least that's what the card said. It was hard to argue with the anniversary part, but "happy"? That was debatable. Lately things between Ryley and Jayden had been decidedly "meh." How did they get to this point? They once had the magical, carefree, and easy relationship everyone wants. They were the perfect couple. Everyone said so. After all, Ryley and Jayden were soul mates, destined for each other. It should have been simple. Except it wasn't.

Ryley and Jayden didn't have any major issues. Neither of them had ever cheated or been abusive in any way. They were content and generally happy, but for Ryley, that wasn't enough. Ryley fully owns the fact that she can be picky. But she also believes that demanding high standards is the only way to get the picture-perfect relationship she sees plastered all over social media. The problem is that high standards are hard to maintain. Ryley is reminded daily of how her relationship with Jayden falls short of perfection. Now she can't help but feel like she's settling for less than she deserves. If they were truly destined to be together, isn't this a bad sign? Where did she go wrong?

CHECKING YOUR BLIND SPOT

We all have expectations for ourselves, benchmarks that we use in order to gauge our progress and accomplishments (or lack thereof). Am I successful enough? Thin enough? A good mother? A good friend? Do I live in the best place for me? Am I making a difference in the world? How we answer these questions directly impacts how we feel. The problem is, we're often unkind to ourselves when making comparisons between our reality and our expectations. We hold ourselves to impossible standards, then lament our shortcomings. We know our hopes might be unrealistic, the byproduct of perfectionistic tendencies.

The Perfection Trap

Yet overly ambitious goals are a blind spot that feels right; we feel we deserve to achieve our ideals.

It's a trap. Sadly, one in which our relationships are easily ensnared.

If we're being honest, we all want the storybook ending, to have the perfect relationship that stands the test of time, to be part of the supercouple that everyone admires and aspires to be. No one aims for mediocrity. We hope for a Mary Poppins future: practically perfect in every way. But that's difficult to achieve, much less maintain. Then again, we've seen glimpses of it in our own love life, especially early on. Back then, everything was exactly how we always hoped it would be. Flawless. It isn't so crazy to want that early relationship bliss to last forever. As our current relationship falls short, doubt creeps in. When that happens it's natural to wonder whether our relationship is living up to our expectations. Careful, though, because that type of thinking is a blind spot that can ruin an otherwise great relationship.

The perfection trap gets set when we start confusing what we consider ideal with what is realistic. Sometimes the difference is easy to see. For example, most of us would ideally like to be multimillionaires and live in mansions by the beach, but we realize this isn't ever likely to happen. When we get our sub-sub-sub-millionaire paychecks, we aren't devastated. We don't think about quitting. Yet, when it comes to our relationships, we're more stubborn about the ideal-versus-real distinction. And we're somewhat unapologetic about demanding relationship perfection. It isn't that we're self-important or entitled. Rather, all the romance we see in the world around us — in life, on-screen, or in books — leads us to believe that relationships should be perfectly magical. We want happily ever after and believe that with the right partner we'll get it. Sadly, fairy-tale endings are more idealistic than realistic. To be an idealist is to be out of touch. We recognize that, but when we reframe our idealism as perfectionism, we convince ourselves that it's a hidden virtue.

The research on perfectionist tendencies is pretty clear.[1] A chapter title from an academic book on the topic says it all: "Deep, Dark, and Dysfunctional: The Destructiveness of Interpersonal Perfectionism." In other words, if we insist on exceptionally high quality in our lives, we're setting ourselves up for misery. Now, the perfection impulse can cut at least two ways. You can expect perfection from yourself in terms of how you treat others. Holding ourselves to unrealistic standards can make life difficult, but it's nothing compared to when we foist our perfectionism on others.[2] Imposing perfectionism involves holding our relationship partner to really high standards, having exaggerated expectations, and critically evaluating our partner. This mindset can make us more distrustful, vindictive, dominant, aggressive, and arrogant, and less empathic. Who wants a partner like that? According to research, no one.[3] Judgy partners are no fun.

Bonus Blind Spot:
Perfectly Vulnerable

When we want near perfection, we believe that our partner desires the same thing. So, any one of our flaws, weaknesses, or vulnerabilities could potentially disappoint our partner, an intimidating thought. A 2018 study asked individuals about their own weaknesses and vulnerabilities, as well as how they viewed vulnerability in others.[4] Researchers had participants think of times they were less than their most perfect, resilient selves, either when they admitted a mistake, asked for help, focused on their body's imperfections, or confessed romantic feelings. Participants also gave their perceptions of others in the same situations. The results revealed that the participants were harsh critics of their own vulnerability, yet viewed others' vulnerability positively. In other words, when we fall short of perfection, we're much too hard on ourselves. Not only are others more forgiving, but they can view slipups as a positive sign, a phenomenon known as the pratfall effect. Mistakes can

---

be humanizing, even endearing. The implication for our relationships is clear. Our partners don't expect us to be perfect. In
fact, when we make a mess of things, they are likely to find
more beauty in our shortcomings than we do.

Wanting to be a perfect couple seems innocent, even helpful. Many people view relationships as a perfect union between
two souls. Sounds magical. To test whether such perfection
was helpful, researchers approached pedestrians walking along
the street in Ann Arbor, Michigan, and asked for their views
on relationships.[5] Those who thought of the relationship as a
perfect union reported lower relationship satisfaction when
thinking about past conflict. Those seemingly magical views
about perfection actually undermined the relationship.

That's the thing. Our best intentions lead us astray. No one
sets out to find a bad relationship, or even one that is decidedly
mediocre. Everyone wants to be better than average. That's
smart, because higher-quality relationships are happier and
more stable. But this "more is better" approach is ultimately
counterproductive. In fact, there is increasing evidence in psychology, particularly within positive psychology, that otherwise good attributes can have negative consequences when
taken to the extreme.[6] In essence, we can have too much of a
good thing. For example, being courageous is good. However,
being overly courageous can encourage risk taking, reckless-
ness, and exposure to unnecessary dangers. In relationships,
wanting a high-quality relationship is good. But taken to the
extreme, as in the pursuit of perfection, that desire can have
detrimental effects, like rigid and unrealistic expectations, fail-

ure to appreciate one's partner, or a persistent feeling of falling short. The key is to seek a happy and realistic middle ground.

If wanting perfection is such a bad idea, why did we acquire such maladaptive beliefs? As social animals, we naturally learn about who we are by comparing ourselves to others. Are you fast or slow? Race other people and find out. We may not take part in these types of competitions, but we run a lot of races in our head. We like to win, so most of the time we compare ourselves to others who are worse off than us. We find people who make less money, are less attractive, experience more stress, and have more problems in their relationship. Winning those mental competitions makes us feel superior. Sometimes, though, we're confronted by others who are doing better than we are. In these cases, we're forced to acknowledge our shortcomings. Our looks, lifestyle, and relationship feel inferior. We lose the race and consequently become envious of the life or relationship we don't have. Our expectations shift upward. We want more. We want to win. We want what others already seem to have.

That feels bad, so we're not eager to acknowledge areas where we fall short. Now, thanks to social media, this is unavoidable. Every day our social media force-feed us idyllic versions of others' lives. We are bombarded with an unending stream of smiling couples doing interesting things together, having fun, and looking very much in love. These images can give us an inferiority complex, along with major guilt over our less-than-picture-perfect relationships. Don't worry; you're not alone. In studying how participants reacted to Facebook posts, researchers found that when couples made their relationships on Facebook highly visible by posting a lot, participants believed that the couples were more committed and happier.[7]

Ready for a dirty little secret? They're not. A study examining the association between posting on Facebook and relationship quality showed that those couples who worked the hardest to craft the perfect image of their relationship actually had worse relationships than those who were less inclined to broadcast their relationship.[8] In fact, people posted about their relationship on Facebook when they felt less confident and secure about their partner's feelings about the relationship. It seems the cure for relationship uncertainty was to seek reassurance by publicly posting about the relationship. Have a fight? Post a picture from a recent vacation or date night to prove to the world (and yourself) that all is well. Refraining from posting the perfect relfie (a term my colleagues and I coined to describe a relationship selfie of you and your partner) never sounded so good.

If we let them, those idyllic couples on social media can warp our perceptions and create unrealistic expectations. And we can't lose sight of the fact that everything we see has been carefully curated. Our friends' and family's relationships could be complete train wrecks, but no one posts the bad stuff. Those seemingly perfect relationships are an overedited false utopia, a mirage. When we see only the greatest hits, it's easy to jump to conclusions. Even offline, what we see isn't necessarily what we get. People put up a facade that masks what's really going on. When couples divorce, others often remark, "But they seemed so happy." That duck smoothly gliding across a pond has little feet kicking like crazy below the surface. It's easy to forget the parts that remain unseen.

Take, for example, a high-profile couple with a seemingly model relationship: Barack and Michelle Obama. From the outside, they seem to enjoy spending time together; they support each other and appear happily married. Despite navigating their relationship in one of the most stressful situations imaginable, they made it look easy. But in an *Insider* article recapping an interview with Robin Roberts, Michelle divulged that their relationship wasn't perfect and, in fact, required a lot of work.[9] The Obamas have even gone to marriage counseling. Michelle explains their relationship reality as follows: "I know too many young couples who struggle and think somehow, there's something wrong with them....I want them to know that Michelle and Barack Obama—who have a phenomenal marriage and who love each other—we work on our marriage and we get help with our marriage when we need it." That type of honesty is rare, but it's real and awfully reassuring. When we see snippets of relationship success on TV or in our own lives, we need to remember that a ton of hard work has inevitably gone into it.

Maximizing the Relationship

Having really high expectations for your relationship feels like the right thing to do. But you must be careful not to be unrealistic, hypercritical, or too picky. Some of us routinely want to have it all, demanding excellence in order to be happy and insisting that the very best option is the only viable one. Researchers refer to people who take this approach as "maximizers."[10] Right about now, anyone with maximizer tendencies is likely wondering, "Wait. What's wrong with being picky?" Maximizers feel like they deserve the absolute best, so the only reasonable approach is to hold their relationship up to a very high standard.

To achieve that superlative relationship, maximizer types

will explore all possibilities to find the flawless partner. This might sound like common sense: demand the best, get the best. But the research paints a different picture. Maximizers not only fail to achieve the best; they report more regret, depression, and feeling more threatened by others who are doing better than them.[11] Maximizers also experience lower self-esteem and less optimism, happiness, and life satisfaction. Because of their desire for perfection and continual improvement, maximizers prefer reversible decisions or outcomes that are not absolute.[12] In other words, they want an easy out if things don't meet their high standards. See the problem? In our long-term relationships, we tend to favor the "until death do us part" over the "until I find something better" approach. The implication for relationships is clear: continually pursuing the very best causes us to fail to appreciate the truly great relationship we've had all along.

The Soul-Mate Solution?

Sometimes we fall into the perfection trap because of our fundamental beliefs about how relationships work. One culprit is a form of perfectionism that masquerades as the ultimate goal in love: finding our soul mate. The underlying assumption is that once we do so, we'll have found our dream relationship. The problem is, soul mates are more mythical than magical. Here's the fatal flaw. Believing in soul mates is an all-or-nothing proposition. Partners are meant for each other or they're not. It isn't up to us; it's up to destiny. When Chip Knee from the University of Houston studied relationships over several months, he found that when partners believed they were meant for each other, those relationships lasted longer, provided the relationship started off happy.[13] That makes sense. When the relationship goes well and everything's working, being with a soul mate is ideal. But there is a downside. Since the partner is meant to be our "one and only," it creates a lot of pressure for things to work out. After all, a soul mate is our ideal match, so perfection is a must. What happens when the relationship inevitably hits shaky spots? Uh-oh. This wasn't supposed to happen. Doubts creep in because perfect fits shouldn't be so flawed.

For this reason, that same study found, when participants believed in destiny and encountered inevitable relationship stressors like money, jealousy, or conflict, they dealt with them by avoiding the issues. That's right. Rather than admit there was a problem or confront it head-on, they dodged the issue. It was almost as if by ignoring issues, they could preserve their partner's soul-mate status. But that tactic works for only so long. The fact that the relationship is faltering can mean only one thing: perhaps this partner isn't really your true soul mate. Research says that rather than sticking around to make it work, those who believe in soul mates are also more likely to end their relationships. They're more likely to move on in search of their "true" soul mate. Of course, this latest quest is bound to fail, too. Time to call off the search.

If we're completely honest, we must know on some level that we're going to fall short of our perfect ideals. It happens all the time. Are we as productive as we would like to be? Do we make as much money as we'd like? Sleep, exercise, or eat healthy as much as we'd like? Live in the house of our dreams? Vacation in the most stunning destination? For most people the answer is "no" (or perhaps more optimistically, "not yet"). The reality is that we routinely fall short of our ideals.

If missing the mark is so common, it may seem harmless. If only that were the case. Unfortunately, having a gap between our perfectionistic ideals and our reality negatively impacts our happiness and self-esteem. How we feel about ourselves depends on how our actual self, or the person we really are, compares to our ideal self, or the person we wish we were and hope to become.[14] The smaller the gap between the two, the better we feel about ourselves. However, when the person we are falls short of who we aspire to be, our self-esteem takes a hit. The same basic principle applies to relationships. Everyone has preexisting beliefs and expectations about what an ideal relationship looks like. But we also have the reality of the relationship we're actually in. When our real-life partner fails to live up to our aspirational ideal, it hurts. Research suggests that the further our relationship falls from our ideal standard, the less happy we are.[15] And the less happy we are, the less willing we are to invest time and energy in the relationship and, ultimately, the less committed we are. There's another insidious angle to all this. If our partner doesn't measure up, we might start to envision a relationship with another partner, one who comes closer to fulfilling our ideals. Now our partner has to compete with an imaginary alternative who not only doesn't exist but is impossible to live up to. All of which undermines the current relationship.

When we recognize our relationship is falling short of our ideals, we experience a range of negative emotions, such as anger, shame, envy, and disgust. We often don't know how to effectively deal with these feelings. We try to cope, but the data suggest that most of the strategies we use aren't helpful and make things worse.[16] We might punish our substandard partner by penalizing or disparaging them, perhaps as a way of enticing them to improve. We might also be critical of our-selves or try to avoid our partner. But these strategies are all strongly linked to negative emotions and lower relationship satisfaction. While no one enjoys failing to meet expectations, this is particularly problematic for those who believe in soul mates. When confronted with their partner's shortcomings, soul-mate believers had especially low satisfaction and dis-played hostility when discussing relationship discrepancies.[17] Missing the mark even by a little bit poses a danger to the relationship.

When the relationship doesn't meet our standards, the rela-tionship itself may not be the problem. The real issue is cling-ing to unrealistic and unattainable expectations. Make no mistake: desiring perfection, or even near perfection, can be ruinous. If our partner can't live up to our expectations, it is easy to start thinking a different partner might. Suddenly, leaving seems like the only reasonable solution. Rather than pulling the plug, rethinking our perspective on perfection will help us avoid undervaluing the relationship we have.

HOW TO SEE YOUR RELATIONSHIP MORE CLEARLY

Here's a basic truth: no one wants to settle. So don't. Everyone deserves to have a great relationship. That said, "great" doesn't mean perfect and "great" doesn't involve a lengthy checklist of "must-have" traits. We convince ourselves that checklists are necessary and even have an innocent-sounding term to match: "relationshopping."[18] When researchers asked online daters to describe how they went about searching for a partner, one explained it this way: "like picking out the perfect parts for my machine where I can get exactly what I want and nothing I don't want." Another described it as "shopping-cart mentality," which the researchers explained could lead to "the tendency to shop for people with the perfect qualifications." When properly calibrated, ideals are a major asset. They perform quality control by clarifying what's important to us and helping us avoid settling for less. Ultimately, ideals give us guidelines of what we need to work on in our relationship to make it better.

Embrace Imperfection

To evade relationship doom, we shouldn't ditch our ideals but do need to fine-tune our thinking. Spoiler alert: no relationship will ever be perfect. Your relationship isn't perfect. Time to face reality and realize that acknowledging and accepting imperfections isn't betraying your partner or giving up on your relationship. It simply means you're being honest. Perfection is a myth. There's no such thing as always or never. Your partner won't always be nice, happy, funny, or attractive. They also can't entirely avoid being annoying, boring, or grumpy. One hundred percent doesn't exist in the real world. Weddings aren't 100 percent full of happiness, and funerals aren't 100 percent sad. Life is messy, complicated, and ambiguous. People are complex. Bad people do good things, just as good people can do bad things. Your job, family, kids, and friends all have their flaws. So does your partner. Even diamonds have their blemishes. That's being realistic.

Appreciating your relationship's value, warts and all, is part of the deal. You need to avoid succumbing to the ostrich effect, where you metaphorically stick your head in the sand to escape your problems. This is like throwing out a credit card bill you'd like to ignore. It always comes back to haunt you. Temporary relief, but long-term regret. Accepting the reality that your relationship is imperfect is the wiser approach.

How Do You Measure Up?
Maximizer/Satisficer

Perfection is a trap that some people are more likely to fall into than others. Are you one of them? While researchers use much more in-depth ways to determine if a person is a maximizer or a satisficer,[19] if you're curious about your own tendencies, here is a quick test:

Which of the following do you agree with more?

1. In whatever I do, I want to get the absolute most out of it.
2. I'm okay with not having the best, as long as it is good enough to meet my needs.

If you picked the first option, you're more of a maximizer; if you selected option 2, you have more satisficer tendencies. Of course, this gives just a glimpse of your general tendency. Your maximizing-satisficing inclinations will vary depending on the context.[20]

Even better, embrace the flaws. Admittedly, that suggestion will be hard for some, especially maximizers, to accept. But there's a better way. Instead of demanding perfection, we need to accept flaws by establishing an achievable benchmark of quality that would satisfy us. This is how a "satisficer" would approach relationships. For satisficers, "good enough" is perfectly acceptable. That's the key. Satisficers want to be happy, but they accept flaws and don't demand perfection. Rather, they have realistic expectations. It's the difference between saying you'll be happy only if you're a millionaire (classic maximizer) and saying you'll be happy provided you're financially stable and don't have to worry about money (classic satisficer). Satisficers have better outcomes as a result.

The key to being a good satisficer is to drop any hint of an "I want it all" mentality. Aim for "perfectly good" rather than "practically perfect."

Perfectly Good

In order to know whether your relationship is "perfectly good," you need to think through what truly matters most in your relationship. The first step in establishing your priorities is to identify key influences. Perhaps the biggest contributor is the culture in which we grew up. To help determine culture's impact, nine researchers from institutions around the world asked nearly ten thousand participants from five continents about the "ideal life that you'd want to live" in domains such as health, intelligence, self-esteem, pleasure, and happiness.[21] Their results have a few important takeaways. First, we are not born maximizers who demand perfection. Rather, the "I want it all" mentality seeps in from our broader environment. The data suggest that respondents from holistic cultures that focus on interconnectedness such as China, Hong Kong, Japan, and India were less likely to maximize than respondents from cultures focused on individualism like the United States, United Kingdom, Canada, Germany, and France.

Second, when respondents from holistic cultures described their ideals, they weren't so perfect. In fact, they were quite modest. When it came to things like longevity and intelligence, although participants could have wished for the absolute best, they didn't. People from holistic cultures didn't want the perfection of living longer or being smarter than 99 percent of others. Instead, they were content with being above average. They were content with imperfection and okay with being perfectly good enough. In other words, growing up in a holistic culture seemed to encourage a realistic satisficer mindset. Regardless of the culture we find ourselves in, the holistic contentment with imperfection will help our relationship. This perspective is consistent with the ancient Greek notion that in between the extremes of inferiority and perfection lies a virtuous golden mean, or place of moderation. When we apply this concept to our relationships, it's easier to accept not getting everything we want and to appreciate, instead, what we already have. When we embrace our relationship's golden mean, we're better equipped to resist cultural pressures that encourage a "more is better" mentality.

But what is our relationship's golden mean? Simple: a relationship that takes a little effort, one that works through problems and seeks continual improvement. In other words, a growth mindset that treats the relationship as a work in progress. In fact, research shows that those who believe that relationships aren't instantly perfect work harder at maintaining the relationship and focus more on long-term happiness than instant gratification.[22] The "we can work it out" crowd is also more likely to use assurances like saying "I love you" and to practice more positivity.[23] Believing that quality relationships are grown over time also helps couples overcome problems and increases partners' willingness to sacrifice by putting the relationship's needs before their own.[24] On the other hand, those who believe in predestined soul mates are more likely to commit relationship violence. Yikes.

We also need to revise the way we think about passion, or the hot-and-heavy aspects of the relationship. One way to think about it is that a relationship either has the spark of passion or it doesn't.[25] If that flame fades, it is lost forever. Rather than believing in irreversible decay, we could believe that when passion begins to fizzle, we can rekindle the heat. Research from 2019 on how these different perspectives impact relationships found that those who believed it was possible to recapture passion were less likely to pursue other partners and were more committed to their relationships.

The Work Makes It Worth It

Our quest to revitalize our relationship starts by changing our relationship mindset. We need to avoid the mistaken belief that good relationships are simple and effortless and should blossom with a naturally occurring ease. Romantic notions, to be sure, but our life isn't a rom-com. And that's okay. Our relationship is worth the effort. Besides, relationships that take a little work are better off than those that seem effortless. Here's an interesting quirk of psychology: we like things less when they're too easy to get. The opposite is also true: we like things more when we have to work for them. This "work hard, like more" phenomenon has been proven repeatedly in social psychology. For example, in one experiment, one set of women read a passage that included highly sexual words to a discussion group, while another read a passage with more mild vocabulary to the group.[26] The women who had the more difficult and embarrassing task (i.e., reading highly sexual words like "cock" out loud) ended up liking their group more than those who had the easy task. The reason this works is simple: we hate being inconsistent.[27] If we're going to endure awkwardness, struggle, pain, or heartache, there must be a good reason. Working hard for something worthless is inconsistent and senseless. For that reason, we convince ourselves that when we expend effort, it must be for something valuable. In other words, our behaviors (effort) and thoughts (perceptions of our effort's results) must align.

This is true in our relationships. A relationship that has overcome hardships will seem more worthwhile. After all, we need to justify the effort we've invested. With this in mind, the secret is to embrace the difficult times because those struggles enhance positive feelings for the relationship. When researchers looked at 795 couples in their first marriage, relationship satisfaction was higher when partners put more effort into the relationship.[28] Couples who worked harder were also less likely to divorce. All that work isn't a sign of what's wrong but rather a sign of their dedication to make the relationship right. High-quality relationships aren't easy. Love is more than just how we feel. Love is the action we take to actively engage with our relationship. Just as a professional singer, athlete, or musician continues to practice, couples need to keep working at it.

See the Bigger Picture by Paying Attention to Patterns

We need to stop wasting time, energy, and effort obsessing over inevitable imperfections. Instead, we should focus on where the real action is: the ups and downs. It's time to keep track of relationship volatility so we can see whether we're heading for happily ever or never after. The research here is clear: couples with more ups and downs experience more distress and negative behaviors,[29] more depression,[30] less commitment, and an increased likelihood of breaking up.[31] Importantly, volatility tends to be higher in newer couples but decreases as relationships become more established.[32]

Being clued in to volatility is a step in the right direction. But relationship ups and downs aren't created equal. Rather, the pattern of changes in satisfaction and commitment also matters. For example, a declining relationship could experience a slow and steady slide, a few moderate bumps in the road, or a major drop-off. Or a relationship could be steady, experience a rough patch, and then rebound to new and improved levels.

Relationship ebbs and flows have important implications for your relationship's health. The problem is that relationship insiders (i.e., us, when we look at our own relationship) have a hard time keeping track of how the relationship changes over time. The solution is simple. You should keep a daily journal of how you feel about your relationship over several months. Each day, consider how fulfilled you are and give it a rating on a 10-point scale (1: Not at All; 10: Completely). If you want to get fancy, you could also chart other aspects, like happiness, amount of conflict, passion, compatibility, or warmth toward your partner. Because any fluctuations are likely to be subtle on a day-to-day basis, a journal will make it easier to look back and see the larger patterns that develop over three- to six-month periods, especially if you include a chart that maps out your thoughts over time. If you want to go more high-tech, as

Bonus Blind Spot:
Watching the Ups and Downs

If you could chart the story of your relationship, what would it look like? A straight, ascending line showing steady improvement? A curvy line showing that you've hit some bumps along the way but remain strong? To determine if partners' different trajectories in commitment to wed influence how the relationship's story ends, researcher Brian Ogolsky and colleagues from the University of Illinois interviewed 376 dating couples in their midtwenties and had them chart what they thought the likelihood of marriage was over time.[33] Researchers analyzed the graphs for the number of turning points, noting any downturns in chances of marriage, and identified patterns—for example, whether relationship dynamics escalated quickly or slowly eroded. Participants updated their graphs over the next several months and provided information about changes in relationship status — such as transitioning from dating to broken up, from casual to serious dating, from serious dating to engaged, and so on. From this data, researchers identified four key patterns of relationship change that fit most participants:

- **Dramatic** (34 percent of the sample) — These participants' relationships were very much up and down, including steeper changes in commitment and more downturns compared to other groups. This group had lower opinions of their own relationship, spent more time away from their relationship, and had less support from friends and family.
- **Partner focused** (30 percent of the sample) — This group approached commitment by making their partner the

center of their universe and reported very few downturns. Changes in commitment were largely due to whether they spent time with their partner.

- **Socially involved** (19 percent of the sample) — This group was very steady and reported fewer downturns compared to those in the dramatic and conflict-ridden groups (described in the following paragraph). However, changes were the result of what friends and family thought about the relationship, as well as how much they interacted with their partner's social network.

- **Conflict-ridden** (12 percent of the sample) — These participants were fighters who experienced a large number of downturns due to relationship conflicts. Though they had numerous dips in their commitment to wed, they were not very steep. Compared to the partner-focused group, these participants had fewer positive things to say about the relationship. They also received less friend and family support than the socially involved group.

Perhaps most telling was that the dramatic group was more than twice as likely to break up compared to any of the other three groups. Those in the partner-focused group were more likely to have their relationship progress (for instance, advancing from casual to serious dating) than those in the dramatic group. In other words, those who experience substantial fluctuations in their commitment should have concerns about the relationship's long-term sustainability.

they say, "There's an app for that." StayGo is a free app that I created with several collaborators that includes a "Relationship Tracker" feature. It operates like a Fitbit for relationships that checks in with you every day, asking a few questions you can answer within seconds on your phone. As you rate your relationship daily, the tracker charts the ratings over time, allowing you to see fluctuations in a more objective way and avoid relying solely on potentially flawed perceptions. Both strategies (low-tech and high-tech) allow you to see patterns and identify volatility. They also give you a chance to appreciate any progress your relationship has made that you might otherwise have missed.

RELATIONSHIP RECAP

- No one should aspire to have a perfect relationship. Perfection is a mirage that can ruin a perfectly good relationship.
- Struggle is real. Embrace it as a secret to a strong relationship. When you experience hardships together, they make your relationship matter to you and your partner.
- People who post more about their relationships on Facebook often have worse relationships.
- You should give up on finding your soul mate. You're much better off planning to grow your relationship.
- Shift your focus to what really matters. Your relationship's ebbs and flows offer a glimpse of your relationship's potential and can predict the relationship's future.

Chapter 4

"I Can't Be Attracted to Someone Who Isn't Gorgeous and Successful"

Stunning. That was the only word that came to mind when Bryce first saw Kayla. She was everything he had ever wanted. She just had that look. Make no mistake, Bryce knew Kayla was way hotter than him, and if he happened to forget, his friends frequently reminded him that she was "out of his league." Bryce relished it because it felt like an accomplishment. Kayla loved it too, fully embracing her role as Bryce's trophy girlfriend. She took pride in her looks and liked that Bryce took notice.

It wasn't like Bryce was unattractive. As Kayla put it, Bryce possessed a charm and magnetic personality that naturally drew you into his orbit. In social settings, Bryce could command a room and reveled in all the attention. He was extremely persuasive and a born smooth talker, traits that Bryce leveraged into a tremen-

dously successful career. His accomplishments, and paycheck, allowed them to live comfortably, although Bryce was rarely around to enjoy their impressive home. In fact, his long hours had become a point of friction between them. That in itself wasn't surprising. Bryce and Kayla had always tended to be a bit like oil and water. Their personalities clashed, and they often seemed to be pulling in different directions. But as they say, opposites attract.

CHECKING YOUR BLIND SPOT

Early on, our partner is a mystery. To solve that mystery, we embrace our inner armchair psychologist by using any available information to uncover what lies beneath the surface. There isn't a lot to go on, so we're forced to look for hints, clues, and subtle signs—anything that will give us the scoop on what this person is really like. Whether it's a glance from across the room at a party, restaurant, or work function, or a peek at a profile picture on a dating app, the first piece of information we have about a person is their appearance. It's the only thing we can know about a person when we don't know them at all.

Looks matter. Brain-scan research has established that seeing a physically attractive person registers in our brain's reward center.[1] But no one wants to think of themselves as shallow or vain. We'd much rather imagine ourselves as deep thinkers who possess hidden virtues, value complexity, and appreciate nuance. We also don't want to feel like we're objectifying our partner. Yet we still have a blind spot because when thinking about our relationships, we're overly reliant on the most superficial information possible: physical appearance.

Beauty Is Bad for Your Relationship

Research confirms that newlyweds want an attractive partner.[2] No surprise there. Here's the problem. Researchers also asked a critical question: Does having an attractive partner help the relationship? Put simply, no. In fact, the only impact of attractiveness on the marriage was negative: attractive husbands were less satisfied. There was no impact for unattractive husbands, and attractiveness didn't matter for wives at all. Okay, but this study focused on the early stages of marriage. Perhaps the benefits of attractiveness become apparent later in the relationship?

Nope. A 2017 paper from researchers at Harvard and other institutions shows that having a hot partner can produce a less stable relationship.[3] In their study, the researchers rated hundreds of men's yearbook photos for attractiveness, then checked their publicly available marriage and divorce records. This revealed that more attractive high school men had shorter marriages and were more likely to divorce. Researchers also checked out photos from male and female celebrities. Once again, being more attractive coincided with staying single longer and being more likely to get divorced. But why? One potential explanation is that attractive people are more vulnerable to relationship threats. In particular, attractive people have a harder time controlling their wandering eye, especially when their relationship isn't going well. In other words, our attractive partner is more likely to check out other potential partners if our relationship gets rocky.

We spend our lives wishing for an attractive partner, then finally get what we always wanted, only to have that threaten our relationship. It's counterintuitive and doesn't seem fair. How could that be? Fatal attraction. Not in a boiled-bunny kind of way, but rather, when a trait or attribute that we initially found attractive later becomes the exact thing about our partner that we despise.[4] Funny how life can sneak up on us that way. But think of the partner whose flirtatious sexuality initially captures our attention. Later, those same qualities are no longer attractive but instead evoke jealousy and insecurity, leading to conflict. Those good things we once found so appealing reverse course to become qualities we wish our partner didn't have. No wonder fatal attractions account for nearly a third of breakups. That smoking-hot partner we were so happy to attract may ultimately reveal himself to be a high-maintenance headache.

Okay, aiming to have a superhot partner isn't the best goal. But it can't hurt to have our partner think we're really good-looking, right? Wrong again. Ready for what might be the biggest surprise of the entire chapter? When our partner cares a lot about our physical attractiveness, it can damage the relationship. A study from 2017 by psychologist Laura Ramsey and colleagues from Bridgewater State University in Massachusetts asked more than one hundred women how much their partner objectified them ("My partner thinks about how I look"), how much the women enjoyed sexualized attention ("I want men to look at me"), and how satisfied they were in their relationship ("How well does your partner meet your needs?").[5] Their results showed that when men gave their female partners more attention for their looks, women were less satisfied with their relationships—even when the same women indicated that they enjoyed the sexualized attention.

Clearly, men should knock it off. But the research also showed that men objectified their female partners more when their partners objectified themselves and reported enjoying sexualized attention. For this reason, both partners need to recognize their role in the problem and realize that objectification isn't romantic, an innocent compliment, or a harmless expression of desire. Rather, objectification is misplaced attention and ultimately harmful to the relationship. All of this points to the tricky nature of attraction in relationships. When we feel sexually desired, we are more satisfied in our relationships. Yet that same sexual desirability can run amok and become objectifying if it becomes too much of a priority.

Beauty Isn't What You Think

Not only does attractiveness have little to do with relationship success; we often read more into others' attractiveness than we should. In some ways we can't help it. We process visual information in milliseconds, which means that physical features leave an immediate and unavoidable impression. Because this is hardwired, we can fool ourselves into believing that making appearance-based inferences is necessary and useful. That type of thinking emboldens us to seek a partner with kind eyes, a trustworthy smile, or a look that we're convinced is a window into their personality.

Yet when we rely on physical features to unlock deeper insights, all we're really doing is using bad information to make a bad decision. A classic social psychology experiment shows just how easily this happens.[6] Under the pretense of testing powers of perception, researchers showed participants photographs of three people, one attractive, one not so attractive, and one average. They then made inferences about their personality characteristics (e.g., outgoing, warm, kind, and sexually receptive) and potential life outcomes in work and marriage. With only a mere photograph to go on, how much could participants really know about the person in the picture? Not much. But that didn't stop them from forming impressions. Participants believed attractive people had more desirable characteristics and felt that they would have more prestigious jobs, be more likely to marry, be good spouses, and have better-quality marriages. All from a single photograph.

When we value one trait, like physical attractiveness, too highly, and it spills over to make other aspects of the person seem positive as well, researchers call this a halo effect. Sounds angelic, but let's call it what it is: stereotyping. As stereotypes go, believing attractiveness makes someone a good person may seem relatively harmless because it's complimentary. The problem is that, as with most stereotypes, our assumptions are wrong, which means decisions based on those assumptions are also wrong. When researchers tested whether attractive people really are the wonderful people we believe them to be, there was only a weak association between attractiveness, positive personality traits, and life outcomes.[7] We're giving attractive people much more credit than they deserve, and we rely too much on physical features when thinking about our partner.

On some level we know that focusing too much on looks is wrong. But we can't seem to help ourselves. It isn't just that we believe "what is beautiful is good."[8] Rather, our inflated perceptions are wishful thinking. Research suggests that when we believe someone attractive might end up as our partner, we convince ourselves that they're not only attractive but wonderful as well. Not only is our partner hot, but they also have a great personality and a bright future. Lucky us. Our great partner (think: trophy spouse) sends a signal to others that we must be pretty amazing ourselves. It's all so self-serving that it's hard for us to see it happening.

We all want the best for ourselves. In fact, a 2018 study of online daters found that most people seek partners who are roughly 25 percent more attractive than they are.[9] But that may be toxic for our relationship. Imagine a mismatched couple. One's hot; the other, not so much. This couple invites instability because the less attractive partner, though proud of how well they've done in the mating game, simultaneously can't help but feel self-conscious because everyone sees the mismatch. It creates vulnerability because the less attractive partner fears that someone else will poach their partner. The natural reaction is to protect the relationship, which amplifies jealousy.[10] This can lead to negative tactics such as monopolizing our partner's time, putting down potential competitors, employing emotional manipulation, and trying to make our partner jealous.[11] In other words, the less attractive partner must devote a lot of emotional labor to keep their good thing going.

It also isn't easy being the more attractive partner. A study of nearly seven hundred women in new relationships found that when women believed they were more attractive than their male partners, it threatened the relationship's long-term stability.[12] That's because the attractive women tended to flirt more with other men, believed they could find a better partner, and thought more about breaking up. However, when women thought their spouse was more attractive, they experienced problems in one key area.[13] A study of more than one hundred newlyweds found that when wives thought they were less attractive than their husbands, they engaged in more dieting behaviors and expressed a higher drive to be thin. All this research on mismatched physical beauty makes one clear point. When there are winners and losers in partners' relative attractiveness, everyone loses in the long run.

Bonus Blind Spot:
Does Mom Know Best?

To see how much we overemphasize physical qualities, we need an objective perspective. To do that, researchers from Eastern Connecticut State University asked women to rate potential relationship partners.[14] Then they asked their moms to rate their daughters' possible partners. Partners' profiles included a picture that was either attractive, average, or unattractive, along with personality information that varied in desirability. Moms and their daughters saw things differently. Daughters focused primarily on appearance and wanted to date an attractive partner regardless of his personality. Moms weren't nearly as picky about appearance and considered a less attractive guy a potential match for their daughter, provided he had a desirable personality. In other words, they were savvier than their daughters because moms were more willing to overlook physical qualities in favor of positive personality qualities such as being friendly and respectful. Moms seemed to realize that looks would be less relevant in the future and instead prioritized qualities that matter more for long-term relationship health.

Problematic Personality Traits That Masquerade as Positives

There's more to beauty than high cheekbones and a slender waist, but even when we attempt to ignore those superficial physical qualities, our natural impulses about attraction can lead us astray. For example, the person who seems kind may turn out to be too meek, the caring and attentive partner might become oppressive and controlling, and the entrepreneurial partner might become distant.[15] That last one highlights a quality most of us want in a partner: success. A go-getting, overachieving partner is desirable because those qualities often coincide with financial security. However, an overly driven partner can be quite costly in other important ways. Time is money, and time making money is time away from the relationship and home. If family time is important, success may be more trouble than it's worth, and potentially disastrous for the relationship. For that reason, a partner's solid but not terribly lucrative career, apathetic approach to working overtime, and disinterest in climbing the corporate ladder may ultimately be better for your relationship.

Success doesn't happen accidentally. It requires a certain kind of person: driven, ambitious, and hardworking. Mix in charisma, intelligence, and creativity, and now not only does financial security feel guaranteed, but we also have the makings of a uniquely captivating partner. The problem is, those qualities, masquerading as positive traits, may in fact be hazardous. Those characteristics fall under three personality traits together known as "the Dark Triad," and if you think that sounds bad, you're right. A person with the Dark Triad exudes *narcissism,* leading them to feel special and superior.[16] They also demonstrate *Machiavellianism,* which makes them socially charming, intriguing, but also manipulative. The final trait is *psychopathy,* characterized by impulsivity as well as antagonism and hostility toward others. Not exactly anyone's dream partner.

The trap we fall into is that these traits can be attractive in small doses. Think of the guy who sweeps you off your feet. Initially his hyperconfident cockiness, charm, and spontaneity are appealing. Those traits are even more alluring to those who

How Do You Measure Up?
The Dark Triad

Given the potential impact of Dark Triad traits on your relationship, you should get a sense of where you (and your partner) stand. For each statement, indicate how much you agree:

1. I like to be the center of attention.
   Strongly Disagree 1 2 3 4 5 Strongly Agree
2. To succeed in life, now and then you need to be willing to get others to do what you want.
   Strongly Disagree 1 2 3 4 5 Strongly Agree
3. When necessary, I can do what needs to be done without feeling remorseful.
   Strongly Disagree 1 2 3 4 5 Strongly Agree

Item 1 measures narcissism, item 2 measures Machiavellianism, and item 3 measures psychopathy. Higher scores indicate a greater tendency toward that trait. Though scoring high in all three is clearly the worst, a high score on any one trait can be problematic. Researchers measure Dark Triad traits with a variety of scales, but if you're interested in a user-friendly version, check out the "Dark Triad Dirty Dozen" scale.[17]

have Dark Triad traits themselves. Of the Dark Triad traits, the trickiest one to identify is narcissism. Narcissists can be particularly attractive. They're self-assured, charismatic, enchanting, socially engaging, and magnetic. In other words, *amazing.* Unfortunately, what captivates us at first may burn us in the long run.[18] In a set of seven studies, a team of European

researchers found that on the one hand, narcissists are fasci-
nating because their confidence excites us.[19] They revel in others' attention. On the other hand, even the most dedicated
admiration fades. We can put our partner on a pedestal for
only so long. Over time, relationship partners need to share
the spotlight. But the narcissistic partner wants to own all the
attention. What was once a partnership is now a rivalry that
ultimately breeds animosity between the partners.

That's bad, but the Dark Triad is also related to the ultimate
relationship sin: cheating. A sample of 884 participants in
their late twenties and early thirties completed Dark Triad
measures and answered the following question: "Have you
ever been unfaithful to your current (or most recent) partner?"[20] The data revealed that all three Dark Triad traits were
linked to greater infidelity in both men and women. A separate study found that women with Dark Triad traits cheated
more, believed they were more susceptible to cheating, and felt
more vulnerable to having their own partner cheat on them.[21]
Not exactly a recipe for relationship harmony.

Opposites Attract, Then Attack

We need to address one of the most pervasive and damaging
myths that exist about attraction: the idea that opposites
attract. Sure, partners have opposing traits and may even find
some of those differences appealing, at least initially. More
often, after opposites attract, they attack. Think about the
dynamic between opposite partners. One likes to go out and
be social; the other is a homebody. One loves the beach; the
other hates sand. One person is neat and tidy, while the other
is messy. Sounds perfect...said no one ever. Competing

preferences create conflict that limits the relationship's potential.

Take, for example, when one partner is a spender who likes to shop, while the other partner is a saver who focuses on being thrifty and having financial reserves. True opposites. Research shows that spenders and savers are often drawn to each other because their counterpart has qualities they aspire to have.[22] Spenders want to be a bit more frugal, while savers want to be more carefree. Sounds like a good plan, but it doesn't work. When researchers studied 112 married couples in their thirties and forties, couples with opposite spending and saving tendencies reported lower marital well-being. A follow-up with 458 married participants revealed that spender-saver couples experienced greater conflict over financial matters (go figure) and that those squabbles deteriorated relationship quality. Overall, the research on attraction suggests that we need to be more careful about what we think we want in our relationship partner. The types of things we most desire, such as beauty, success, confidence, and charisma, aren't ideal for the long-term relationship happiness we seek.

HOW TO SEE YOUR RELATIONSHIP MORE CLEARLY

Make no mistake: we need to get this right because whom we're attracted to lays the groundwork for whom we ultimately fall in love with. The solution isn't to ignore physical qualities or seek out unattractive partners with no future prospects for success. Those are overreactions. Instead, we can remind ourselves what is truly important for long-term relationship success. The fact is that barring extreme measures or great expense, year after year our partner will become less and less physically attractive. So will we.

Clearly, we shouldn't love our partner just for their looks. Similarly, we should be wary of a partner who values us primarily for our physical features. This is not to say that our partner shouldn't find us attractive. They should. However, it's one thing to think we're cute and another to love our looks but merely tolerate our personality. We have to ask ourselves: When we inevitably lose our looks over time, what does that mean for our relationship? The best answer is: nothing. Not sure? Start rebuilding the relationship's infrastructure.

When Physical Attractiveness Matters

It's clear that placing too high a premium on appearance hurts our relationship. But at the same time our looks aren't entirely irrelevant. We need to know how to focus on physical attractiveness in a way that helps our relationship. The key is that similar attractiveness levels in partners result in a better relationship.[23] Researchers call this the matching hypothesis. We shouldn't be surprised, then, that a study of nearly seven hundred women found that in most couples, partners had similar attractiveness levels.[24] That's probably what happened in your relationship, and it's a good thing because matched partners are more likely to stay together.[25]

Even so, there's some wiggle room. Though matching is best, in heterosexual relationships if one partner is going to be more attractive, it's better if it's the woman.[26] Research shows that in married couples where the wife is more attractive, couples have an easier time being supportive and positive with each other. In contrast, husbands' attractiveness doesn't seem to affect wives' relationship satisfaction.[27] Much of this is also true for partners' physical fitness. A study of newlyweds found that when wives were more fit and had a lower body mass index than their husbands, both partners were more satisfied initially and remained so over the four-year study period.[28]

There is an interesting wrinkle to this research: being a bit out of shape speaks well of the relationship. That's right; when men and women felt satisfied and stable within their relationship, they tended to gain weight. You don't hear this too often, but being thinner wasn't better! Instead, gaining weight, which we associate with being less attractive, was more helpful. What gives? When you feel secure in your relationship, you aren't worried that eating that bowl of ice cream will threaten your relationship. However, if the relationship seems tenuous, being optimally fit is more important, because there is a greater possibility of needing to attract a new partner. All of which goes to show that good relationships may be bad for our waistlines. In this context, a few extra pounds could be a good sign because it may suggest that we're not worried about looking our best to attract other potential partners.

Personality Goes a Long Way

If all this emphasis on appearance has felt shallow, that's because it is. For the good of any relationship, we need to look beyond skin deep. Surely we've all had this experience: We see someone at a distance and find them absolutely stunning. Then we meet, and as soon as they start talking, their attractiveness plummets. It goes the other way too. Someone who initially isn't physically alluring reveals an infectious personality and instantly becomes more attractive.

> ## Bonus Blind Spot:
> ## Timing Is Everything
>
> Clearly, looks matter. How much can depend on how long partners knew each other prior to forming the relationship. Researchers speculated that when partners didn't know each other that well, they would rely more on physical attractiveness and be more matched.[29] But when couples were more familiar with each other pre-relationship, they would rely less on appearance and be less similar in physical attractiveness. As hypothesized, couples who got serious soon after meeting tended to have more similar physical attractiveness levels, suggesting that they put more emphasis on appearance. However, when couples knew each other for a longer period of time pre-relationship, they were less matched on physical attractiveness, suggesting they put more emphasis on personality. In fact, if partners knew each other for nine months or more before becoming a couple, partners' physical attractiveness was hardly related. This study suggests that a good way to de-emphasize physical attraction's role is for partners to spend time getting to know each other before becoming romantically involved.

Having had both experiences in college and graduate school, I was curious if personality really altered perceptions of attractiveness, or if it just felt that way. To test it out, I had participants come into my lab and rate pictures of dozens of highly attractive, moderately attractive, and unattractive faces.[30] Next, because I didn't want participants to remember their ratings, I had them do a math task where they counted

backward from a high number like 9,366 by 13s: 9,353...
9,340...9,327. Then, a few minutes later, they had to count
back up by 7s. Mind-numbing. After that experience, it was
nearly impossible for them to remember their earlier picture
ratings (or anything else, for that matter). Next, the participants saw the same pictures again, but this time they included
information about each person's personality. Sometimes that
personality information was positive (this person is smart,
funny, and kind); other times it was negative (this person is
unintelligent, boring, and rude). After reviewing the pictures
and personality profiles, participants again rated the individuals' physical attractiveness.

As I expected, personality mattered. When participants read
about positive personality traits, that person became more
physically attractive. Learning about negative personality traits
made people less attractive. Awesome, right? Remember, nothing changed about the picture. But participants perceived those
pictures differently. Other researchers replicated the same phenomenon with body attractiveness, finding that men rated a
wider range of women's body sizes physically attractive when
they learned about the women's positive personality traits.[31]
Yet when men read about negative personality traits, they were
pickier about the body sizes they found attractive. Once again,
personality goes a long way.

For better or worse, we live in a culture that emphasizes
superficial aspects of our appearance, whether it's the perfect
smile, biceps diameter, thigh gap, or V shape of our lower abs.
It's refreshing to know that enhancing our attractiveness doesn't
require expensive makeup, excessive hours at the gym, starva-
tion, or surgeries. Instead, we can find comfort in the fact that
our stellar personality makes us more attractive. Similarly,

when we can appreciate all our partner's wonderful qualities, they will become more beautiful to us.

Personality is complex. It can feel like there are so many facets to consider that it's hard to know what really matters. To help you better appreciate your partner's good qualities, the

Top 20 Most Valued Personality Attributes in a Potential Marriage Partner

What Men Value	What Women Value
1. Reliable	1. Warm
2. Warm	2. Reliable
3. Fair	3. Fair
4. Intelligent	4. Intelligent
5. Knowledgeable	5. Knowledgeable
6. Conscientious	6. Trusting
7. Trusting	7. Secure
8. Hardworking	8. Hardworking
9. Secure	9. Emotionally Stable
10. At Ease	10. At Ease
11. Emotionally Stable	11. Perceptive
12. Perceptive	12. Lenient
13. Even-Tempered	13. Conscientious
14. Energetic	14. Energetic
15. Practical	15. Generous
16. Curious	16. Sociable
17. Sociable	17. Curious
18. Creative	18. Well Organized
19. Well Organized	19. Flexible
20. Relaxed	20. Relaxed

facing page presents a list of research-backed qualities that many find most desirable in a marriage partner.[32]

Take a moment to peruse this list. Are there valued qualities that your partner has that you've neglected to notice? Maybe it's time to start giving credit where credit is due and focusing more on qualities that are potentially more important than appearance.

Pay special attention to all the traits you share with your partner. That may be difficult at first because similarities fade into the background, while differences are easier to notice. We also like to emphasize our individuality, particularly in Western cultures, which can make acknowledging all the qualities we share with our partner difficult. But make no mistake: if there were a golden rule for how to promote attraction between two people, finding similarity would be it. We like people who are like us. That's good news, because we're probably a lot more similar to our romantic partner than we recognize. Most likely, our partner is similar to us on demographic variables like age, ethnicity, religion, socioeconomic status, geographical location, and family values. Partners also share similar personalities, hobbies, and interests. How alike partners are initially matters a lot.[33] As the relationship progresses, research shows, that kind of similarity isn't nearly as important as believing our partner is similar to our ideal self, or the person we want to become.[34] So, if we currently aren't similar to our partner, that's okay. It's more important that our partner have qualities that we hope to have in the future. For example, if our partner is very responsible but we're not, as long as we want to be more responsible in the future, it helps our relationship. We value partners who are similar to the person we want to be.

Use Your Illusions

In our pursuit of aspirational qualities that our current partner possesses, things can get tricky. It's entirely likely that how we view our partner is a love-induced illusion fueled by self-deception. Is "self-deception" just a fancy way to say that we're lying to ourselves? Definitely. It seems as if it would be hard to deceive ourselves, because we're so close to our partner. Certainly, we have ample opportunities to fact-check any false perceptions. At some point the truth should smack us right in the face. Yet it doesn't. In fact, people in romantic relationships routinely hold positive illusions about their partners' qualities, which encourage them to see their partners more positively than the partners see themselves.[35] To test this, researchers had both members of a couple rate their own facial and body attractiveness, as well as their partner's.[36] Husbands rated their wives more attractive than the wives considered themselves to be. For example, wives considered themselves a 7, but when their husbands looked at their wives, they saw a 9. Not to be outdone, wives were equally kind toward their husbands. The same thing happened when partners evaluated each other's personality.[37] Once again, partners held overly kind illusions. The result was that partners believed their counterparts were kinder, funnier, smarter, and generally just better than their partners thought they were themselves.

It's a nice lie. But is it also a recipe for eventual disappointment? It seems that inevitably we'll see the error of our ways. The research begs to differ. In fact, the research suggests we should continue deceiving ourselves, and if we aren't already lying to ourselves, we should start. Though we might assume this type of self-deception is bad, holding on to positive illusions enhances relationship quality, even over long periods of time. In one study, researchers found that as newlyweds, couples who held more positive illusions were more in love.[38] Okay, but early on everything is great, so being positive is easy, right? True, but the researchers also found that those positive illusions protected the relationship over the next thirteen years by resulting in less loss of love. It may seem impossible to continue lying to yourself for so long or to do so purposefully, but partners don't realize it's happening or that their illusions are false.

What's the secret to the benefits of positive illusions? Their powers come from a simple piece of advice found in one of the most widely read self-help books of all time. In *How to Win Friends and Influence People,* Dale Carnegie suggests, "Give the other person a fine reputation to live up to."[39] When we hold positive illusions, we're giving our partner credit for desirable traits and qualities they don't actually have. Our partner knows we're wrong and now has a choice: be revealed as a fraud, or start living up to our high regard. Praise feels good, but it feels even better when it is properly earned. Our partner doesn't want to disappoint us and must work to live up to our charitable perceptions. This makes them a better partner. Consider this permission to lie to yourself. If you don't, you may be putting your relationship at risk.

RELATIONSHIP RECAP

- Attractive people have more relationship problems.
- Having a partner who highly values your appearance can undermine the relationship.
- Your mom wouldn't pick a hot partner for you, and this time, she's right.

- Confidence and charisma are attractive but may be signs of the Dark Triad, which can lead to major relationship threats like cheating.
- Your partner's personality goes a long way to making them more attractive.
- It's good to lie to yourself a bit about how wonderful your partner is.

Chapter 5

"If We're Not Having a Lot of Sex, We're Not in Love"

It had been a little over three weeks; twenty-four days, to be exact. Certainly not a world, or even a personal, record as far as sexual dry spells go. But other downtimes had happened while Heidi was single and were largely by design. Sexual fasting helped Heidi get her head straight after a rocky relationship. All that changed when she met Cole. They hit it off immediately, began an intense love affair, and fell in love completely. Everything was amazing. Their conversations, the trips they took, and the sex. The sex was great. After living together for a year and a half, Heidi and Cole got married. It was perfect.

That was then.

Now, after being married for several years, things feel different. Not bad, but certainly not as exciting. Heidi has given up cocktail dresses and clubs for baggy pajamas and binge-watching Netflix. She likes their easy, low-pressure lifestyle, and she really cherishes *spending time with her best friend, Cole. Comfortable. That's probably the best word to describe it. But twenty-four days is still twenty-four days, their longest drought by far. The weird thing is that Cole hasn't said a word about it. Heidi wonders if he just hasn't noticed, or worse, doesn't care. It's hard to understand because Heidi has never felt more secure and at peace living the life she always envisioned. Yet she feels like she accidentally traded in her husband for a housemate.*

CHECKING YOUR BLIND SPOT

Who doesn't want to be one of those made-for-TV couples who are perpetually flirty and have lots of super-witty, double-entendre-laden banter? Clearly, those couples have lots of amazing sex and are supremely happy as a result. The hard part is that no real relationship can compare. Our banter with our partner is boring and stale, the sex is infrequent, and it spells trouble. If sex is the ultimate expression of love, what does this say about our relationship? As Carrie Bradshaw from *Sex and the City* put it, "Some people are settling down, some people are settling, and some people refuse to settle for anything less than butterflies."

What if I told you all the focus on sex and butterflies is overrated?

That gives us all permission to stop being so hard on ourselves, our partner, and our relationship. Those of us who worry we're not having enough sex are focusing on the wrong thing. But it's not our fault.

Blame the media. Songs, TV shows, and movies send us clear signals about love. Those signals just happen to be wrong. Take, for example, Disney's *High School Musical* movie. What could be more innocent than a Disney movie? Researchers found that, compared to girls who watched *Over the Hedge* (an animated movie about forest animals who gather food among humans), girls who watched *High School Musical* identified with the characters, reported more idealistic beliefs around the importance of love, and believed in things like love at first sight.[1] Sure, *High School Musical* may not be your movie of choice. But these results demonstrate that what we watch can leave lasting impressions. Whether it's *Grease, Twilight, The Notebook, Fifty Shades of Grey, Love Actually, Friends,* or *This Is Us,* what we watch shapes our thoughts about love. In fact, we gravitate toward those shows because of how the brain reacts to love.

At the mere sight or thought of someone we love, our brain displays an interesting pattern as areas rich in dopamine, a neurotransmitter linked to motivation and reward, become activated.[2] The affected parts of the brain include areas key to the processing of emotions, memory, and learning. In the initial stages of love, we also experience heightened levels of nerve growth factor, which facilitates neuron development (critical for brain connectivity and functioning), as well as increased feelings of connection with others and euphoria.[3] No wonder falling in love makes us feel so good.

The Pleasure and Perils of Passionate Love

These brain chemistry changes make the exciting aspects of love, or what researchers call passionate love, feel more important.[4] Passionate love is where those butterflies are born. This type of love is highly sexualized, full of ecstasy, arousal, and preoccupation with your partner. It borders on obsession. We also idealize our partner and see them as more perfect and flawless than is humanly possible. It's intense. It's fun. When deeply in passionate love, we feel like we can't control our thoughts, like we want our partner physically, emotionally, and mentally.[5] As you can see, passionate love is an all-encompassing experience that captivates our thoughts, feelings, and motivations.

Sounds great, but here's the problem. Those passionate feelings aren't sustainable. Research consistently finds that passionate love has a short shelf life. It's great while it lasts, but it simply doesn't last that long.[6] Why? We habituate. Try to think of the most fun and exciting activity possible. One that comes readily to mind: skydiving. Much like falling in love, jumping out of a plane gives you a mixture of anticipation, uncertainty, exhilaration, and a healthy dose of terror. Especially the first time you do it. If you have the opportunity to keep jumping out of airplanes, the intense feelings persist for many of the early jumps. But if you keep diving from the sky, what happens? Well, contrast the experience as a first-time skydiver with the experience of the instructor who is awkwardly strapped to your back. As you're about to leave the plane, you're *freaking out.* Your instructor? Calm, cool, and joking around. ("What's the hardest part about skydiving? The ground. Ha!") It's just another day at the mile-high office. Your instructor has habituated; you have not.

Our bodies are designed to adapt, even to the life-threatening thrill of skydiving. In other words, we'll get used to practically anything. It's no wonder that we acclimate to passionate love in our relationships. See the issue? Overemphasizing the importance of passionate love is like banking on a dying industry. Just as you wouldn't put all your life savings into a new videotape/DVD rental store, you shouldn't invest too much of your relationship's capital in passionate love.

Bonus Blind Spot:
Love Conquers All

Many people feel that a relationship truly begins when we fall in love. Until that point, we're just not serious. It's the defining feature of a real relationship, but it's easy to misinterpret just how important that milestone is. Don't get me wrong, love is important — just not as important as we've been led to believe. We must keep things in perspective and realize that it is merely one of several important ingredients for a healthy relationship. For our relationship to truly work, we also need mutual respect, kindness, trust, caring, shared interests, and common goals, among other things. We shouldn't expect love to compensate for shortcomings in other important areas. Yet, all too often people willingly tolerate poor treatment from their partners, simply because they're in love. It's worth repeating, because it's that important: a partner who truly loves us is also respectful, kind, trusting, and caring. Love is important, but by itself it isn't enough to sustain the kind of great relationship we deserve.

Focusing on passion seems innocent because we rely on those feelings to answer the key relationship question: "Am I in love?" The problem is that we then risk overemphasizing the importance of sex.

Enough Sex?

Think back to when you felt most in love with your partner. During that time, you were probably also having the most sex.

When you saw or thought about your partner, your knees went weak, your palms sweaty. When it came to sex, you always felt ready.

Early in relationships, sex and love are virtually one and the same. You fall in love and connect with your partner sexually. The sex you have is new and amazing, your bond strengthens, and you feel more in love. It's no surprise that you're motivated to have more sex. The payoff is enormous. Your brain is swimming in feel-good neurotransmitters.

Then, life happens. The world gets in the way. Work, kids, a mortgage, bills, and family obligations. In one word: stress. It chips away at your time and energy. Your sex life suffers. You can't quite shake the feeling that if you're really in love you should always want sex, and the sex should be amazing. While that is true in a perfect world, who lives there? As we discussed in Chapter 3, it's better to realize that perfect is the enemy of good. If you're not having as much sex as you did in the past, it doesn't mean all is lost. You may be expecting too much of your relationship and need to acknowledge the good that is still there.

First, it is important to realize that our own insecurities encourage us to assume others are doing much better. We then seek out clues and make assumptions that seemingly confirm our suspicions. When we see friends in relationships post on social media about their date night, it doesn't mean they are having sex more frequently. It's just as likely that after a rare night out they collapse from exhaustion. If we're feeling self-conscious about our sex life, it's easy to assume that everyone else is doing it more than we are. But we need to see the facts as they are and not rely on assumptions.

To get a sense of what other couples are doing, we could be brazen and simply start asking around. Awkward. But this is where relationship scientists have a major advantage. Not only are they willing to ask awkward questions, but they'll ask thousands of people. One such study from 2004 from researchers at Dartmouth College and the University of Warwick in England asked sixteen thousand Americans how often they had sex.[7] The answer: not a lot. Most of the respondents had sex slightly less often than once a week, or about two to three times per month. Younger respondents (under forty) had more sex, which probably isn't surprising, but "more" was only slightly more: a whopping once a week.

Now, it's easy to think, "That study is a bit dated and the world is more sexualized than it was fifteen years ago." Wrong. In fact, according to a 2017 study by Jean Twenge from San Diego State University, Americans are averaging less sex in their relationships.[8] Twenge and colleagues compared data from more than twenty-six thousand American adults and found that married and cohabitating couples had sex sixteen fewer times per year in 2010–2014 than they did ten years earlier, in 2000–2004. In other words, sexy time has become less frequent. Sexual frequency also consistently heads downhill with age, with an average decrease of 3.2 percent every year after age twenty-five. This means that by age forty we're having roughly half as much sex as we did when we were twenty-five. As we get older and our relationship withstands the test of time, it is natural for sex to become less frequent.

Finding out how much other couples hit the sheets is informative, but be careful. Comparing ourselves to others may undermine how happy we are with our relationship.[9] The truth is that the amount of sex we have in our relationship is open to interpretation. Partners count differently. Not the exact number of times couples have sex per se; after all, both partners were present and accounted for each time. Rather, partners might agree on how often they had sex ("twice last month") but reach wildly different conclusions about what that means. Take, for example, this exchange from the classic movie *Annie Hall*. In the movie, Alvy (played by Woody Allen) and Annie (played by Diane Keaton) experience relationship trouble, and each seeks out the help of a therapist. Alvy's therapist asks, "How often do you sleep together?" Alvy responds with a sense of lament, "Hardly ever. Maybe three times a week." Annie visits her own therapist, who asks her, "Do you have sex often?" Annie responds, almost with exasperation, "Constantly. I'd say three times a week." While they agree on the frequency of sex, their interpretation varies considerably.

Doesn't it feel like all this number crunching misses the most obvious point that sex, even mediocre sex, still feels pretty good? If sex is so great, having it must make the relationship feel good, right? When researchers tracked newlyweds over two weeks, they found that on days they had sex, couples felt more sexually satisfied, with that feeling lasting for forty-eight hours post-sex.[10] Scientific proof of an afterglow. Those who reported a stronger afterglow also reported higher marital satisfaction. Of course, because those positive feelings linger, they can give us a false sense of how much sex really benefits our relationship. Fight for a day, have makeup sex for fifteen minutes, and the relationship feels fine. To understand how sex impacts a relationship, we need to look past the afterglow and take in the bigger picture.

Our Sex Life Is Sinking Our Relationship

To study the life of a relationship, we need time. Ideally lots of it, along with the ability to measure couples through the years.

A 2017 study by Elizabeth Schoenfeld, Tim Loving, and colleagues from the University of Texas at Austin kept tabs on one hundred couples who answered questions about their sex life two, three, and fourteen years after their wedding day.[11] When the researchers looked for the link between sexual frequency and marital satisfaction, they didn't find it. That's right; how often a couple had sex did not impact their marital satisfaction.

Though it's surprising, other research backs up this finding. For example, in a large-scale 2016 study done at Florida State University that followed more than two hundred marriages over a four-year period,[12] couples from Ohio and Tennessee completed surveys about their relationship every six to eight months. The goal was to see how sexual frequency during a particular time frame influenced marital satisfaction six months or several years in the future. As before, couples who had less sex at any given point were not less happy later on. Researchers also tested the opposite possibility, that current happiness predicts later sexual frequency. They didn't find that connection either. Those who were happier did not have more sex in the future.

When researchers measure couples this often, they gain a significant scientific advantage because they can explore the factors surrounding increased or decreased sexual activity. Funny thing, the findings are completely counterintuitive. Couples who initially reported having worse marriages also reported increases in sexual activity. Bad marriage now, equals more sex later. Though this finding was unexpected, the researchers speculated that "spouses who are less satisfied with the marriage overall focus on the sexual aspects of the relationship, either in attempts to improve the relationship or maximize their current benefits." This interpretation may not be equally accurate for both husbands and wives. Other research shows that when husbands are in love, they engage in more affection and try to initiate sex with their wives more often.[13] For wives it's the opposite. When they felt less in love, they were more likely to seek sex with their partners. Not only does more sex not make relationships better; this research suggests that one potential reason wives initiate sex may be that they think the relationship is in trouble.

Though this research shows that people have sex for different reasons, the underlying assumption seems to be that more sex is always good for the relationship. Prepared to be surprised. The data from both sexual-frequency studies show that men's sexual frequency and satisfaction did not predict their marital satisfaction.[14] For women *and* men, having more sex isn't the secret to marital bliss. Still not convinced? I get it. The truth is that these studies use correlational data from surveys, which means there could be other explanations. For example, couples under a lot of stress may not have a lot of sex and may also have an unsatisfying relationship. Perhaps what we really need to test is a relationship hack or easy technique to help ignite a couple's sex life. Introducing a mini-intervention pushes couples out of their existing routines and forces them to try something different. You've probably heard of "sex challenges," where couples intentionally ramp up their sex lives to help save their relationship. Some require couples to have sex seven days in a row. For the more ambitious, there's the 30-Day Sex Challenge. The basic logic is that if couples have more sex, they'll be happier and their relationship will improve. Does it work?

To really know, we'd have to round up lots of couples and flip a coin to determine which ones would have a lot more sex, and which ones would not get as lucky, maintaining the status quo. Researchers from Carnegie Mellon University did just this with more than one hundred middle-aged couples.[15] The researchers told couples to either double the amount of sex they were currently having (e.g., if they typically had sex once a week, they now had to have sex twice a week) or continue having sex as they normally did. Over the next three months, researchers routinely checked in with the couples to make sure they were playing by the rules and to ask about their relationship. The results? Men and women in the "more sex" group reported a decline in their mood across all three months of the study, especially when it came to excitement and energy. Not only does artificially increasing how much sex we have not give us any discernible benefit; it carries negative consequences, possibly because the mandated sex we're having is less exciting.

So if more sex isn't the answer, what is?

HOW TO SEE YOUR RELATIONSHIP MORE CLEARLY

If we're worried that we aren't having enough sex, perhaps sex isn't the problem. Maybe our expectation of what constitutes "enough" is a blind spot. Really, any amount of sex can count as "enough." Even no sex at all. Though it's relatively uncommon, for some couples sex is highly infrequent, sometimes to the point of being nonexistent—in what one part of Reddit calls a "dead bedroom."[16] But as researchers from Georgia State University found in one of the few studies on the topic, even within sexless unions, partners are not inclined to leave, and the relationships are stable. Although these couples may remain hopeful that they will resume having sex at some point, they also seem to have found that other aspects of their relationship make staying together worthwhile. Couples also occupy themselves with other activities like work or hobbies or focusing on self-growth. If a completely abstinent relationship isn't the goal, it's worth exploring what science has to say about what counts as "enough."

When Is Enough, Enough?

Perhaps the most compelling question people have about their relationship is "How much sex should we have?" To answer this, a group of researchers from the University of Toronto Mississauga dug into the sex lives of more than thirty thousand Americans.[17] Turns out, there is a magic number. The researchers' analysis found that couples who had sex at least once a week were happier than those who had sex less than that. Importantly, though, having sex more than once a week didn't carry any noticeable benefits. The same was true for life satisfaction beyond the relationship.

There it is. Once a week; fifty-two times a year. That's the magic number. Seems kinda low, right? Wait, there's more magic. Once a week happens to be the gold standard for pretty much everyone. There weren't any differences based on gender (men and women were the same), age (young and old were the same), or relationship length (short and long were the same). As Amy Muise, the lead researcher of the SHaRe (Sexual Health and Relationships) Lab[18] and a rising rock star in the world of sex research, explained, "Our findings suggest that it's important to maintain an intimate connection with your partner, but you don't need to have sex every day as long as you're maintaining that connection." You've been beating yourself and your relationship up about nothing. Once a week is a completely reasonable and attainable number. #realisticgoals. Now, you may want to discuss this with your partner so that you're both on the same page in terms of your expectations.

If your relationship just isn't there yet and is falling short of that once-a-week threshold, remember that a relationship's current state isn't its destiny. Things change. Your sex life is no exception. Improvement is simply a matter of putting in the effort. There are two types of people. Those who believe what I just said about effort and those who don't. If you believe in the power of hard work, you have sexual-growth beliefs. If you think sexual satisfaction comes from finding a naturally compatible partner, you hold sexual-destiny beliefs.[19] Here's the thing. According to the data, one of them is much better for your relationship: growth. A series of six studies from 2017 by a group of Canadian researchers with nearly two thousand people from the United States and Canada found that those who held sexual-growth beliefs had more satisfying sex, partners who were more satisfied, and higher relationship satisfaction. The destiny believers? Not so much. When their sex life got bumpy, it harmed their relationship quality. If the sex isn't great, you may question your sexual compatibility, which leads to questions about the relationship's viability. That's a dangerous line of thinking because your sexual experiences with your partner won't always be perfect. When those inevitable issues come up, be careful not to overreact. Imperfect sex isn't a sign that a relationship is doomed. Rather, it's a sign of a typical relationship. The key is to realize that and be willing to put in the effort to improve your sex life.

The research is also clear on where we should direct those efforts. While quantity doesn't matter, quality does. Think about it: all else being equal, would you rather eat a huge meal of poorly cooked food or a smaller portion meticulously prepared by a Michelin-star chef? The same is true for our sex life. A study of nearly ten thousand older adults (ages fifty to eighty-five) revealed that more sex didn't equate to more enjoyable sex.[20] In fact, those who had the most enjoyable sex had sex fewer than once or twice a week. Their secret? "An expansive sexual repertoire." Sounds fancy. Essentially, the more tricks they had up their sleeves (or wherever else they kept their tricks), the better the sex. Others were having more sex, which seems good, until you learn that the sex they were having was routine and boring. Quality counts, quantity not so much.

How Do You Measure Up?
Sexual Novelty

A key to keeping sexual satisfaction high and your relationship going strong may be your ability to keep things new and interesting in the bedroom (or kitchen, living room, etc.). A group of researchers at Southwestern University, in Texas, led by Sarah Matthews developed a Brief Measure of Sexual Novelty to see if a couple's sex life is boring and routine or more unpredictable.[21] To get a sense of where your relationship's sex life stacks up, indicate how much each statement describes you and your partner, using the scale provided:

1. When having sex, we try to mix up what we do to keep things interesting.
    Strongly Disagree 1 2 3 4 5 Strongly Agree

---

2. We like to try new things sexually to make our sex life more exciting.
   Strongly Disagree   1   2   3   4   5   Strongly Agree
3. We try to inject novelty into our sex life by trying new positions and places to have sex.
   Strongly Disagree   1   2   3   4   5   Strongly Agree

Those who agree more with each of the items have more sexual novelty in their relationships. When researchers gave participants the full-length official scale, those with higher sexual novelty scores had higher sexual satisfaction, higher relationship satisfaction, more frequent sex, and less sexual boredom.

The disconnect between quality and quantity is important because it means having more sex won't necessarily make us happy with our sex life; but if we are able to improve sexual satisfaction, we have a higher chance of being happy with our relationship. In fact, when researchers tracked participants over thirteen years, couples who were more satisfied sexually also reported happier marriages.[22] What led to increased sexual satisfaction? Not how much sex they had, but rather how they treated each other. That is, whether they were nice to each other, showed physical affection, and didn't try to annoy or antagonize each other. As the authors put it, "When it comes to feelings of marital satisfaction, therefore, a satisfying sex life and a warm interpersonal climate appear to matter more than does a greater frequency of sexual intercourse."

Essentially, what everyone wants is an intimate connection. But where does this intimacy come from? That seems like an easy question—it obviously comes from attraction and physical connection. Wrong! Once again, common sense doesn't match the research.[23] When relationship scientists look at the most central aspects of an intimate relationship, guess what's not on the list? Sex and passion. Don't get me wrong, they're important, just not more important than other qualities. The true driving forces of a satisfying intimate relationship are trust, understanding our partner, caring, and having a greater sense of "we" and "us," rather than "I" and "me." Though these aspects are critical, they are underappreciated and taken for granted. We don't focus on them and don't always see the nourishing intimacy our relationship really does provide.

It's clear that relationships are best served by not focusing on sex so much. But people have a harder time shaking their misguided beliefs about love. Some are overly romantic. Not in a candlelit-bedroom-with-rose-petals-on-the-sheets kind of way, but in a love-is-magical kind of way. Do you tend to agree with these statements: "True love is perfect," "I have only one true love," "Love conquers all," and "Love is possible at first sight"?[24] If so, you're more romantic. Though those beliefs may sound harmless or even helpful, they're not. For example, research confirms there's no such thing as love at first sight.[25] What the highly romantic person may consider love is often physical attraction, which has little to do with feelings of intimacy or commitment.

Moving Beyond Butterflies: The Love That Truly Matters

Holding ill-informed beliefs about love leaves us vulnerable to missing out on what matters most. Once we shake those misguided notions, we can learn to embrace what researchers call companionate or friendship-based love.[27] This love involves a

---

**Bonus Blind Spot:
Share the Love on Your Next Date Night**

When you finally get to have a date night, your first impulse may be to spend that time alone with your partner. But research suggests that spending time with other couples may boost feelings of love.[26] In one study, couples participated in a "getting to know you" activity, either alone or with another couple, responding to questions like "What is the greatest accomplishment of your life?" When couples answered questions by themselves, their passionate love stayed the same, but they reported greater passionate love when they did the activity along with other couples. Having another couple may boost passion because there are more opportunities for learning new and interesting things, which helps keep the sparks flying. As you plan date nights with your partner, be sure to plan a few couples' date nights as well.

"comfortable, affectionate, trusting love for a likable partner, based on a deep sense of friendship and involving companionship and the enjoyment of common activities, mutual interests, and shared laughter." If the excitement of jumping out of an airplane is akin to passionate love, our parachute is companionate love. It might be less flashy, but it provides a reassuring and grounding experience.

When our relationship's foundation is in companionate love, our partner is our BFF. That's great, because if we want kindness, caring, and trust, there may be no better relationship to use as a model than a best friend. But do people really think of their romantic partner as their best friend? I asked a national sample that question, with the help of the Monmouth University Polling Institute.[28] For those in a relationship, the vast majority (83 percent) said their romantic partner was their best friend. For married couples, 88 percent said the same. Older respondents were also more likely to report having a best-friend partner. However, there were no gender differences. Men and women were equally likely to report best-friend romantic partners.

Some may think, "I already have a best friend; I don't need that from my romantic partner." Well, we asked about that in our poll as well. Those who had best-friend romantic partners were more satisfied compared to those whose romantic partner wasn't their best friend. Other research corroborates this finding. When relationships have more companionate love, they are more satisfying and last longer.[29] Remember, that second *F* in "BFF" stands for "forever," and companionate love helps our relationship make it over the long haul. This really isn't surprising considering that a study of 622 married individuals found that those with more friendship-based love reported that their relationship was more important to them, that they felt closer to their spouse, and that they had more respect for their partner.[30] Couples who have been happily married for more than fifteen years back up these findings. Researchers asked more than 350 of these "expert" couples what the secret was to their success.[31] Secret number one? My partner is my best friend. Secret number two? I like my spouse as a person.

It's easy to see how companionate love facilitates relationship satisfaction,[32] but does it really do anything for the lusty aspects of the relationship? In fact, companionate love helps your sex life too. In one study of nearly four hundred people, when participants highly valued their friendship with their partner, they also reported feeling more in love, more commitment, and greater sexual fulfillment.[33] An added bonus: they were less likely to break up. Companionate love wins again.

Companionate love is the love that matters most. The best romantic partners are best friends. So perhaps it's time to start holding your partner to the same standards that you have for a best friend. Stop putting up with behaviors from a romantic partner (e.g., disrespect) that you would never tolerate from a best friend. Pick partners based on how good a friend they are, rather than how good they are in bed. Put another way, if your best friend was routinely grumpy, argumentative, nagging, unkind, rude, unwilling to talk or hang out, or just generally shady, what would you do? You wouldn't put up with it. Yet when our romantic partners do these types of things, they all too often get a free pass. No more. Having companionate love in our relationship is too important. Rather than worrying about whether we're having enough sex in our relationship, we should consider whether we have enough mutual respect, kindness, and friendship. The best way to achieve true love forever is to be best friends forever.

RELATIONSHIP RECAP

- You're focusing too much on how you feel when your partner kisses you and not enough on how you feel when you hold your partner's hand.
- Couples aren't having sex as much as you think, and sexy time in relationships has become less frequent over the past few decades.

- How much sex should you have? The magic number for keeping your relationship going strong is once a week.
- Having a lot of sex isn't always a great sign. Research shows that when people feel their relationship is vulnerable, they increase sexual activity.
- Simply trying to have more sex to fix your relationship will likely do more harm than good.
- When it comes to your sex life, quality is more important than quantity.
- True intimacy doesn't come from partners' physical connection. Other qualities, like your partner being your best friend, are much more important.

Chapter 6

"If You Loved Me, You'd Change"

When it came to love, Maddie always enjoyed a bit of a project. Carson was her latest. There was something enticing about recognizing untapped potential, then embracing the challenge of molding Carson into the person she knew he could be. It wasn't always easy. Carson wasn't fond of change and resisted losing some of his comfortable old ways. Maddie insisted that he should focus on how she was helping him grow and bringing them closer together. Maddie believed in love's transformative powers and knew she was helping Carson develop into the best version of himself.

Carson begrudgingly saw the wisdom of Maddie's ways and decided to embrace the change. He didn't want to simply become a better person; he wanted to become the man that Maddie saw in him. He made sacrifices and willingly transformed himself to strengthen their relationship. When it came to Maddie, Carson accepted her for who she was and loved her unconditionally. It seemed they both believed the saying "Women marry men hoping they will change. Men marry women hoping they will not." In *fact, Maddie was making great strides on her partner improvement project, especially on Carson's transformation from the stereotypical 1950s "housework is women's work" type of guy into the progressive modern man he was becoming.*

CHECKING YOUR BLIND SPOT

Who are you? Though that's difficult to answer, think back to the person you were five or ten years ago. You might be surprised by how much you've changed. Life has a funny way of doing that. But you haven't just changed; you've grown. You're different now. As couples grow together on life's journey, we expect love to transform us. It doesn't disappoint.

How Relationships Impact the Self

When we fall in love, our world seems to shift. Maybe what changes isn't really our world but us. To test the power of love to alter who we are, researchers followed more than three hundred undergraduate students over a ten-week period.[1] Why undergrads? To see how falling in love impacts the self, it helps to focus on a group that is highly likely to fall in love. During the ten-week study period, researchers checked in to see if people fell in love and to ask, "Who are you today?" For those who had fallen in love (about one-third of the sample), their answers became fuller and included additional self-concept content, such as new traits, skills, interests, roles, abilities, and perspectives. They experienced a literal expansion of the self and, as a result, had more to say. In contrast, those who didn't find romance provided less detailed information about themselves.

As much as relationships build us up early on, over time they may shape who we are in other ways. To understand this, we need to see the full picture of how relationships impact who we are. Along with my colleagues Brent Mattingly and Kevin McIntyre, I created a "Two-Dimensional Model of Self-Concept Change."[2]

Though the name is a bit of a mouthful, the model reveals the full spectrum of how relationships shape our self. True, relationships can hold us back by introducing negative qualities we never had (e.g., we were never so insecure or messy) or can steal our good qualities (e.g., we used to be so carefree and spontaneous). But we also need to give credit where credit is due and recognize how our relationship helps us. For example, our partner can enhance us by adding good qualities (e.g., we're much more cultured and a better listener) and can prune away some of our bad qualities (e.g., we're much less flaky and irresponsible).

Our relationship's impact on the self, both good and bad, helps determine relationship quality. If the relationship holds us back or encourages us to add negative qualities, we're more likely to cheat. When our relationship encourages us to develop good qualities and shed the bad ones, the relationship becomes stronger and more filled with love. Over time, being part of a self-enhancing couple encourages us to nurture the relationship by being more forgiving, sacrificing our own needs for the sake of our partner, and being more accommodating by doing things like seeking to reconnect when there's conflict.[3] However, if we're in a self-diminishing relationship, we're more likely to do damaging things like seeking revenge when our partner hurts us, paying greater attention to other, potential partners, and thinking more about breaking up. We rarely pause to appreciate how our relationship molds us, but focusing more on how it shapes our identity can help us thrive.

Helping Our Partner Change Isn't Helpful

The fact that relationships shape us makes it seem as if we should do our best Chip and Joanna Gaines impression and give our partner the fixer-upper treatment. If relationships change us, it seems logical that we should play a key role in guiding our partner's change, right? Wrong. Though it may seem like giving our partner little nudges down the path of improvement is a good idea, we're basing that belief on several faulty premises: (1) change is always good; (2) we know what changes are best; (3) we should help initiate the change; and (4) we have the skills to pull it all off. When we put it this way, our "Partner 2.0" plans sound more than a bit presumptuous.

Our biggest assumption is that change is automatically good for our partner. Yet when researchers studied thousands of adults over a ten-year period, those who experienced changes in their levels of personality traits (e.g., becoming less consci-

Bonus Blind Spot:
It Depends on Us

Our relationship's power to change us makes who we pick to be our partner an awfully important decision. That's because, for better or worse, we're likely to adopt some of our partner's traits. While it seems obvious that we should take on only traits that make us a better person, we don't always do what's best for ourselves. A 2019 study from Erica Slotter and a colleague at Villanova University sought to find out why this happens. Under the guise of a new online dating service, they had people describe themselves before and after reviewing a potential romantic partner's profile.[4]

When those who had a high opinion of themselves described themselves after viewing the profile, they incorporated positive traits from the potential partner. In a twist, those who held unflattering self-views voluntarily took on a potential partner's negative attributes. Though willingly incorporating undesirable traits is counterproductive, it shows just how strong the drive is to verify or reinforce one's current self-views. That is, if we have a low opinion of ourselves, a partner who adds to our negative attributes helps us maintain our self-view. Of course that relationship isn't changing us for the best and may, in fact, alter us for the worse.

entious or more open to new experiences) also reported lower life satisfaction, lower well-being, and worse overall health.[5] The negative impact of shifts in personality traits on physical health was even larger than the influence of age, ethnicity, smoking, and a history of cardiovascular disease. Not only is it bad for our partner's health; it's also bad for our relationship. Simply believing our partner needs to change can be enough to hurt the relationship.[6] And the more people tried to change their partner, the more the relationship suffered. Ironically, what helped the relationship was focusing on our own improvement and recognizing that a partner was also taking steps to improve. Trying to strengthen the relationship by changing the partner only made things worse.

Why are our attempts so counterproductive? Well, it's often a case of having a decent plan but lackluster implementation. The strategies we use to encourage our partner's improvements simply aren't very nice. Common tactics include expressing displeasure with the partner through yelling, cursing, and showing signs of irritation, frustration, and anger. We might also put our partner down by ridiculing, belittling, criticizing, insulting, and teasing them or try to control them by making them feel guilty, imposing demands, using bribes, and making outright threats. Not exactly a greatest-hits list of loving behaviors.

It's important to recognize when we're prone to using antagonistic techniques. For example, we're more likely to implement tactics like inducing guilt or being critical when we're feeling insecure about our relationship or bad about ourselves.[7] Again, those tactics are linked with lower relationship quality. Not only that, but we tend to pick on partners who are particularly vulnerable.[8] Our attempts to change a loved one who is sensitive to rejection or wants a lot of closeness are especially hurtful. This isn't lost on our partner, who fights back by attempting to make us feel guilty for trying to change them. If that works, they feel better, but we're less satisfied with the relationship. If their guilt inducing doesn't work, they're less happy. We can't win, and the relationship loses either way.

As bad as these negative strategies are, we convince ourselves that they're necessary. Our desire to help our partner make positive changes justifies a little discomfort and tough love. But we need to remember that bad tactics make the relationship worse. Perhaps a more subtle and positive approach would help? Instead of being mean, we could encourage our partner's transformation by "killing them with kindness."

Rather than punishing the bad, we could reward the good by being extra-supportive, loving, affectionate, and accepting when our partner acts the way we want them to. Going positive is better than going negative, but according to one study, positivity can also be problematic.[9] First the good news. On days when partners used positive strategies, relationship quality was higher. However, when looking at the relationship's overall quality over time, using positivity to manipulate partner change ultimately damaged the relationship. The problem? Good behavior comes with strings attached. When we put specific terms and conditions on our love, our good intentions seem anything but.

Embrace the Resistance

What if our partner-improvement plan isn't the problem? We've done our due diligence and have crafted a master blueprint of what needs to happen. Now we just need our partner to cooperate.

It's tempting to want a perfectly pliable partner who embraces change, happily follows our suggestions, and gratefully accepts our input.

Reality is quite different. All too often our biggest improvement-plan roadblock is a stubborn partner who doesn't want to change. Though having our plans thwarted can be frustrating, we should instead embrace the resistance. Our partner's reluctance is a good sign. People are less willing to change when they have high self-esteem, are less anxious, and aren't willing to adjust their behavior to fit in.[10] In other words, they don't require a lot of reassurance and attention to feel comfortable in the relationship. Relationships with these self-assured partners are more satisfying, are more committed, and have less cheating.[11] Clearly, our partner's stubborn streak has some hidden positives.

Similarly, those stoic partners are quite sure of what they believe and who they are.[12] Although that makes them less likely to change who they are as a person by taking on qualities from those around them, it helps the relationship. My own research finds that when people are clear and confident about who they are, they report higher satisfaction and commitment in their relationships.[13] These kinds of people engage in more helpful behaviors like listening or helping their partner consider problems from a new perspective.[14]

When our partner allows us to shape and craft them into who we want them to be, we get what we think we want. We convince ourselves these modifications are for their own good and are best for our relationship. If our partner is uncertain, they can lean on us to figure themselves out, or vice versa. Isn't that what good partners do? The truth is that having a hard-headed partner who is completely comfortable with who they are makes our relationship better.

HOW TO SEE YOUR RELATIONSHIP MORE CLEARLY

So, trying to change our partner into the person we want them to be is a blind spot that no longer seems like a good idea.

How Do You Measure Up?
Self-Concept Clarity

We like to think that we understand ourselves, are clear about who we are, and are confident and consistent in those conclusions. The more correct we are in those beliefs, the greater our self-concept clarity. To determine how clear you are about who you are, consider the following items:

1. My opinions about myself rarely conflict.
   Strongly Disagree 1 2 3 4 5 Strongly Agree

2. I know myself and am clear about the type of person I am.
   Strongly Disagree 1 2 3 4 5 Strongly Agree

3. My thoughts about myself are consistent and don't change often.
   Strongly Disagree 1 2 3 4 5 Strongly Agree

4. I find it easy to describe my beliefs, personality, and preferences.
   Strongly Disagree 1 2 3 4 5 Strongly Agree

Higher scores suggest greater clarity about who you are. Researchers find that those with lower self-concept clarity also report lower self-esteem, more neuroticism, chronic self-analysis, and more dwelling on self-thoughts.[15]

Instead, we need to think about our relationship differently. In many ways, the best change is no change at all. Rather than playing puppet master, we should welcome a little serenity and accept the things we cannot change. We need to love and appreciate our partner for who they are.

Accept the Things You Cannot Change

Imagine if the love of your life will fully love you only if you're willing to fix a few things about yourself. It feels wrong because our partner is supposed to love us for who we are. We should love them for who they are, too, unconditionally, no strings attached.

This is also the smart approach because when it comes to personality change, we're working against tremendous inertia. Findings from more than 150 studies with more than three thousand participants confirm that personality is largely stable and, importantly, only becomes more entrenched over time.[16] In other words, if we're hoping our partner becomes more outgoing, more thoughtful, less emotional, or less neurotic, not only is that unlikely to happen, but any improvements become less and less likely with each passing year. And this is good news because people who expect that their personality will remain consistent over time are happier and more satisfied later in life.[17] If we want what's best for our partner's happiness and well-being, not only should we not try to change them, but we should support their status quo and discourage them from trying to alter their personality.

Accepting our partner is important, but if they don't measure up to our expectations, we can feel stuck. Rather than forcing our partner to conform to our notion of a picture-perfect person, we need to be more realistic. In his eye-opening book *The All or Nothing Marriage: How the Best Marriages Work*, relationship scientist Eli Finkel argues that we demand too much from our romantic partner.[18] As part of his "suffocation model," Finkel argues that we require our partner to fulfill all our needs in ways that are historically unprecedented; one person can't possibly live up to these high standards.

Instead, we should diversify our relationship portfolio. We need to allow other relationships (with friends, family, and co-workers) to help pick up the slack. For example, our relationship partner may not need to help us solve every problem at work. Instead, we can rely on a close work friend to help us deal with our overbearing boss or passive-aggressive co-worker. Doing so will give us the freedom to stop insisting our partner meet every expectation and enable us to accept them for who they are, shortcomings and all.

Support the Partner's Change

Though we may accept our partner as is, they may not. The fact is that most people aren't content sticking with the status quo.[19] Instead, they want to grow for their own benefit. Our loved ones are no exception and deserve that opportunity on their own terms, with our full support. That starts with us stepping aside. If we're not able to do that, we might need to look in the mirror. Research from 2018 found that we fail to support our partner's desires to improve when we're unclear and confused about who we are.[20] If we don't know ourselves well, our partner's wish to change can feel threatening because we think we'll need to change too. However, if we're nurturing and supportive when our partner wants to take action, it not only helps them grow but also helps our relationship.[21] It's a win-win.

But we can do even better than just stay out of the way. The first step, and this is crucial, is to realize that what our partner chooses to improve is completely their call and has nothing to do with our preferences. What changes, when it happens, and how it's done are entirely their decisions to make. We're merely along for the ride, playing a supporting role and helping however we can along the way. That is, we need to be our partner's "sculptor." If that sounds a little too hands-on, you'll see that it's actually more passive and supportive when you consider Michelangelo's perspective on sculpting. Sculptors aren't builders who create things. Rather, sculptors are artists who help reveal the existing art form encased in stone. While working on the sculpture *David,* Michelangelo described it this way: "I saw the angel in the marble and carved until I set him free."[22] That's the role we need to play for our partner, through a process researchers have dubbed the Michelangelo phenomenon.[23] The process starts with our partner identifying their ideal self. That's the person she or he really aspires to be, keeping in mind that it's likely hidden underneath the considerable "marble" of our day-to-day lives. If it wasn't for work, kids, bills, family, daily hassles, and errands, who would our partner ideally want to be? Remember, this isn't about actively promoting what we want for them or for ourselves, but rather championing what our companion authentically wants.

When we've done our part successfully, we become an ally rather than an adversary. If our partner wants to be more adventurous, we can point out a new paddleboarding group they can join or help them find nearby hiking trails. If they want to be more outgoing, we can join them in attending social functions. If they want to become more organized, we can take notice when they make efforts to tidy up and declutter. That's playing Michelangelo and helping our partner reveal their inner angel. When we affirm our partner's ideal self, our partner experiences greater life satisfaction and better psychological health.[24] The relationship also benefits from increased satisfaction, commitment, and trust. All of which only becomes more important as our relationship matures. Research from 2018 shows that as we grow older and our sense of self becomes better defined, having our partner validate our ideal self is increasingly critical.[25]

Change What You Can — Yourself

Helping our mate achieve their ideal self is fantastic, but we shouldn't overlook a more direct strategy to help our relationship. We can simply direct our attention inward and start our own self-improvement plan. A major advantage of this approach is that we're the literal worldwide expert on ourselves. No one knows us better than us. Consequently, we're in a great position to know what we think is best for us, what we are truly willing to change, and what the best approach might be.

That all sounds good in theory, but can we actually put it into practice? To answer that question, researchers from the University of Illinois at Urbana-Champaign had participants indicate their change goals (e.g., wanting to be more talkative, agreeable, thoughtful).[26] Over the sixteen-week study, many people improved, with those who expressed a greater desire for change making more progress. In a follow-up, researchers helped one group of people develop a change plan in which they devised highly specific actionable steps to meet their goals. For example, instead of saying, "I want to be more sociable," they said, "I will smile more" or "I will start a conversation with a stranger." The other group simply described traits that were already true of them (an outgoing person would describe how talkative they were) and how those traits were beneficial. As predicted, those with a clearer change plan were more successful and experienced greater improvements. Not only is change possible, but it's especially likely when we want to improve and have a plan with clear, specific, and concrete steps.

Change the Relationship, Not Each Other

Relationships are full of moving parts. As we've seen, our partner may change, we may change, and both of those will shift our relationship's dynamics. This emphasizes the importance of partners getting on the same page about their plans for improvement. A 2017 study confirms that when partners' changes are aligned (both partners staying the same or both partners changing), couples have better relationships, are more stable, and experience more personal growth.[27] Partners are less satisfied with their relationships when they don't plan on changing themselves but think their mate is going to change.

We can become more aligned by focusing on a common goal. Instead of concentrating on each other's individual change, we can join forces to work on what we have in common: our relationship. This "relationship work" includes anything a couple does to maintain the relationship.[28] Although the word "work" makes it sound laborious, it's simply about making small changes that improve relationship harmony. Relationship work includes behaviors done for the partner's benefit like adjusting one's daily sleep or work schedule, adopting diet or exercise plans, improving spending habits, communicating with the partner, doing household or childcare tasks, spending time together, and being physically intimate with each other. When couples work to improve the relationship, the relationship benefits from greater closeness, satisfaction, and commitment. Importantly, relationship work helps all relationships, not just those that are in trouble or already broken.

Perhaps the most important work we can do is to uncover the origins of the "if you loved me, you'd change" impulse. If we stop to think about it, requesting that someone alter who they are is bold. That brazenness comes from the relationship's underlying power dynamics. We expect others to change only when we feel some level of superiority or authority over them. Case in point: an employee would never march in and ask their boss to change, but it's natural for a boss to ask or coax a subordinate to improve. We need to disrupt any hint of that imbalance in our relationship and acknowledge a basic truth: relationships function best when partners get fair and equal treatment.[29] Problems arise when one partner gains more benefits than they deserve, while the other gains fewer than they deserve.

How Do You Measure Up?
Equity in Your Relationship

Relationships require that partners work together. At different times, one partner may give while the other takes, and vice versa. Those instances accumulate over time to reveal general patterns in partners' relative contributions. To get a sense of your relationship's overall give-and-take, answer the following questions as honestly as possible.

1. In terms of what each partner contributes versus the benefits they receive, who is getting the better deal?
    __ Me __ Neither / It's Equal __ My Partner
2. In terms of decision-making, who is getting the better deal?
    __ Me __ Neither / It's Equal __ My Partner
3. In terms of showing affection toward each other, who is getting the better deal?
    __ Me __ Neither / It's Equal __ My Partner

---

4. In terms of receiving support and acceptance, who is getting the better deal?

___ Me   ___ Neither / It's Equal   ___ My Partner

Researchers measure equity in two ways. One is by getting an overall sense of who gives more to the relationship (e.g., item 1). The other, a "multitrait" approach (items 2–4), is by assessing equity in specific areas (e.g., appearance, intelligence, appreciation, household maintenance, finances).[30] In terms of scoring, the best answer for all four items is "Neither / It's Equal," but that's probably unrealistic. Instead, work on evening things out across all relationship areas (e.g., you do more in two categories while your partner does more in the other two so that you have a fair balance).

When we have the upper hand, it can embolden us to be more demanding. Not only do we expect our partner to fix things, but we feel compelled to supervise the process. That isn't fair. To balance things out we need to make the relationship more equal, which will ultimately make it stronger. Research that followed couples over a twenty-year period found that husbands and wives both reported worse relationships when they thought they "gave more" to the relationship than their spouse.[31] Similarly, a 2018 study found that among US couples, when relationships weren't equitable and fair, they had a greater chance of divorce, especially if the wife felt she received less than her fair share of benefits.[32] In contrast, when women felt more equal to their partners in terms of social status and love for each other, they were more satisfied.[33] Not only that, but the women's male partners experienced more intense and passionate sex.

The Division of Labor: Should That Change?

To help restore balance and keep things fair in the relationship, there are many facets to consider, such as finances and parenting duties. To appreciate how imbalance affects relationships, it can help to highlight a commonly researched area that every couple struggles with, one that has traditionally been unequal: housework. Nobody truly enjoys doing the dishes, cooking, doing the laundry, and cleaning up after the kids. But it's a necessary evil that couples need to navigate. For a number of reasons, it's also a breeding ground for inequity. The first issue is that everyone overestimates his or her contributions. When researchers asked participants what percentage of the housework they did, partners' estimates added up to over 100 percent.[34] Obviously, that's mathematically impossible, so someone is fooling themselves.

Though both partners may overestimate their individual contribution to household chores, the research is clear about who does more: women. Though estimates vary from study to study, one put women's weekly contributions at eighteen hours, easily outpacing men's ten hours.[35] Think about that. Women put in an entire eight-hour workday more each week than men! When women work outside the home, they put in less time around the house, making things a bit more equitable. However, in an unfair twist, when women earn more than their husbands do, their hours dedicated to housework increase. Worse, research shows that each week husbands create seven extra hours of housework for their wives, while wives actually save their husbands an hour of work each week.[36] Not surprisingly, once couples have children, wives' workload increases even further. In a sample of more than nineteen thousand participants, women reported doing more housework than their husbands when there was a young child at home.[37]

All this may seem unfair, but does anyone in the relationship care? At least according to one study, no.[38] To really understand what was going on, a researcher conducted in-depth interviews with couples regarding their household's division of labor. Importantly, these couples had the financial means to establish highly equitable roles. Yet, although they all claimed to value equality and considered it ideal, the vast majority didn't have equitable arrangements. You'd think that would be upsetting, but they were okay with it. Participants had several reasons (or rationalizations) for why unequal roles worked for their relationship. Mostly it came down to logistics based on partners' work schedules, or women being more adept at completing household chores. Though couples didn't seem to specifically negotiate their respective roles, women reported naturally "falling into" the role of primary household caretaker. Despite that being a rather stereotypical and uneven outcome, both men and women in the study reported feeling comfortable with the unequal roles.

Ready for a shock? Simply having guys make dinner or do the dishes more often to even things out may not help the relationship. That's because what is truly equal and what feels equal are worlds apart. The research shows that though it's still objectively unfair, if both partners consider the imbalance to be a good arrangement, it can benefit the relationship. A 2018 study that analyzed data from more than one hundred thousand men and women found that as couples were together longer, women's housework contributions decreased, while men increased their contributions over the years.[39] Though that made the division of labor fairer for women, women were less satisfied, while men were more satisfied. The reasons why the division of housework can impact relationships in this way could fill a sociology textbook. For our own relationships, the takeaway is that relationship success doesn't necessarily require every aspect of the relationship to be perfectly fair. As long as partners feel that everything balances out overall, the best change may be no change at all.

RELATIONSHIP RECAP

- Love changes us, and you need to see the full picture of how your relationship shapes you.
- It isn't your job to fix your partner. Change may not be good for them, and the techniques you might use to encourage change may be doing more harm than good.
- Be careful about being too pleased that your partner is willing to change for you; it could be a bad sign.
- You need to accept the things about your partner you cannot change.
- If you really want to make a difference, you can play Michelangelo and help sculpt your partner's ideal self.
- You should focus on what is easiest for you to change: yourself.
- You and your partner need to get on the same page about change, starting with making the relationship more equitable.
- Your relationship's division of labor may not be fair, but the imbalance may be good for your relationship.

Chapter 7

"It's Wrong to Be Selfish in a Relationship"

*C*onnie was a planner who chased her goals with a blueprint for who she wanted to be next week, next month, and next year. When she met Brian, everything changed. Connie was in love, so her master plan took a back seat. She made Brian her top priority, dedicating herself to making him happy. Not just for him, but for them.

Though Connie realized she was trading in some of her own happiness for the sake of the relationship, it felt right. Relationships were about giving, and Connie was willing to do her part. There was no denying it, being selfless wasn't always easy. Sometimes Connie felt unappreciated and a bit empty. In those moments of doubt she wondered, "What about me?" But she guiltily pushed those feelings aside and distracted herself from the creeping sense of dissatisfaction. Their relationship had stagnated and become boring. Rather than confront that fact, Connie made excuses and convinced herself that was normal.

CHECKING YOUR BLIND SPOT

The prevailing wisdom seems to be that true love requires endless devotion to our partner. What if it didn't? Prioritizing our partner feels noble, but it's a romanticized belief and blind spot that we've taken too far, all to our relationship's detriment. If we become our partner's personal Giving Tree, eventually there won't be anything left of us to give.

You Before Me, for Us?

In some ways, we can't help it. Our strong feelings toward our partner encourage us to put them first.[1] Along the way and in the name of love we may alter our career ambitions, live somewhere we don't particularly like, decide to have kids (or not have kids), change religions, or buy a house we don't really want. We may cede decisions to our partner, like which friends we hang out with, how much time to spend with each other's families, who takes care of the kids and the house, what we do for fun, where we vacation, what car we buy, how much sex we have, how much we talk, and how much time we spend at work or working out.[2] In each case, we're neglecting ourselves to bolster the relationship. Sadly, we may be doing more harm than good.

Bonus Blind Spot:
Why Too Much Giving in the Bedroom Is Bad

Sex requires a natural give-and-take, with each partner balancing their own interests with their partner's potential pleasure.

To explore sexual selflessness, a 2019 study tracked 122 cohabiting couples for three weeks, asking about two types of sexual giving.[3] The first focused on being attentive to the partner's needs (e.g., "During sex, I was focused on meeting my partner's needs"). The second took it one step further and focused on prioritizing partner needs to the exclusion of one's own (e.g., "During sex, I put my partner's needs ahead of my own needs").

Putting the partner first might seem like the ultimate selfless act and expression of love. Except that participants who took that "you before me" approach had lower sexual satisfaction. By focusing too much on their partner's needs, they noticed more negative aspects (e.g., their partner appearing distracted) and sex was less enjoyable. The researchers summed it up this way: "While meeting a partner's needs with responsiveness and care is crucial in romantic relationships, it is important, especially in the domain of sexuality, that people do not neglect their own needs when meeting the needs of their partner."

Admittedly, it's tricky because sacrifice does benefit our relationship in one major way: we're more committed.[4] Giving more of ourselves creates a stronger bond, making us more reluctant to leave. Sounds good so far, but that greater sacrifice doesn't make people any happier with the relationship or make them feel closer to their partner. In other words, putting our partner first keeps us together but doesn't necessarily make us better. And really, what's more important, a quality relationship or a long-lasting one? No one wants to get stuck in a bad relationship. The same study found that sacrifice increased commitment only on days when participants weren't stressed or experiencing hassles. Ever have one of those days? No? Neither do I. Not only that, but the partners who gained from the sacrifices weren't more committed. That's right, those benefiting from their partners' selflessness didn't feel more dedicated to the relationship.

Our partner isn't necessarily ungrateful, just oblivious. They miss about 50 percent of the sacrifices we feel we're making.[5] It's also legitimately difficult for anyone to know when we selflessly hold back opinions, interests, or emotions. That makes it hard for our partner to realize all the times we mute our frustration or disappointment with them, stifle our own positive emotions when they had a bad day, or hold back our true feelings about spending so much time with their family. The result? Both partners experience fewer positive emotions and lower life satisfaction, making the relationship less close and satisfying and encouraging more thoughts about breaking up.[6] When our attempts at generosity combine with our partner's apparent apathy and lack of acknowledgment, it's a recipe for resentment.

It's even worse if we're ceding our own interests for the wrong reasons, for instance, out of obligation, to feel less anxious, to avoid guilt, to have our partner think more positively about us, to keep our partner from being angry, or to feel more deserving of our partner.[7] Those types of selflessness lower life satisfaction and relationship quality, while increasing negative emotions, relationship conflict, and the chances of the relationship ending. While putting the love of our life first sounds like the right thing to do, our relationship doesn't need that kind of help.

Sacrifice's Fatal Flaw

There's an assumption that the more we give in our relationship, the more we get. In the spirit of hard work paying off, we romantically deny self-interest and prioritize our partner. Though the inclination is well intentioned, when we sacrifice the self we undermine the single most powerful determinant of our everyday experience: who we are. Our self-concept includes everything that describes us, including our roles (e.g., father, mother, employee, boss, caretaker, boyfriend, girlfriend, husband, wife), skills (e.g., good cook, fast runner), traits (e.g., skinny, athletic, smart, rich, pretty, funny, healthy), and hobbies and interests (e.g., hiking, painting, scrapbooking). Our self-concept influences every thought, memory, emotion, motivation, experience, interaction, and relationship. To ignore the self is to compromise everything.

Our best intentions can easily get the better of us, allowing us to give up too much. When we relinquish or silence our sense of self, our sacrifices take their most harmful form.[8] We give ourselves fully to the relationship by playing the role of deferential partner who puts personal needs aside in favor of the relationship's needs. Holding ourselves back can leave us feeling angry, inauthentic, or like we're putting on an act. That sounds bad, but we rationalize that we're altruistically devoted to the relationship's greater good. Ironically, it has the opposite effect.[9] Despite self-silencers holding themselves back to minimize relationship problems, their partners still express aggravation and frustration with them. Not surprisingly, self-silencing increases conflict as well as depression.[10] In all this, our relationship doesn't emerge unscathed.

There are countless academic books and research papers documenting how the self impacts relationships.[11] Suffice it to say that who we are is a critically important driving force for relationship success. When we sacrifice our self, we're making a mistake that can be fatal for our relationship. That's because depriving the self contradicts a fundamental human motivation: self-expansion, or our innate desire to grow and improve to become more capable, competent, and knowledgeable.[12] The self-expansion model was created by my mentor and graduate school advisor, Art Aron, and his wife, Elaine, two PhDs who met as students at Berkeley in the sixties. The model was born at the confluence of Eastern and Western philosophy and grounded in psychological science. With self-expansion, Art and Elaine tapped into an essential truth: we all want to be better people. When we bolster the self, we increase our sense of competence. That empowers us to seek out future challenges, which further expand the self. In other words, building and sustaining the self are crucial. But not just for ourselves.

Ignoring our own interests is also a recipe for relationship failure. For example, our sex life can suffer. Research from 2019 on 122 long-term couples in their early thirties found that on days when people spent less time focused on improving the self, they had less sexual desire and were less likely to have sex.[13] Worse, there was a carryover effect: failing to grow on a particular day made people less satisfied with the relationship on the following day. Deny ourselves self-expansion today, experience more problems tomorrow.

Forsaking our own self-development may even push us to commit the biggest relationship sin of them all: cheating. To escape that fate, we have to remember that providing ourselves with sufficient self-expansion is fundamental. Though we may try to convince ourselves that we can accept an unfulfilling relationship, there are consequences. Because self-expansion is so essential, if we don't get it from one source, we'll find another. If our current relationship partner can't meet our expansion needs, we may seek out someone who can. I studied this along with colleagues Laura VanderDrift Machia at Syracuse

University and Chris Agnew at Purdue University.[14] First, we asked people how much self-expansion they experienced in their relationship, then gave them a chance to interact with someone they felt was attractive. In reality, that someone was a computer giving preplanned answers. As we predicted, those with less fulfilling relationships enjoyed the scripted interaction more and wanted to ask more questions that gauged the potential partner's ability to provide self-expansion. Remember, these were people who were in relationships; paying extra attention to an attractive person who isn't their partner represents a significant threat to the relationship.

When people feel like they are getting insufficient self-expansion, there can be even more dire consequences. In a surprising follow-up, nearly 150 participants in long-term committed relationships did what they thought was an in-person "get acquainted" activity, where they could chat with other participants who happened to be attractive and single. Based on photographs alone, participants selected as many people as they wanted to as well as questions to ask them. Remember, as before, our study participants were already in long-term committed relationships. Given that, how many superhot singles should they try to get to know? *Zero!* However, those with less self-expanding relationships wanted to meet more people and planned on asking them questions like "Are you currently in a relationship?"

Maybe that doesn't exactly qualify as outright infidelity, but I think we can agree that having a wandering eye and seeking out conversations with attractive singles isn't good. Rather, it's a gateway behavior that brings us one step closer to crossing the line. The fact is that no one immediately jumps from "I would never consider cheating" to secret weekly hotel trysts with a new lover. Instead, infidelity starts with a series of seemingly innocuous behaviors. Sacrificing our self sets us on that path. In fact, research that I've done with my former student Rob Ackerman, now a professor at the University of Texas at Dallas, found that when participants thought their relationship wasn't providing enough self-expansion, they admitted to being more susceptible to cheating on their partner.[15] And a 2018 study by Brent Mattingly and colleagues found that if our current relationship doesn't sustain our sense of self, we'll end it so we can find another one that will.[16] When we willingly make sacrifices for the benefit of the relationship, we may ultimately end up sacrificing the relationship itself.

HOW TO SEE YOUR RELATIONSHIP MORE CLEARLY

Here's a piece of science-backed relationship advice that you never saw coming: be more selfish. Although it sounds like a crazy drink-more-wine-to-get-skinny fad diet and violates everything you have ever learned from Disney movies, wedding vows, and Drake songs, focusing more on yourself can help your relationship. The key is to meet your own needs in a way that doesn't harm your relationship. It's time to realize that the Giving Tree approach to love is a blind spot that leaves us feeling like a hollowed-out stump. No more martyrs. Instead, we need to spend more time focusing on our needs. Pull down that oxygen mask. Me before you.

Stop Accepting Less

Putting yourself first starts with refusing to accept less than you deserve. The problem is that you've been underselling yourself without even realizing it. Happily ever after. That's the relationship dream, right? It's the fairy tale we're all chasing. But when our relationship falls short, it's discouraging. Worse, when it happens repeatedly, it's easy to grow complacent.

It turns out we're focusing on the wrong goal. Happiness has a fatal flaw: it has a short shelf life.[17] Sure, when your partner gives you a kiss when you get home, puts a note in your lunch, snuggles with you on a chilly morning, encourages you, or simply remembers to take out the trash, it feels good. But that same partner may also be forgetful, grumpy, picky, nagging, lazy, emotionally distant, aggressive, unadventurous, unromantic, quiet, messy, inconsiderate, boring, difficult to live with, and an uninvolved parent, and, on top of it all, may snore. We learn to live with these shortcomings by finding happiness in other places: sunshine, warmth, drinking our morning coffee, hitting lighter-than-normal traffic during our commute, an afternoon nap, a snuggly blanket, our pets, a walk in nature, getting likes on our social media post, a lower-than-expected credit card bill, a good meal, or even a quiet house. Because we look outward to compensate for our less-than-satisfying relationship, we never solve the underlying issues.

We've been hopelessly and romantically seeking happiness from our partner and in our lives. But the truth is, life shouldn't be about merely being happy; we deserve to be a little selfish and demand so much more. We've earned the right to seek fulfillment, which far surpasses mere pleasure or satisfaction. While happiness is an ephemeral state, fulfillment is a way of life that impacts our whole self. Happiness is how we feel after spending a week at an all-inclusive resort. Fulfillment is how we feel after completing a 5K race. The resort gives us immense pleasure, and though it feels good, it doesn't take up much energy or initiative. The resort-inspired good feelings evaporate on Monday morning when we head back to reality. However, a demanding race requires greater determination, facing up to challenges, and a lot more effort. When we cross the finish line we're happy, but we experience a sense of growth and achievement that is deeper and more enduring. Though fulfillment demands more from us and involves less lounging around and fewer daiquiris, the experience sticks with us.

Fulfillment is meaningful. When researchers tracked 397 adults over several weeks, they found that people were happy when they were healthy, had their basic needs met, had an easy life, and had enough money.[18] Yet those things didn't make their lives any more meaningful. Those who found more meaning in their lives spent more time in deep thought, expressed themselves more, and established their own identity. If those activities sound a little self-absorbed, they are. But maybe that's the point; being a little selfish and focusing on themselves helped them find meaning in their lives, which benefited their relationships. Everyone wants what's best for the relationship. But forsaking our own need for fulfillment or focusing too much on superficial happiness has greater costs for our relationship.

Embrace the Suck

When you prioritize finding deeper meaning and fulfillment, you unburden yourself from needing to solve every little problem by working harder, doing more, dedicating more time, giving more, and, yes, sacrificing more. Attempting to reclaim lost happiness is a natural impulse, but trying too hard to make things better can backfire, a phenomenon known as the *cobra effect.*[19] The name comes from India, where during British rule, government officials sought to curb an overpopulation of venomous snakes. Their solution: place a bounty on the cobras' heads to incentivize residents to become snake killers. It worked, perhaps too well. In fact, snake heads became so valuable that breeding snakes became a decent side hustle. When the government caught on, it canceled the program. This left entrepreneurial snake breeders with a bunch of worthless snakes that they then released into the wild. Ultimately, the snake buyback program ended up exacerbating the original problem. The cobra effect's key lesson? Some problems are best left alone.

A 2018 study suggests that, rather than try to make things better, we should simply accept that we're annoyed, disappointed, frustrated, sad, angry, or hurt.[20] When we embrace negative feelings, we don't stress out as easily, have higher life satisfaction, and experience greater psychological well-being. The fact is (as we discussed in chapter 3), life isn't perfect, and neither is our relationship. When we acknowledge this reality, negative feelings can't sneak up on us and make us overreact. Understanding that it's okay to feel bad in small doses gives us permission to leverage those feelings in search of deeper fulfillment. We can do that by "embracing the suck." This Buddhist-military hybrid philosophy advocates the use of negative experiences as pivot points that set us on the path for improvement. The first steps on that journey need to focus on you.

Why Not Me?

It starts by looking in the mirror and being truthful with yourself. What if you're looking outward simply to avoid gazing inward? It's the perfect excuse. You convince yourself you can justifiably neglect yourself because you're fine. Honestly, it's a lie that disguises the fact that you find self-improvement intimidating. Sure, you acknowledge that growth is valuable, but when things get hard, you put it off. It's the perfect storm for procrastination.[21] Achieving growth takes grit, or a sense of passion and perseverance toward important long-term goals.[22] If you're not gritty enough, you take the easy way out and distract yourself with easier endeavors.

You hit the snooze button on yourself by claiming that you're too busy, that it's not important, that it's overly indulgent, that others need you more, or that you're completely happy as you are. There's another problem. According to research by Lydia Emery, a rising star in the field of the self and relationships, you're reluctant to pursue self-improvement out of fear of failure.[23] It's like calling in sick for the test you didn't prepare for. If you don't know where to start, pursuing personal growth feels impossible to navigate. It's also difficult because improvements may make you even less clear and confident about yourself. That makes it all too easy to selflessly shift your focus onto others around you, like your kids, spouse, pets, extended family, and friends. However, you can't leave yourself behind.

Me Time

You need to put yourself first, and that's going to require being a little selfish. As uncomfortable as that sounds, believe it or not, our partners want this for us. As researchers who study sacrifice in close relationships stated, "People might prefer that their partner chooses not to sacrifice for them and instead, that their partners independently pursue their own interests."[24] That's right, this is our free pass to take some me time.

When we do, we want to optimize our me time to make it as beneficial as possible. The key is to make sure we're doing NICE things—*n*ovel, *i*nteresting, *c*hallenging, and *e*xciting things. Importantly, these elements are subjective, so what checks all four boxes for one person (e.g., working on the Sunday crossword) may not be as interesting or exciting for another who requires something more intense (e.g., rock climbing). Incorporating self-expanding NICE qualities is as easy as taking on new hobbies, exploring new interests, building new skills, and contemplating new ideas. We could simply read a book from a new author or on a new topic, check out a podcast we've never heard, watch a YouTube clip to teach ourselves a new skill, start a brand-new series on Netflix, take a class at a local college or community center, go to a newly opened restaurant (bonus points for sampling a cuisine we've never tried), take a different route to work, have a conversation with someone who sees the world differently than we do, or take a trip to an unfamiliar place. We have a lot of choices and the choice is ours.

Here's the part where we start feeling guilty because all that me time seems self-absorbed, egotistical, and neglectful. But that's being unnecessarily harsh. Sure, solo activities require time away from our partner, but the net gain is well worth the temporary absence. Our me time has a trickle-down effect because research shows that when one person expands the self, provided their partner is supportive, everyone benefits from a more satisfying relationship.[25] This suggests we should also embrace our partner's selfishness. Not only will they grow and reap the personal rewards, but they may be more likely to support our selfish pursuits as well.

Us Time

If all that me time still feels overly selfish, here's some welcome news: you can also be selfish while doing things with your partner. That is, you can selfishly focus on improving yourself, building up your capabilities, adding to your knowledge and perspectives, and growing as a person by having the right kind of "us time." It's as simple as continuing to date your partner.

Dating...sounds vaguely familiar. Early in your relationship it was part of your routine. Over time it's easy to get a little lazy and take the relationship for granted. To counteract any potential apathy, you need to selfishly preserve your relationship by unapologetically giving it the care and attention it deserves. Step one is not to become comfortable with boredom. Cheryl Harasymchuk, one of the least boring people I've ever met, has done research showing that couples rightfully consider boredom a clear sign that they need to pay more attention to their relationship.[26] But how? They could focus on doing familiar and well-liked activities that they know will restore a sense of security. Or they could try something new that might be interesting and promote self-growth. It turns out couples don't play it safe. Despite the risk involved, when confronted with boredom they choose to do NICE self-expanding activities together. That's really smart because the science makes it abundantly clear that people who self-expand more have better, more passionate, more satisfying, and longer-lasting relationships.[27]

As you get ready for date night, you'll inevitably ask your partner, "So what do you want to do?" Their likely response is either "I don't know" or "Whatever you want to do." Looks like it's up to you. To be fair, "What do you want to do?" is a tough question because there are endless possibilities. If only someone could identify activities and rank which are best. Relationship scientists have you covered. They contacted adults over a three-week period to see how much self-expansion they

---

How Do You Measure Up?
Self-Expansion

In light of self-expansion's importance, you may wonder how your relationship stacks up. To gauge how much self-expansion you're currently getting from your relationship, consider the following sample items from the Self-Expansion Questionnaire (SEQ), which I developed:

1. How much has knowing your partner made you a better person?
    Not at All 1 2 3 4 5 6 7 A Great Deal
2. How much does being with your partner result in you having new experiences?
    Not at All 1 2 3 4 5 6 7 A Great Deal
3. How much has being with your partner resulted in you learning new things?
    Not at All 1 2 3 4 5 6 7 A Great Deal
4. How much does your partner help to expand your sense of the kind of person you are?
    Not at All 1 2 3 4 5 6 7 A Great Deal

Each of the four items taps into how much your relationship helps you expand your sense of self, with higher scores indicating more self-expansion. If you want another way to see how

---

self-expanding your relationship is, just look at your Facebook page.[28] When a relationship helps to grow and nurture the self, partners mention similar interests in their profiles, tag each other in status updates, or appear together in pictures. The first step to making sure you get to where you want to go is knowing how self-expanding your relationship is.

experienced each day and what led to that growth.[29] They found that the most common NICE activities were going on outings together (e.g., going to dinner or a special event), doing things together around the house (e.g., painting a room), and engaging in leisure activities (e.g., watching TV together at home).

But we also want to know which activities will help us reap the most benefits. The top three activities were having sex and experimenting with new positions, showing affection by cuddling or massaging each other, and sharing humorous or funny experiences. Other highly ranked activities were planning for future events, supporting each other, engaging in physical activity (e.g., exercising together, going on a hike), attending religious services together, learning something new from the partner (e.g., they teach you how to garden), and having in-depth conversations and self-disclosing feelings. Surprisingly, the researchers found that even negative experiences like having an argument can produce self-expansion. That's because fights give us an opportunity to communicate, work things out, and ultimately overcome the source of conflict. When we do that, we feel a sense of accomplishment and develop skills that will make future disagreements less likely or less severe.

Bonus Blind Spot:
Partners Who Play
Together Feel Good Together

One of the perks of being in a relationship is hanging out with someone we love. There are plenty of activities couples can do together, so the million-dollar question is: what kind are best? Though activities that stretch our comfort zone promote self-expansion, more mundane activities have their benefits as well. A study from 2019 explored whether it was better to stay in or go out by randomly assigning married and cohabiting couples one of two activities:[30] playing games like Battleship, Boggle, Connect 4, Jenga, Monopoly, Risk, Scrabble, Sorry!, UNO, or Yahtzee; or taking a group art class in which they sat next to each other.

Both the game and art-class groups had similar levels of social interaction, and all couples experienced a spike in oxytocin levels (the so-called cuddle hormone) from doing an activity together. However, couples in the art class released more oxytocin and engaged in more touch, despite communicating less. The art class was especially beneficial to male partners, with their oxytocin levels shooting up twice as high as all the women's and as the men's who played games. Why? It was more distinct and novel than the couples' everyday activities. Helping our relationship obviously doesn't require a smock and paintbrushes, but this research shows that we need to step outside of our comfort zone if we want to give our relationship a boost.

Ultimately, sacrificing self-interests for our relationship isn't good or bad but somewhere in between. It comes down to dosage. Some selflessness is helpful, but we can go too far and lose ourselves along the way. When we do make sacrifices, they should ideally be minor, like letting our partner decide which TV show to watch, what color carpet to buy, or what to have for dinner. Sacrifices should also be mutual, and not fall primarily on one partner, or require anyone to compromise their own pursuit of meaning, fulfillment, and self-discovery. Rather, to keep the relationship going strong, both partners should be able to be a little selfish and indulge themselves without guilt.

RELATIONSHIP RECAP

- Sacrificing yourself to benefit your partner feels romantic, but it undermines the relationship.
- Failing to properly nurture yourself has a fatal flaw: self-sacrifice puts the relationship at risk by increasing the chances of cheating.
- To really help your relationship, you should feel empowered to be more selfish. That starts with refusing to accept less than you deserve by focusing on finding fulfillment, instead of merely being happy.
- You should "embrace the suck" and use negative emotions as a pivot point to start spending more me time. Putting me before you helps both of you.
- Couples who are selfish about the relationship, by dating and expanding together, stay together.

Chapter 8

"We Need to Be Closer"

*Y*ou know that feeling you get when a puppy or kitten is so impossibly cute that you want to squeeze it and never let go? That's how Annabelle felt about Benjamin. He was her everything. In their circle of friends, they were the couple. Everyone jokingly referred to them as "Benanna." It was a bit cringey; Ben tolerated it, but Annabelle loved it. By practically any standard, Benanna's relationship was amazing. Good thing because, for perhaps the first time in her life, Annabelle was officially all in. Everything was going well, almost too well, which was a little terrifying. If it didn't work out, Annabelle knew, she would be devastated. It all left her with a nagging sense of vulnerability.

Naturally she was protective of their relationship, and lately Annabelle had felt Ben drifting away. Sensing the growing distance, Annabelle insisted they spend even more time together. Still, Annabelle never quite felt they were close enough. Wary of threats, she constantly looked for signs of trouble. And she found *them. Benjamin pushed back against the new demands on his time, Annabelle's neediness, and her constant checking up. Annabelle insisted it was romantic, a well-intentioned sign of how much she cared, and simply what good couples do. She thought he should feel flattered but, more important, loved. Ben just felt smothered.*

CHECKING YOUR BLIND SPOT

When we picture romantic relationships, we often envision two people happily snuggling by a fire, enjoying every moment together, and pondering their shared destiny, side by side. In reality, a relationship is more about two individuals desperately trying to sync up whenever possible, only to spend much of the time apart, tired, stressed out, and living in what feels like two different worlds. When our relationship feels like it's falling short, doubt creeps in because we don't want to lose something we care so much about. Rather than indulge our overprotective impulses, we're better off putting our faith in our relationship's inherent strength. That's easier said than done.

Many of us want more closeness. According to a large-scale longitudinal study of more than 1,500 adults primarily in their midthirties, 57 percent felt too distant and wanted more closeness.[1] That's a big problem, because when people don't get the closeness they desire, they feel more depressed; their relationship suffers from lower satisfaction and commitment; and they think more often about breaking up. Sure, that sounds bad, but don't take this as a suggestion to solve any perceived intimacy gap by insisting on greater closeness.

We Don't Want to Lose Our Partner

We all yearn for a loving relationship that feels safe, reliable, and comfortable. Feeling unsure about something as important as our relationship can leave us unsettled. Our partner is our person, the one we depend on. If our confidence in that bond is shaken, we feel threatened and worry about being abandoned. We can respond in two ways. First, we focus on self-preservation by putting up walls. It feels right because we're keenly aware of how unbelievably devastated we'd be if our relationship faltered. We do whatever we can to avoid those bad feelings ever happening. The concern over being hurt and abandoned overtakes our natural desire for connection. We all have concerns and exhibit self-protective impulses at times. However, when this guarded approach to intimacy is pervasive, researchers consider it an avoidant attachment style.[2]

Second, when we start to feel the relationship slip, we hold on tighter. In other words, our sense of vulnerability encourages us to be hypersensitive to any signs of drifting apart. To curb uncertainty, we double down on our connection by seeking ways to get closer and strengthen our bond. Doing so allows us to feel more confident in our relationship and worry less about potential abandonment. We figure if we're super-close to our partner, it would be difficult to miss them, feel neglected, feel lonely or sad, or worry about who else our partner may spend time with. This is a common strategy for those with an anxious or preoccupied attachment style.

It's logical to want to build a stronger bond in response to feeling less close. But when this desire becomes more oppressive or one-sided, some very real problems can occur. Wanting to be closer can morph into increasingly attention-seeking, clingy, and demanding behaviors that quickly start to feel stifling, suffocating, and oppressive to our partner. It's immensely counterproductive because we don't like needy partners. In fact, when a multinational team of researchers sampled more than five thousand Americans about their top relationship deal breakers, being "too needy" was number three on the list.[3]

Optimal closeness is a slippery goal because it's difficult to define. Without any clear criteria, every time we achieve a benchmark for greater closeness, there's the tantalizing possibility that if we were just a bit closer, our relationship would be even better. Tempted by this thought, we become preoccupied with our relationship. Our closeness concerns also encourage us to become hypervigilant. Now we start focusing on our partner's actions and mannerisms, all in an attempt to pick up subtle clues about how our partner is feeling.[4] Fueled by an intense desire to be with our partner, we can spend a lot of time contemplating our anxieties about the relationship's future.

When our partner starts feeling distant, it even hinders our ability to think clearly.[5] The real problem is what all this misplaced attention does to the relationship. According to a 2018 study, when people regularly felt their partner didn't "want to get as close as I would like," their relationship was more volatile.[6] In other words, caring too much about closeness is a destabilizing force that leads to more ups and downs, more daily conflict, and lower relationship quality. Ultimately, trying to hold on so tightly leads to bigger problems than the one we're attempting to solve.

Protecting What's Ours

We may use more subtle strategies to bolster confidence. For example, we could get reassurance by making sure everyone in our life knows we're a happy couple. There is perhaps no better place to broadcast our relationship's strength than on social media. When we're scrolling through posts on our phone, it's easy to assume all the smiling couples, with their exciting date nights and perfect family portraits, are completely confident in their relationship. But research from 2019 shows that those with concerns about their relationship's closeness were more likely to use Facebook to maintain their relationships and solicit positive attention from others.[7] People were also more likely to make their relationship visible when they felt less secure in their partner's feelings about them and less sure about the relationship.[8] They made their relationship more noticeable by including their partner in their profile picture, posting more couple pictures, mentioning the partner in updates, and disclosing more about the relationship in posts. Those who were less secure were especially likely to post about their relationship on days they felt more uncertain about the relationship. These kinds of posts are meant to show strength and certainty, when the reality is they reveal anything but.

There's also a darker side. Those seeking greater closeness in their relationship are more likely to stalk or engage in surveillance of their partner's social media (e.g., Facebook page).[9] Sure, spying or checking in on our partner to see what they've posted recently might be harmless, but it can suggest deeper problems like jealousy. When we sense threats to the stability of our relationship, it sets off alarm bells. Thinking about the potential loss of something we hold so dear breeds jealousy.[10]

Ironically, jealousy emanates from uncertainty, yet research from 2018 finds that we often combat those feelings by trying to make our partner jealous.[11] We don't want to lose them, so we set out to make them worry about losing us.

What's even more ironic, not to mention counterproductive, is that we commonly use distancing as a jealousy-inducing technique. We might create artificial space in the relationship by being too busy to see our partner, ignoring our partner, or making plans without our partner.[12] The hope behind our manipulative strategy is that our partner senses the distance, starts to worry, and becomes motivated to close the void so we don't leave — that they'll now do whatever they can to improve the relationship, including getting closer to us to cure their own jealousy.[13] If only it were that simple.

There are three potential responses to induced jealousy. Our partner might try to improve the relationship, might become aggressive (e.g., throwing things, punching a wall), or might withdraw. So, not only are we twice as likely to get a bad response, but one of those responses — withdrawal — is the antithesis of the enhanced closeness we originally sought. By playing games and trying to bait our partner into getting closer, we actually push them further away. If strengthening the relationship is truly the goal, increasing jealousy is more likely to do the opposite. In fact, jealousy is one of the most common reasons for couple violence and even murder.[14] Not only are relationships with more jealousy less satisfying; jealousy's harmful effects on the relationship are magnified for those who are anxious about being close.[15] Jealousy also triggers repetitive thought processes about the partner, increased surveillance of the partner, and ultimately lower relationship satisfaction.[16] We have a blind spot that encourages us to see our jealousy as a plea for greater closeness and a positive sign of our devotion, when in reality it is a red flag for our relationship's future. Not only do we need to recognize the negative implications of our own jealousy, but we should also realize how a jealous partner threatens our relationship.

What Does It Mean to Be Close?

Perhaps inducing jealousy feels a bit extreme, or passive-aggressive. Instead, to achieve the closeness we desire, we might seek a more obvious solution: undivided attention. We can simply spend more time together, without anyone else around.[17] Not in a creepy way. We might just want more alone time, more quality time together. The possibilities are endless because we can hang out together doing almost anything: laundry, grocery shopping, cooking, eating, watching TV, going out, cleaning, exercising, working on the house, and so on.

It's a good start, but if we're desperate to deepen our bond with our partner, those everyday behaviors are focused only on the time we spend together, which can feel superficial. To get the full closeness experience, just hanging out isn't enough. We also want to form a deeper connection by defining ourselves as part of an "us." That is, we seek to merge our identity with our partner's, willingly losing parts of ourselves along the way. Sounds romantic, but it can backfire. When this blending happens, we have a hard time knowing where one person ends and the other begins, which leads us to confuse our own traits with our partner's.[18] Because we want so badly to have a close and loving relationship, we're willing to potentially sacrifice who we are to make it a reality. Relationship scientists Erica Slotter and Wendi Gardner study how who we are as a person influences our relationship, and how our partner shapes our sense of self. Their notable study "How Needing You Changes Me" found that when people worried about being close enough, they wanted to have their sense of self more fully merged with their partner's.[19] To make that happen, participants happily adopted their partner's traits as their own. That is, to get closer, they sacrificed their own identity and willingly changed who they were. By itself, that isn't necessarily a bad thing, but it is risky. We can change for the better with our partner's help, but allowing ourselves to be so malleable puts us in jeopardy. Though we hope to take on only each other's best qualities, the reality is that our real-life partners come with a mix of positive and negative traits. Rather than judiciously sorting the good from the bad, the desire for greater closeness encourages us to incorporate all a partner's traits, including the negative ones, into the self.[20] For example, our partner may be ambitious, funny, and adventurous, but also pretentious, materialistic, and rude. As we grow closer and take on their qualities, we may get more negative traits than we bargained for. When we prioritize greater closeness, we can forget what's best for us and willingly sacrifice who we are. As Marc Chernoff (not Ernest Hemingway, as the Internet would lead you to believe) put it, "The most painful thing is losing yourself in the process of loving someone too much, and forgetting that you are special too."

Careful, You Might Just Get What You Want

Clearly, we're willing to go to great lengths to get the closeness we desire. However, there's a potential unintended consequence of spending more time together and blending our identity with our partner's: we may be successful. By asking our partner to meet our needs, we run the very real risk of pushing past their comfort zone. That is, we may want more closeness than our partner is willing, or able, to comfortably provide.

When I started studying relationships in graduate school, I had the pleasure of sharing a research lab with Deb Mashek. A native Nebraskan, Deb is one of the most delightful and genuine people you could ever meet. Deb is now the executive director of the Heterodox Academy, but during our time in grad school she was busy pioneering research exploring how partners can feel too close. Deb's insight wasn't just that we can go overboard with what's typically a positive component of healthy relationships. It was also that how close we are to our partner isn't nearly as important as how close we want to be.

Think of it this way: both relationship partners could have identical scores indicating how close they currently feel (e.g., a 6 out of 7). However, both partners may not feel the same about the relationship. One person could be perfectly content with their 6, while the other is miserable. To really know how someone feels, we need to know how the closeness they're getting compares to how much closeness they desire. A 6 can feel insufficient if we want more closeness or oppressive if we want less. In other words, the reality of how close we are to our partner doesn't matter. Whether we're content with our closeness depends on whether we're getting what we want. We can have too much of a seemingly good thing.

Feeling too close is more common than we might think. When Deb collected data from more than six hundred participants, nearly 60 percent reported feeling too close to their partner at times in their relationship.[21] Her research also revealed that the feeling of wanting more space was unpleasant. People described being too close as feeling "locked down," "caged up," "overwhelmed," "oppressed," "trapped," and "suffocated." The root cause seemed to be that excessive closeness infringed on participants' sense of personal control and threatened their identity. That is, they weren't feeling like themselves and felt like they were losing their freedom.

Not surprisingly, people pushed back by increasing distance. The top ten most common responses to wanting less closeness included "needing time alone," "needing space," "spending less time together," "spending more time with friends," "needing independence," and "pushing the partner away."[22] Participants felt "trapped," "smothered," and "like the partner wanted too much," which led to "withdrawing," "wanting freedom," "needing space," and "thinking partner is 'not the one.'" The relationship naturally suffered, resulting in less passionate love, satisfaction, and commitment. Wanting greater closeness comes with a clear risk: it may compel our partner to seek greater distance and potentially push us away forever. It hardly seems fair. We were only trying to make our relationship stronger. Maybe we didn't need to.

HOW TO SEE YOUR RELATIONSHIP MORE CLEARLY

When people feel disconnected from others, they can sulk and retreat further away. But that's not what they do.[23] Instead, research participants sought a stronger bond by making themselves seem more similar to those they wanted to be closer to. They even lied a bit to do it, presumably because they felt it was for a good cause. They simply wanted to reconnect. When our partner pulls away, we reflexively pursue connection.

However, our instincts about fixing the distance dilemma fail us. Rather than seek greater closeness, we need to realize a bit of space isn't a problem worth fixing.

A Little Distance Goes a Long Way

We're sensitive to any signs of aloofness in our relationship because we all have a fundamental need to belong and maintain a connection with the people who are most central in our lives.[24] Any glitch captures our attention, but if we react to those glitches by not overreacting, we give our partner a chance to step forward.

That tiny bit of a buffer does something very practical: it allows our partner to miss us. The key is to understand "miss" for what it is. Research I've done with my friends Ben Le and Tim Loving shows that while missing makes us feel separate and sad, it also creates a sense of longing, of wanting to be with the partner and thinking more about the partner.[25] All of which can encourage us to reunite. Thus, missing our partner isn't the red flag we might think. Rather, missing is a positive sign of our commitment and how much we value the relationship.[26] That dedication encourages us to sustain the relationship by being nice to our partner, talking more, and telling them how much we care. However, if we continue to insist on omnipresent closeness, neither partner will get a chance to miss the other. As a catchy power ballad from the eighties hair metal band Cinderella once suggested, we don't always have the wisdom to see what we have until it's gone. By embracing a little more breathing room, we can use missing as a secret weapon to energize behaviors that will strengthen our relationship.

A little time apart also provides an opportunity to gain perspective and more fully appreciate what we have together. It's easier to forget than we may think. That's because we have a natural tendency to adapt to experiences that provoke happiness, a phenomenon researchers call hedonic adaptation.[27] We start taking the positives in our lives for granted. The good parts just don't seem as good as they once were because we've grown accustomed to them. Relationships are especially prone to hedonic adaptation. A great relationship is really satisfying early on, but its impact lessens over time. Those fantastic experiences quickly become the new norm, and we subsequently need even greater levels of positivity to be equally satisfied. If our relationship is somehow superhuman and able to provide a constant stream of experiences that only increase in amazingness over time, hedonic adaptation isn't a concern. But that's asking a lot. Realistically, at some point, it becomes impossible for partners in any relationship to have the time and energy to keep up the pace of providing endless positivity.

To avoid this trap of taking what you have for granted and constantly needing more, we can draw a lesson from massage research. As positively satisfying experiences go, a full-body rubdown from someone who knows what they're doing is way up there on the list. Want to know what makes a massage even better? A little break. When people paused and took a rest partway through their massage, it made their experience more enjoyable.[28] Taking a bit of a breather allowed them to come back fresh and ready to better appreciate the overall experience. The same is true in our relationship: a little space can go a long way toward avoiding apathy and sustaining good feelings.

To keep our positive relationship momentum going, we can elude complacency by learning from long-distance relationships.

That may seem like an odd suggestion, but most people have the wrong idea about long-distance relationships and assume they're inferior to relationships where partners routinely spend time together. In fact, they have a key benefit. When romantic partners live apart, their relationships naturally include breaks that disrupt the hedonic-adaptation cycle. When couples are physically apart, their communication patterns must adapt, so that the couples are video chatting, calling, and texting more.[29] Despite the technological divide, their interactions are of higher quality and focus more on key issues like future plans. When those partners are physically together, they make their time count by doing fun and interesting things. It seems that having little breaks not only helps these couples avoid falling into a rut but also makes them savor their time together.

With that in mind, it probably won't be surprising to learn that long-distance relationships can be stronger than relationships where couples see each other all the time. In fact, data from a national sample of nearly one thousand people found that people in long-distance relationships were more in love, had more fun with their partner, had better conversations, were more dedicated, were less hostile, felt less trapped, and felt less likely to break up than couples who regularly spent time together.[30] In commuter marriages, partners live separately for work and see each other on the weekends. Though they are untraditional, a 2017 study of these marriages found that spouses felt the distance made them more reliant on the relationship, and they were more integrated in their partner's life.[31] It's a bit counterintuitive, but for many, living separately enhanced their closeness and strengthened their bond. The benefits of long-distance relationships are so pronounced that research out of Ohio State University shows that when long-distance couples no longer have to be apart, their relationships often suffer.[32] The takeaway isn't that partners must live separately for the relationship to survive. Rather, giving each other a little space and time apart and demanding less closeness give us the best of both worlds and provide our relationship the room it needs to thrive.

Closeness Done Right

At the heart of every relationship there's friction between each partner's need to be connected and their need to be distinct. We fear losing our relationship, but we also don't want to lose ourselves. To master closeness, we need to find the balance, an equilibrium researchers call "optimal distinctiveness."[33] In couples, optimal distinctiveness means creating harmony between each partner's need to express their individual "me" and their desire to be part of a "we."[34] For that to happen, we need to give each other space to breathe and move. When we balance me time with we time, we allow each other the room each of us needs to sprout. As Kahlil Gibran writes in *The Prophet,* "Let there be spaces in your togetherness.... / And stand together, yet not too near together: / For the pillars of the temple stand apart, / And the oak tree and the cypress grow not in each other's shadow."

To achieve optimal growth, we must stop romanticizing persistent closeness and neediness. Rather, we need to see insecurity for what it is: a relationship threat. When we're too needy, we become overprotective in ways that can make our partner feel smothered. Too often in the quest for closeness we take aim at the low-hanging fruit: the amount of time we spend together. But that's misguided because it's possible to spend a lot of time with our partner and still feel we're not as close as we'd like to be. We need to trade in quantity for quality by emphasizing the psychological connection we have with our partner. This means focusing on how much who we are aligns with who our partner is—researchers call this "inclusion of other in the self."[35] When this happens, our self-concept begins to blend with our partner's and we think less in terms of "I," "me," and "mine," and more in terms of "us," "we," and "ours." Again, there's a balance to strike between sharing ourselves with our partner and becoming too close and losing ourselves completely. Instead of thinking "I like pizza" and "My partner likes pizza," inclusion makes us think "We like pizza." Research shows that focusing more on this type of couple identity ultimately benefits the relationship.

This may sound like it is easier said than done, but there are ways for partners to create closeness between their self-concepts. A few years ago, a classic psychology study went

How Do You Measure Up?
Closeness

To get a sense of how close a person feels their sense of self is to their partner's, researchers use two key measures. The first is Art and Elaine Aron's Inclusion of Other in the Self (IOS) Scale, which features seven pairs of overlapping circles (shown here as hearts). These Venn diagrams represent how much our sense of self overlaps with our partner's. They range from no overlap at all to nearly complete overlap. Your job is to pick the one set of circles / hearts that "best describes your current relationship with your partner." Circles / hearts with greater overlap represent greater inclusion of other in the self.

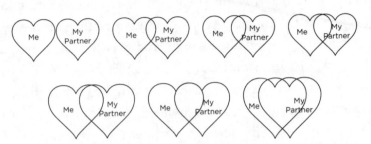

Despite the IOS Scale's simplicity, it effectively and reliably captures both how much time we spend together in shared behaviors and how much our sense of self is blended with our partner's.[36]

The second approach, developed by Chris Agnew and his colleagues, provides an even subtler test of closeness by focusing on the language we use when describing our relationship.[37] In this test, you "share some of your thoughts concerning your relationship." These can be any thoughts you have about your partner or the relationship. Taking no more than fifteen minutes, write down as many or as few positive or negative thoughts as you want. You can write anything, but your responses should be full sentences. To see how close you feel to your partner, look back at your statements and count up the number of plural pronouns (e.g., we, our, us) and compare it to the number of singular pronouns (e.g., I, me, mine, he, she). Greater use of plural pronouns suggests greater closeness and integration of our self with our partner, while more singular pronouns indicate less closeness and merging of identities.

viral. It all started with a *New York Times* article by Mandy Len Catron entitled, "To Fall in Love with Anyone, Do This." The contents caught fire and quickly spread across the Internet. The study even made a cameo on *The Big Bang Theory,*

169

where Sheldon and Penny tried their hand at accelerating intimacy. Needless to say, psychology studies rarely gain this type of popularity, especially research that is two decades old. Yet the study's lesson is timeless.

The original paper's title was actually "The Experimental Generation of Interpersonal Closeness."[38] That's right, the study was about enhancing feelings of closeness, not about making two people fall in love (though that was a side effect for at least one pair of participants). Importantly, the activity featured in the study didn't require that people spend more time together. Instead, it required only a conversation.

Researchers had everyone take turns responding to thirty-six questions. Half of the participants had closeness-promoting questions such as "Is there something that you've dreamt of doing for a long time? Why haven't you done it?" The other participants' thirty-six questions focused on small-talk topics like "What is your favorite holiday? Why?" As predicted, the first type of question increased intimacy and made partners feel closer to each other.

If you're curious and want to try the original thirty-six questions from the study, a quick Internet search for "36 questions" will surely lead you to them. However, the magic isn't in the exact wording of the original questions but in the themes that the questions evoke, such as disclosing important personal information and sharing in a way that creates vulnerability. Topics included personal traits, past experiences, family relationships, hopes for the future, things partners have in common, and sensitive areas that expose personal weaknesses. Here are ten questions I created that follow the original thirty-six questions' themes:

1. When you were a kid, what did you want to be when you grew up?

2. Think of someone you consider a mentor; what qualities do you most admire in them?
3. If you could wave a magic wand and change one thing about your life so far, what would it be and why?
4. What are three traits you like about yourself? What are three things you'd like to improve?
5. When have you failed?
6. Describe something in your life that made you cry.
7. What are your parents like? How are you similar to or different from them?
8. Describe something you did in your life that made you proud.
9. What key experiences have made you the person you are today?
10. Think about the person you're doing this activity with; what about them do you admire?

Armed with these questions, you're ready for your next dinner conversation or date night. Now, the natural impulse would be to have this intimate conversation alone as a couple. But this seemingly logical assumption can hold your relationship back. To strengthen the thirty-six questions' power, you may want to take the show on the road. In a study cleverly titled, "When Harry and Sally Met Dick and Jane," Rich Slatcher, now at the University of Georgia, wanted to see how having couple friends impacted a relationship.[39] He did this by having sets of couples either engage in a thirty-six-question-style activity or engage in basic small talk. As Rich expected, the thirty-six-questions activity improved relationships for several reasons. First, the activity introduced new and interesting information as each person learned not only about their partner but about the other couple as well. These high-quality interactions intensified positive feelings. Second, answering the thirty-six questions built stronger connections and friendships between the couples. Not only did they expand their social circle, but the quality of that new bond was better because it came from deeper and more meaningful conversations. The next time you plan a date night, you should probably make it for four instead of two. When promoting closeness, the more the merrier.

Rather than focusing on reclaiming closeness when we feel our partner slipping away, we're better off doing whatever we can to strengthen our relationship's bond in the first place. So what can couples do on date nights to build intimacy and keep their relationship going strong? In two studies, researchers asked couples about their shared hobbies, fun activities, and regular date nights to learn the secrets to their success.[40] The most commonly mentioned activities were going on trips, doing sports or recreational activities together (e.g., tennis, hiking), going out to eat, sharing hobbies (e.g., photography), watching TV or movies, shopping, talking, or working around the house together. Although the activity's exact nature didn't impact relationship quality, the couples' reasons for doing the activity mattered. Date nights were more helpful when partners purposefully had them to benefit the relationship and when partners felt that their counterpart authentically wanted to participate. That is, having a date night out of obligation or dragging our partner along isn't going to work. To get the most benefit, couples should intentionally plan dates or activities with their relationship in mind and make sure both parties are on board.

RELATIONSHIP RECAP

- Desiring greater closeness seems romantic and feels like proof of your love and devotion. Except it isn't and it doesn't.
- The tactics we use to keep our partner close are often bad, and a little distance is good.
- When it comes to closeness, you can have too much of a good thing.
- You can learn a lot from long-distance relationships, which are often stronger than traditional relationships.
- Missing your partner can ultimately improve your relationship.
- Striking the right balance with closeness is as simple as answering thirty-six questions.
- Want to optimize your time together as a couple? Have other couples join you.

Chapter 9

"The Less We Argue, the Better"

*T*aylor and Campbell had never had a fight. It was a point of pride, so they kept the streak alive by dodging sensitive topics and not pushing each other's buttons. Sure, it wasn't always easy, but they were in love and completely invested in each other. That said, they were both self-diagnosed conflict avoiders who walked on eggshells around each other, never fully comfortable sharing how they really felt. There was always a lingering fear that any disagreement could turn into a fight and do irreparable harm. Instead, they became well versed in saying things like "Let's just drop it," "I don't want to argue with you," and the remarkably versatile "Whatever…"

It worked for them, until one day it didn't. It all started innocently enough. Campbell had asked Taylor to record her favorite show. Taylor forgot. When Campbell sat down after a long day to watch her missing show, the floodgates opened. Like a lawyer presenting her case, she unloaded a long list of Taylor's infractions, which she'd been "trying to ignore for far too long." Caught off *guard, Taylor got defensive. Campbell doubled down. Sensing futility, Taylor shut down, left the room, and refused to talk any more. The next morning, they both pretended that nothing had happened. It was awkward, but neither of them wanted to make it worse. Besides, they had a spotless "no fighting" record to maintain, and neither wanted to be like those couples who argue all the time.*

CHECKING YOUR BLIND SPOT

"I don't want to fight." We've all said it, because few of us truly enjoy conflict. Arguments are upsetting and make our stomach fluttery. They're confrontational, so we feel threatened. We worry about the sanctity of our relationship, so it feels safer to keep the peace. Afterward we think about all the great things we should have said. But we don't give ourselves, or our relationship, enough credit.

What Are We (Not) Fighting About?

Let's get a simple fact out of the way: all couples argue. Whether you see it or not, everyone has disagreements. You may think that happily and unhappily married couples argue about different things, but according to a 2019 study, they don't.[1] Everyone argues about kids, money, in-laws, and intimacy. When it comes to relationship friction, that's quite the greatest-hits list, but it's still rather broad. Curious about the top three conflict triggers that upset, irritate, hurt, or anger partners?[2] They are:

1. Condescension (i.e., you are treated as stupid or inferior; your partner acts like they think they're better than you)

2. Possessiveness, jealousy, and/or dependency (i.e., your partner demands too much attention or time or is overly jealous, possessive, or dependent)
3. Neglect, rejection, and/or unreliability (i.e., your partner ignores your feelings, doesn't call or text, doesn't say they love you)

Other high-ranking contenders were inconsiderate, self-absorbed, and moody partners. That's quite the minefield to navigate. Here's the good news: if your partner acts in any of these ways, we know it's normal and doesn't necessarily reveal flaws in your relationship.

With everyday issues like who snores, what we're having for dinner, who needs to take out the trash, or how we're going to coordinate kid coverage, we're willing to engage and problem solve, even if it creates a little friction. But what about the topics we avoid? The conversations where we know "not to go there," so we dodge, duck, dip, and dodge again to avoid conflict? While we sidestep thorny areas such as past partners, our past and present sex life, and outside relationships, there is one topic we avoid altogether: the relationship itself.[3] Didn't see that one coming, did you? In fact, the study revealed that the state of the relationship union was the number one taboo topic for one out of every three people and was included among the top topics to avoid for seven out of ten people.

To better understand why, think about what that conversation meant: what partners felt, what they wanted, and where they thought the relationship was going. Heavy stuff. People dodged the relationship discussion because they considered those conversations inefficient and ultimately futile. Then again, they might have just been making excuses; they also admitted to skipping relationship chats because those conversations were risky and potentially destructive. Much like parents who avoid the "sex talk" with their kids, partners avoid discussing the relationship because it provokes anxiety. Never have we paid so little attention to something so important. When couples believed that conflict was a bad sign, they had worse relationships.[4] Those who believed "arguing should not be tolerated" were less satisfied and more aggressive, and the female partners were more depressed.[5] Clearly, the anti-argument approach does more harm than good.

Dealing with Disagreements

Rather than embrace the "relationship talk," we revert to inertia and let things slide.[6] We pat ourselves on the back for avoiding any unpleasantness, convinced we're doing what's best. But there's more to the story.

Our protective impulse doesn't come from the best place. What seems caring is actually a sign of insecurity in ourselves and the relationship.[7] Those doubts get the best of us, so we avoid anything that might threaten the relationship. But there's a fatal flaw in this thinking. Talking less about the relationship makes things worse and creates even more relationship uncertainty. For those in truly solid relationships, relationship conversations shouldn't be intimidating. In fact, more committed couples tend to attack problems head-on and confront their partners about problems.[8] If a relationship is strong, a bit of disagreement should pose no threat.

Relationship uncertainty makes us question everything, including whether we can communicate effectively and whether

177

How Do You Measure Up?
Relationship Uncertainty

Life is hard enough when it's just you. But add a relationship partner, and now you have to contend with two people's thoughts, feelings, hopes, and dreams, as well as how you're doing together as a couple. There's a lot that can go right, and a lot that can go wrong. Regardless, the more confident and assured you are about all of it, the better off your relationship will be.[9]

To get a sense of your relationship uncertainty, think about the following questions:

1. How sure are you that you want to be in your current relationship?

    Totally Certain 1 2 3 4 5 6 7 8 9 10 Totally Uncertain

2. How sure are you about your partner's feelings about the relationship?

    Totally Certain 1 2 3 4 5 6 7 8 9 10 Totally Uncertain

3. How sure are you that you and your partner have similar goals for the relationship?

    Totally Certain 1 2 3 4 5 6 7 8 9 10 Totally Uncertain

4. How sure are you about what is okay for you to say and do in the relationship?

    Totally Certain 1 2 3 4 5 6 7 8 9 10 Totally Uncertain

5. How sure are you about your relationship's future?

    Totally Certain 1 2 3 4 5 6 7 8 9 10 Totally Uncertain

Scoring here is like golf: the lower the better. While these five items take a big-picture approach, we can also look at certainty in key areas. Among those areas, greater uncertainty in the relationship's sexual health, the ability to talk things out with your partner, or your own feelings about the relationship is most directly tied to lower marital quality.[10]

our partner can, too.[11] We can also worry about conversations making things worse, especially if we get defensive, criticize our partner, or show contempt when discussing issues. Those behaviors are three of John Gottman's "Four Horsemen of the Apocalypse."[12] However, as bad as criticism, contempt, and defensiveness are, at least partners are talking. The fourth "horseman," stonewalling, involves completely shutting down and refusing to respond to the other person. We can stonewall by walking out of a room, hanging up on someone, or not responding to texts. Our refusal to engage can be a response to our partner's actual or anticipated negativity. However, stonewalling halts all progress, with research on more than five hundred married couples finding that stonewalling was the worst "horseman" of them all.[13] When we feel like we "can't even," skipping the fight feels good in the moment. But problems don't magically go away. Instead, they grow and intensify. This leaves us vulnerable to experiencing a flood of negativity over minor transgressions. A misplaced pair of socks, a messy countertop, or a mother-in-law's offhand comment is enough to set us off. How has our relationship come to this?

We simply believe that disagreements are destructive. We fall for this trap because nearly every relationship launches in an argument-free state of blissful harmony. Early on everything is

Bonus Blind Spot:
Shaky Conflict-Resolution Skills?
Blame Your Parents

Where do we learn how to deal with conflict? Our resolution skills (or lack thereof) come from many places, but research by my former student Rob Ackerman and his colleagues suggests that how you grew up matters. Specifically, your family climate during adolescence impacts not only how you manage conflict as an adult but your marital outcomes as well.[14]

Using data from a longitudinal study of 288 individuals and their spouses, researchers videotaped families with adolescent kids each year while family members attempted to resolve a common source of conflict (e.g., chores at home). Approximately twenty years later, the researchers observed the now-grown adolescents interacting with their spouses. They wanted to see how they spoke to their spouses, looking for signs of positivity and hostility, as well as assess the couple's marital quality. Those who had more positive interactions in their families as adolescents displayed and received more positive engagement in their marriages, expressed less hostility toward their spouses, and had better relationship quality. In essence, a positive family upbringing benefits our relationship because it encourages us to have a supportive and caring style, which our future spouse reciprocates. It's also possible that growing up in a family that deals with conflict in a supportive and constructive manner predisposes us to seek a spouse with a similar approach. It's win-win because either way, our relationship is better off.

new and wonderful, and partners are on their best behavior. But once the honeymoon stage fades, a perfect "no argument" streak is unrealistic. The reality is that two adults with their own independent feelings and thoughts are not going to agree about everything. We are going to have bad days when we're tired, cranky, or stressed out, and moments when we lose our patience and say something we shouldn't. So will our partner. That's why the "we never fight" relationship is a myth.

The Case of the Missing Arguments

We don't always do what's best for us, especially when it's difficult. That's why we don't look forward to starting a diet, getting up at 5 a.m. to hit the gym, or going to the dentist. We can safely add arguing with our partner to that list. Tough conversations help a relationship grow, but we'll never know if we continue to tiptoe around uncomfortable conversations. We may not even realize we're doing it.

The easiest way to skip an argument is to never see problems in the first place. When we see no evil and hear no evil, there's no evil to speak of to our partner. Being super-easygoing allows us to let everything roll off our backs, as if nothing bothers us. That may sound enlightened, but if we can't be bothered to fight for something, how much do we truly value it? We willingly jump into disputes about politics, religion, standardized tests, sports teams, and the best local pizza place because we care about those topics. What does it say if relationship issues don't make us a little feisty?

On the other hand, we may have our eyes wide open, fully aware of what's going on, but refuse to engage. We may ignore problems, avoid mentioning them, and hope our partner drops the issue.[15] We may keep quiet, suppress our feelings, stifle our reactions, defer everything to our partner, pretend that our concerns are unfounded or that our partner's flaws are minor, and generally convince ourselves that it's best to steer clear of our relationship's hot spots. But this isn't good for us. When researchers from the University of Michigan and Penn State University followed more than 1,500 adults for more than a week, they found that while people felt better on the day they avoided an argument,[16] the next day they had diminished psychological well-being and increased cortisol, which can lead to weight gain, mood swings, and trouble sleeping. Short-term gain, long-term pain.

What if we could solve problems, minus the fight? To do that, we could use a few carefully placed sighs and eye rolls or a bit of conspicuous silence to get our partner to notice there's trouble. Then we sit back and wait.[17] Sure, this approach relies on our partner doing a bit of mind reading to know what's wrong, but if our partner truly loves us they should know what we're thinking, what we need, and what we want fixed. If only it were that easy.

The other way to avoid fights is to be a very forgiving person. Our partner goes low; we take the high road. Giving our partner a pardon may arise from the best intentions but can easily make us a doormat. When we're too quick to forgive unrepentant partners, it erodes our self-respect and makes us less sure of ourselves.[18] Besides, our forgiveness doesn't always help the relationship.

We assume that after we forgive our partner for messing up, they'll be on their best behavior. But partners have a way of taking advantage. When researchers followed newlywed spouses for a week, they found that after being forgiven, partners were more (not less) likely to start arguments and to be moody, nagging, or critical.[19] Not only that, but forgiveness enabled further misdeeds. If those wrongs are also forgiven, it creates a cycle that emboldens partners to engage in worse conduct.

There's an even darker side to this. Among married couples, spouses who were more forgiving encountered more aggressive behaviors from their partner, such as yelling, threatening harm, smashing items in the house, and pushing, grabbing, or hitting, compared to those who were less forgiving.[20] As much as we might look the other way in an attempt to preserve our relationship, letting things go can invite bigger, less forgivable problems.

These conflict-avoidance techniques produce the same result: Avoid conversations now, make the relationship worse later.[21] In fact, a 2017 study found that when partners avoided important relationship topics, they had worse communication, were less happy, and were less dedicated to their relationship seven weeks later.[22] Rather than alleviate tension, pretending that there aren't problems and refusing to open up creates stress that harms relationship satisfaction[23] and increases secrecy.[24] Not only that, but when we avoid conflict we miss the opportunity to help our relationship improve. The key is knowing what works best.

HOW TO SEE YOUR RELATIONSHIP MORE CLEARLY

We give conflict too much credit. It's a blind spot because disagreements don't have as much power over our relationship's fate as we think. We need to realize that our relationship is strong enough to weather the occasional argument, especially if we're ready to approach it in a way that sets us up for success. Conflict isn't a threat; it's an opportunity to better understand each other. Without arguments there is no progress.

Break Out of Bad Patterns

We need to argue more. To be clear, we shouldn't seek friction and intentionally find reasons to fight. However, we should willingly embrace naturally arising conflict. Don't worry, there will be plenty of opportunities. Relationship success isn't about conflict frequency but, rather, conflict severity. With that in mind, we should embrace frequent low-stakes disagreements and occasional arguments and have few, if any, big confrontations. Major fights are major red flags. When we allow ourselves to have lots of little skirmishes, we can avoid big battles and all-out war. Letting things go enables animosity to build.

Bonus Blind Spot:
Should You Discuss
Relationship Problems with Friends?

At this point the need to discuss our relationship issues with our partner is obvious. But couldn't we just talk things out with our friends? That seems safer because our friends are supportive and easy to talk to, aren't emotionally invested in our relationship, and won't leave us. Sounds good, but when researchers looked at the potential benefits of discussing our love life with a friend, they found choosing to have those conversations with a friend instead of the romantic partner led to relationship damage in the form of less love, happiness, and commitment.[25] Sure, those friend talks make us feel better because we're getting things off our chest, but ultimately it's a cop-out that does little to actually improve the relationship. Makes sense. After all, how

---

> many times have you actually solved a problem you had with your boss by talking with a co-worker? We need to go to the source.

It all starts with "kitchen thinking," whereby a current transgression conjures up thoughts about other similar or even tangentially related wrongs we've previously tolerated.[26] Sure, right now it's about the dry cleaning our partner forgot to pick up, but we can't help but note that this is all part of a larger pattern of forgetfulness, irresponsibility, and simply not caring about us. It escalates quickly. When we kitchen think, the inconsequential feels monumental. A cascade of negative thoughts inundates us, making it feel like we have more than our share of big problems. With that swirling around in our head, we spring into action. Our kitchen thinking morphs into kitchen sinking, where we confront our partner by throwing every complaint, shortcoming, and hurt feeling we can think of at them.[27] We've been saving up for a while, so we have plenty of ammunition to take our partner down. Our partner never sees it coming because we never bothered to mention any of it before. Even if they wanted to fix things, where would they start? Naturally, they get defensive and fight back with their own complaint list. Whether we're the aggressor or the target, it's overwhelming and leads to negative-sentiment override, which is just a fancy way of saying we're no longer able to give our partner the benefit of the doubt.[28] At this point, if we aren't careful we can get into the habit of perpetually dwelling on the negatives, unable to see any positives.

Impulsivity is the enemy of good communication.[29] To avoid knee-jerk responses, we need to recognize our trouble spots, anticipate the conversation's possible directions, and prepare our comeback. Planning ahead lets us choose our words more carefully by focusing on specific problematic behaviors (e.g., "Can you please pick up your clothes?") instead of attacking or blaming the partner ("Can you stop being an inconsiderate slob?"). It helps us avoid making a bad situation worse. By minimizing impulsivity, we can take a more measured approach and avoid saying things we'll later regret, which ultimately benefits our relationship.

Us Versus Us

The strongest couples think in terms of we, us, and ours, not you, me, and mine.[30] Therein lies the secret to dealing with conflict: you and your partner are on the same team. We're not fighting against each other; both of us are confronting the problem for the good of our relationship. The first rule of relationship-conflict club is that disputes aren't about winning. Sure, it might feel good to win every argument and show our partner why they're wrong, but if we win, our partner must lose. We need to remember that we're connected, so their loss is also our loss. If either of us gets embarrassed, frustrated, or hurt, it impacts the other person and the relationship. When we commit to this mindset, we're better at minimizing argument-induced negativity, allowing us to keep our relationship's positive aspects in mind.[31]

To embrace the "us," it helps to see the world as our partner does. Henry David Thoreau asked, "Could a greater miracle take place than for us to look through each other's eyes for an instant?" If we paused and took that instant to consider how our partner sees our actions, hears our words, thinks and feels about our relationship, what might we see for the first time? What have we been missing? Asking these questions forces us to take the other's perspective, which brings us closer.[32] Similarly, if our partner points out something we did wrong, rather than getting defensive or debating what we actually did, said, or meant, we try to understand our partner's point of view, by asking things like "Why do you believe that I did/said/meant that?"; "What about it bothers you?"; and "What could change in the future so that this doesn't happen again?"

We need all the help we can get because marriage is challenging. A study of married couples found that in the first year, couples uniformly experienced a decline in marital quality in terms of passion, trust, commitment, satisfaction, love, and intimacy.[33] The researchers followed up by trying to stymie the declines. They gave half of the couples a writing exercise that Dr. Eli Finkel calls "the marriage hack." The seven-minute hack allows couples to view the relationship through the eyes of a complete outsider who wants only what is best for them. It's possible, then, for couples to see how others view the disagreement and how they might find a hidden benefit. Here's what they found: Couples who used the simple marriage hack prevented continuing declines in marital quality and even bounced back a bit, regaining some of what they had lost. Spouses who didn't use the marriage hack continued experiencing declines in marital quality. If you're interested in trying out the marriage hack, check out Eli Finkel's TEDxUChicago Talk (the key piece starts at 8:15).

The marriage hack is quick and relatively easy, but if you're not interested in a relationship writing assignment, there is another option that allows you to gain new perspective on your relationship. Building stronger relationships and dealing with conflict may be as easy as having a movie night. Researchers tested this by having one group of newlyweds watch and reflect on one relationship movie (e.g., *Love Story, Sleepless in Seattle,*

The Notebook) each week for a month.[34] This task allowed couples to consider relationship hot spots, like conflict, in the context of a movie. Another group did nothing. Fast-forward three years later, and the "Netflix and spill" movie-night couples were less likely to have broken up compared to couples who maintained the status quo. Because the movies didn't carry the emotional baggage of the relationship, watching rom-coms gave couples neutral ground and allowed them to discuss thorny issues like expectations, conflict, support, and forgiveness. That is, by approaching conflict-provoking topics from the movie characters' viewpoint, rather than from the point of view of their own relationship, couples could gain greater awareness and perspective.

Building the Better Argument

For the good of the relationship, every argument needs to start the same way: partners need to give each other the benefit of the doubt. Rather than start off assuming your partner is wrong, is hopelessly flawed, has bad intentions, or is trying to hurt you, you give them what psychologist Carl Rogers calls "unconditional positive regard," or the belief that at their core, everyone is a good person.[35] What better starting point for any discussion with the person we love, care for, and respect? With that foundation, coming up with solutions is easier. Research from 2019 backs this up, finding that when we assume the best of our partner, we're less likely to see malice in their actions, which makes the argument less stressful and more likely to be resolved.[36]

For successful conflict resolution, next you need to know what type of problem you're dealing with.[37] For serious problems like infidelity or substance abuse, it's better to be direct by demanding change, taking a nonnegotiable stance, and showing anger, especially if your partner is able to change. If the problems are more mundane (e.g., divvying up chores at home), you're better off taking a cooperative approach by using love, humor, affection, and optimism. This is also the better tack for unsolvable problems (e.g., a meddlesome mother-in-law) or a partner who is hopelessly stubborn. Careful, though; techniques like humor and optimism are potentially counterproductive for serious problems (e.g., the death of a family member).

Regardless of the problem, there's no substitute for listening to your partner. Sounds simple, but we rarely truly listen. Sure, we know our partner is talking, and we may hear some of what they're saying, but often we're not fully listening as much as we're waiting for our chance to speak. That needs to change.

How do we become good listeners? Give a "CRAPO":

1. Clarifying. When your partner talks, you need to be sure that you're clear about what they're saying. No assumptions, mistakes, or misinterpretations allowed. Sounds easy, but there's a lot of false confidence to go around. We are too confident in our ability to understand our partner, and they overestimate how clear they are. To remove all doubt, you should ask questions like, "When you say _____, what exactly does that mean?"; "Am I correct that _____ is the key issue?"; and "Can you give an example of _____?" Sure, it's possible you'll get it wrong, but then your partner can set the record straight and they'll appreciate that you cared enough to try. The fact is, conflict isn't necessarily bad; its impact depends on whether people feel understood.[38] Anytime someone feels heard, communication and the relationship improve.

2. Reflecting feelings. This one should really be named "empathy," but I needed the letter *R* in "Reflect Feelings" to spell out CRAPO, so I took artistic liberty. Of course, the *R* could also stand for "Really Important" because of the five keys, this one is the most critical to get right. Mastering empathy starts with a simple realization: behind everything our partner says, there's an emotion they're dying to have us notice. Sometimes they know exactly what they're trying to convey (e.g., "My boss's narcissism makes it hard to feel appreciated at work"); other times it's fuzzy (e.g., "I can't stand my job"). When you give a CRAPO, your job isn't to give advice, make jokes, blindly agree, get defensive, or escape the conversation. Instead, you try to move beyond happy, mad, and sad by reflecting the deeper feelings your partner expresses: hurt, embarrassment, confusion, disappointment, frustration, annoyance, nervousness, bewilderment, apathy, or feeling overwhelmed, undervalued, lost, and inauthentic. When acknowledging your partner's feelings, you should hedge a bit with phrases like "You seem...," "It sounds like...," or "Are you feeling...?" If you're wrong, your partner knows you're trying to understand, and empathy research shows your effort is more important for relationship satisfaction than accuracy.[39] When you do get it right, your partner will light up. Who among us hasn't come home from work and complained about the commute's traffic, lights, delays, and other people's general annoyingness? Imagine if, instead of "That sucks" or "Yeah, commuting is rough," our partner said, "That sounds really frustrating" or "Wow, that's probably the last thing you felt like you needed after a stressful day." Mind blown.

3. Attending. We spend most of our time trying to find the right thing to say. But that's only half the battle. You also need to watch your nonverbal signals, or all the ways you communicate that go beyond the words you're using. For example, you need to show you're listening by maintaining eye contact and sitting squarely facing your partner in a relaxed and open position, with just the slightest lean toward them. Appearing fully engaged and present, without nearby distractions like your phone or other screens, conveys to your partner that the conversation is important. Prioritizing nonverbal signals also helps you pay attention, which is important because you need every ounce of mental bandwidth to master the other four keys to giving a CRAPO.

4. Paraphrasing. When listening, we need to show our partner that we "get it." To demonstrate your understanding, you should be able to recap what your partner is saying, using your own words. Mind you, this isn't some type of thesaurus challenge where you swap out every single word. Rather, your goal is to listen intently so you can capture the essence. The process of rephrasing and summarizing has two big benefits. First, it shows your partner that you're deeply invested in the conversation. Second, knowing you need to paraphrase forces you to pay extremely close attention. Just in case you're not totally understanding, hedging a bit helps: "It feels like you may be saying...," "What you seem to be stating is...," or "Sounds to me like..." Paraphrasing makes it abundantly clear that you're listening and you care.

5. Open-ended questions. If we're being honest, in most conversations we're waiting to turn the focus back to ourselves. Your partner deserves better. When giving a CRAPO, you keep the spotlight on your partner by giving them the space to talk through how they feel. To do that, you should ask open-ended questions that help your partner process their feelings. Instead of focusing on factual details like who, what, when, and where, you lead them toward deeper analysis by asking questions like "What would you suggest to someone else in this same situation?"; "How did you make this decision?"; "What would make things better?"; "Why do you think this happened?"; and "How do you see this turning out?" Each question focuses on the problem, helps our partner gain perspective, and allows greater insight into the issue at hand. Now all you have to do is give a CRAPO and really listen to your partner's answers.

Every relationship has flaws, but those imperfections can be intimidating. We need to realize that problems won't just disappear and that talking things out is our only hope for improvement. We must see those conversations for what they are: difficult but necessary steps that help a strong relationship get stronger.

RELATIONSHIP RECAP

- Your strategies to prevent arguments and dodge disharmony are doing more harm than good.
- The more you try to avoid conflict, the more likely you are to have real problems in your relationship.
- Embracing minor skirmishes allows you to prevent the major battles.
- You should never try to win an argument. Ever.
- Sometimes a little TV is just what your relationship needs to gain new perspective.
- The key to better communication is simple: you have to give a CRAPO.

Chapter 10

"I Need You to Always Be There for Me"

I t had been an awful day, just the worst. Maelyn should have been numb to it by now. As she walked through the door looking defeated, Jarron launched into his best British accent, "'Ello, 'ello, well, aren't you a cheeky li'l lass." Classic Jarron. She gave him a look. He pressed on: "This call may be recorded for training purposes, mate." Despite cracking a smile, Maelyn wondered when he'd grow up. Sensing a tough crowd, Jarron skulked away to make dinner. When they sat down to eat, he insisted that "everything would be okay" and that she "shouldn't worry." Maelyn explained that she wanted to quit and pursue her dream job across the country. Jarron wasn't on board. Maelyn felt betrayed.

Truth be told, Maelyn recognized that Jarron was constantly building her up with reminders like "Who's my superstar?" and "You've got this." He was by her side, but mostly when things went *well, not when she truly felt she needed it. Jarron was the king of thoughtful celebrations for every career accomplishment, birthday, or anniversary. Maelyn appreciated those gestures but still felt that he didn't get it. His funny greeting earlier and annoying optimism were so typical. It was just like him to be clueless about how to make her feel better, how to alleviate her anxieties, and how to give her the kind of help she needed. He should be there for her more, yet he was often invisible.*

CHECKING YOUR BLIND SPOT

We're not in this alone. That's the point of being in a relationship, right? You want your partner to be your rock, the one you can always count on to protect you from the maelstrom of life. Clearly, having a completely unsupportive partner is hugely problematic. However, when we feel we aren't getting enough support, it's likely that we're not giving our partner enough credit for all the ways they are there for us.

Why So Serious?

Like it or not, we all hit the point where the "adulting" begins and we need to grow up. There are bills to pay and a life to manage. We can't do it by ourselves and need the right partner to make it work. What kind of person is that? According to Gwendolyn Seidman, a relationship scientist at Albright College, there are five research-backed qualities that are essential in a relationship partner: kindness, loyalty, conscientiousness, stability, and a serious willingness to build a relationship.[1] Note what isn't on her list: funniness, spontaneity, and goofiness. The most important traits all emphasize dependability, seriousness, and maturity. It's what we want when it's time to be a grown-up.

So, when our partner approaches meaningful moments by making jokes, we may feel unsupported. It's a lesson I learned firsthand. In college I dated an amazing woman. One day, we talked about what our first fight would be. We were falling in love and feeling so compatible, an argument seemed unthinkable. Unable to stifle my inner scientist, I hypothesized that I'd say something I thought was funny, but she wouldn't agree. Boy, was I right. Fast-forward several weeks: With all the kindness and affection in the world, she complimented my blue eyes. Perfectly matching her gentle and heartfelt delivery, I responded, "Your eyes are the most beautiful shit brown I've ever seen." Hilarious!

Nope, dumb. Like, super-dumb. In an instant that deserved warmth, sincerity, and gentle attention, I brought jokes. She sat there stunned and rightfully upset. I nervously chuckled and backpedaled by noting the accuracy of my previous prediction: our first fight was the direct result of my reckless sense of humor. That made it worse. I apologized profusely. I thought it was clear that I was joking. She thought it was clear that I was an oblivious dolt. She called out my insensitivity. Lucky for me she was the nicest and most warmhearted person I had ever met, and she forgave me. Not only that, she became my wife. Over the years, I've gotten better and even, I think, a little funnier. But if I'm honest, I'm still working on my timing.

Make no mistake, being serious and mature has its place in our relationship, but we don't want to overdo it. There's also a time for humor. Although joking around can backfire in certain circumstances, we need to recognize that there are lots of ways to "be there" for our partner, and humor is one of them. Though a goofball partner seems like the exact opposite of the caring and supportive partner we want, that sense of humor actually helps in underappreciated ways. When Jeffrey Hall from the University of Kansas did a comprehensive review in 2017 of humor's impact on relationships, he found that a funny partner who goes for the laugh and makes light of situations boosts relationship satisfaction.[2] When partners use jokes to foster connection, couples report being better at resolving problems.[3] That's because laughter puts us in a good mood, creating a sense of intimacy.[4] As a result we feel closer to our partner and more supported.[5] A partner's sense of humor also provides benefits in the bedroom. Men with a better sense of humor have sex more often and their female partners have more orgasms.[6] Though ill-timed humor can make it seem like our partner isn't fully there for us, humor plays an important role in supporting the relationship, even if we don't realize it all the time.

What You See Isn't All You Get

A fun-loving partner who jokes around is one thing. But a partner who blatantly fails to back us up is a much bigger issue, right? It feels like betrayal because our partner should be there for us, no matter what. You know, "in sickness and in health," and "till death do us part."

But this expectation blinds us to a surprising fact: in certain contexts, a seemingly unsupportive partner can be a good sign. That's right, we should have a greater appreciation for the times our partner doesn't fully endorse our ambitions, and even an appreciation for partners who sabotage our progress.

Researchers call this phenomenon the "Manhattan effect."[7] The name comes from the movie *Manhattan,* in which Woody Allen's character, Isaac, attempts to navigate a relationship with Tracy, who is considering a move to London. Isaac doesn't take the relationship seriously, so he's extremely supportive of Tracy's fantastic overseas opportunity. He even encourages her move, despite the obvious consequences for their relationship. However, when Isaac later has a change of heart and gets serious about their relationship, he rescinds his support and implores Tracy to stay. Paradoxically, as he becomes more committed, his support for Tracy dwindles.

In our own relationship we'd never guess that our partner's failure to support us came from a good place. Certainly that isn't always the case, but there are instances when our partner is so invested in our future as a couple that they become especially wary of any potential threats to the relationship. Taking a class or starting a new hobby is good for us, but it means spending less time together. Sure, our partner's less-than-enthusiastic reaction feels bad, but it's a tacit admission of how important we are to them. It's also their way of being there for the relationship, even though it might not feel like it at the time.

In fact, the best kind of support is the kind we don't see. Our partner might be working in the background, silently making our lives easier without us noticing.[8] This subtle support helps us even when we're super-stressed. For example, consider law students taking the highly stressful bar exam. When asked about support, the students had no idea how much their partners were doing for them. Yet, despite being completely unaware, their partner's invisible support reduced students' anxiety and depression levels.

Bonus Blind Spot:
I Can't Even

Being that A-plus super-supportive partner isn't easy. To support or not to support? Well, it depends. If we believe we have only so much energy to give, we may think we have to choose between helping our partner and helping ourselves. The other way to look at support is that exerting energy in other areas (e.g., our career, work around the house, parenting) encourages us to keep the momentum going by doing other things, like helping our partner.

Research from 2019 found that when participants believed they had only a limited amount of energy, they were better at picking up signs that their partner was tired.[9] Recognizing fatigue encouraged partners to want to help more. Sounds good so far, but there was a problem. Believers in limited energy were also much more attuned to their own poor mood. The result: despite being better at noticing their partner's need for help and wanting to help more, they were actually less supportive. Ultimately, they didn't feel they had the reserves to help out. Instead, this research suggests that being there for our partner by providing support can energize us and make us more likely to continue providing support in the future.

That unseen support can also help us feel more capable and competent, as well as less angry.[10] Remaining blissfully ignorant is part of what makes invisible support helpful. Research from 2018 shows that when we realize our partner is helping, that support damages our mood.[11] With invisible support, these negative side effects don't occur, allowing us to have more enjoyable and less moody interactions, which benefit the relationship. In other words, what we don't see is more helpful than we ever realized. And insisting on the visible support we think we want can have a dark side.

The Dark Side of Support

When we play the martyr and become overly supportive of our partner, it wears us out, leaving us exhausted and resulting in sacrificing our own goals.[12] And it's all for nothing because anytime we jump in to assist, our partner pays an emotional cost.[13] Accepting our help forces them to acknowledge that they need support, which can make them feel inadequate and undermines their self-esteem. Not only does over-helping put us in a bad mood;[14] it also increases anxiety,[15] depressed feelings, and anger.[16]

Okay, but when we're stressed out, dealing with problems at work, parenting hassles, the tedium of everyday tasks, or family drama, having our partner step up, without us needing to ask them to, has to be helpful. Wrong. Though we like the idea of having someone there for us, when we're stressed, unsolicited support makes us feel worse, not better.[17] It's tricky because early in our relationship, our partner's hyperattentive nature gave us confidence that they would be there when we needed them.[18] However, when the relationship matures, getting help we don't need or didn't ask for feels intrusive and condescending.

Problems arise for a few reasons. One, our partner's attempts at backing us up may be well-intentioned but poorly executed. For example, they might make us feel worse by saying the wrong thing, minimizing our experiences by suggesting we "get over it," or offering ill-advised solutions like "just find a new job." Two, our partner's support may be fantastic, but it throws our relationship out of balance, and the asymmetry is associated with depressive symptoms and health problems.[19] If we notice such an imbalance, it means we're keeping track of who's helping whom. And that means there may be other issues lurking.

Keeping Score: Losing by Trying to Win

Keeping a tally can be self-serving. Pointing out what our partner isn't doing draws attention to all that we do. That can make us feel superior, which helps us feel better about the relationship. But being the alpha partner comes with a catch.[20] Alphas tend to be insecure and to feel the need to outperform their partners.[21] This emboldens alphas to expect more from their counterparts. If their partners don't rise to the occasion, it can lead to a feeling of "After all I've done for you..." Expecting reciprocity creates a "relationship scorecard," where we keep track of each partner's contributions in order to keep things even.[22] This "exchange" approach leads us to focus more on ourselves than on our partner[23] and, according to 2019 research, encourages overreactions to relationship conflict.[24]

When we believe we're holding up our end of the deal, we notice when we're not getting our fair share of support. Of course our partner may not notice everything we're doing or how little they're helping out. But here's a shocker: being unaware of each of your relative contributions doesn't mean they don't care. It suggests they don't focus on who is giving or receiving benefits.[25] When we take a "communal" approach, we provide support with "no strings attached." If one person does more than their fair share for a while, that's okay because we trust that it'll all balance out in the long run.

Not only does a "we're in this together" mentality sound

nice; it's good for the relationship. Communally oriented partners share resources more, give their partner credit for success, resent their partner less, and have greater marital satisfaction.[26] When we see the relationship as a team effort, doing a little extra for our partner feels good because we care about their outcomes as much as our own. In fact, we feel better when our partner outshines us.[27] Rather than focusing on who is more supportive, we're better off putting the relationship first by tearing up the relationship scorecard.

How Do You Measure Up?
Communal Strength

How responsive are you to your partner's needs? The answer depends on what your motivation is to help them, or what researchers call your "communal strength."[28] It's a concept that taps into what you're willing to do for your partner and what you're inclined to sacrifice. To get a sense of your communal strength, consider the following:

1. How happy would you be to make a sacrifice for
   your partner?
   Not at All 1 2 3 4 5 6 7 Extremely
2. To what extent is helping your partner a priority?
   Not at All 1 2 3 4 5 6 7 Extremely
3. How willing would you be to take on negative consequences
   for yourself in order to benefit your partner?
   Not at All 1 2 3 4 5 6 7 Extremely

Those who score higher on this measure do more for their partner and are more in love. When one partner has high communal
strength, the other partner tends to have it as well. That's good
because high communal strength is linked with higher marital
satisfaction.

HOW TO SEE YOUR RELATIONSHIP MORE CLEARLY

What if we've been thinking about support all wrong? The
support we want may not be the help we really need. Support
comes in all shapes and sizes, so when we address our blind
spot by knowing what to look for, what truly matters, and how
to value it, we'll see how our partner has always been there for
us, in ways that we haven't fully appreciated.

Own It

The first step is to take responsibility for our feelings and try
to be less needy by adjusting our expectations. It just isn't fair
to require our partner to constantly pick up our emotional
baggage, meet our every need, reassure us, validate us, and be
a constant unwavering and perpetually supportive presence.
We're putting too much pressure on them. These expectations
are a sign that we're insecure and concerned about our partner
abandoning us.[29] And if our partner responds by being super-
supportive, there's a fatal flaw. While getting too little support
deteriorates satisfaction, a longitudinal study of marriage
found that receiving too much support was even worse, resulting in even steeper declines in satisfaction.[30]

Instead of looking to our partner for support, we can start by doing a better job of handling our own emotions. When life threatens to make us feel mad, upset, stressed, frustrated, unwelcome, hurt, worn out, unappreciated, embarrassed, or incompetent, we don't have to give in. How we appraise a situation has tremendous influence over our response to it.[31] In *Man's Search for Meaning,* Viktor Frankl writes, "Everything can be taken from a man but one thing: the last of the human freedoms—to choose one's attitude in any given set of circumstances, to choose one's own way." In our relationship, we could take our partner's lack of support personally. Or we could consider the extenuating circumstances that make them less attentive. Research from 2018 suggests that doing so helps short-circuit problems before they get out of hand, keeping relationship quality high.[32]

Tough times are still inevitable, so we should proactively bolster our resources by stockpiling positive relationship experiences.[33] Accruing emotional capital doesn't require grand gestures or relationship overhaul. Rather, we gather resources by loving each other, having fun together, and simply focusing on all the good times we've had in our relationship. It might help to create a scrapbook, memory box, or slideshow of your relationship's greatest hits; watch your wedding video every year; or take a trip to revisit the site of your first date. Each of these activities allows you to bank that goodwill to draw upon when needed. When our relationship hits the inevitable rough patch, our emotional capital reserves allow us to weather the storm and leave us more satisfied and committed.

More important, our banked capital helps us avoid overreacting to the times when our partner isn't as supportive as we'd like them to be. That's because emotional capital makes it easier to give our partner the benefit of the doubt. According to 2019 research from Courtney Walsh and Lisa Neff of the University of Texas at Austin, banked capital changes how we see our partner, including how we interpret and explain their behavior.[34] For example, when our partner seems to ignore our stress and doesn't offer help, we could easily conclude, "I have a terrible partner." However, if we have a backlog of good times to fall back on, we understand their neglect in kinder and more forgiving terms. That helps protect our relationship's health.

Finding Our Partner's "Why"

When considering relationship support, it's almost as if what our partner does isn't important, and what really counts is how we perceive their actions. True and true. We're constantly playing the role of armchair psychologist, trying to understand why our partner acts and feels the way they do. In the end, our interpretation is everything. As Shakespeare wrote in *Hamlet,* "For there is nothing either good or bad, but thinking makes it so."

Consider the following: After a stressful week, you wake up Saturday morning to find that your partner ventured out early, in the cold, to get your favorite cup of coffee. Sitting by its side is a chocolate croissant full of flaky buttery goodness from the local bakery. Perfect, and completely unexpected. Naturally, you wonder…what's up? How you answer that question is critical to your relationship's success.[35]

Researchers have identified two key patterns. First, the bad one: "distress-maintaining," or "conflict-promoting."[36] Here, we find a way to turn positives, like surprise coffee and croissants, into negatives. Perhaps our partner felt guilty about something they did (e.g., Are they cheating?) or have bad news to share (e.g., What did they mess up?). Or maybe our partner simply felt obligated. This thought pattern weaponizes our partner's kindness by reminding us just how rare and out of character these gestures are. Rather than giving our partner the credit they deserve, we turn their benevolence against them and use it to emphasize their negative qualities. It is called "distress-maintaining" because if we keep dismissing or devaluing our partner's attempt to help us, we virtually guarantee future misery.[37] Sensing this, our partner may give up trying. Who can blame them? If their efforts at being kind, thoughtful, and supportive aren't acknowledged or, worse, are twisted into accusations or dismissed, it's easier not to bother. And their apathy may encourage the same from us (e.g., "If you're not going to help me, I'm not going to bother helping you"), creating a downward spiral.

There's a better way. In the second, "relationship-enhancing" pattern, we don't see an unexpected breakfast; we see further proof of our partner's kind and considerate nature. Sure, it's just one Saturday morning, but it reminds us of all the ways our partner is there for us. When our partner isn't as supportive and doesn't check in about how our day went, we know it's rare and we cut them some slack. Perhaps they're busy, stressed, or caught up doing something really important. In other words, we consider extenuating circumstances. Even if they were at fault, we'd recognize it wasn't intentional. We can see our partner's failure to provide support as the exception that proves the rule of just how considerate they typically are.

There's a bit of magic that happens when we take this approach. Positive behaviors get magnified, while negative behaviors recede into the background. Sure, at times we may give our partner more credit than they deserve, but there's no doubt it's good for the relationship.[38] When both partners adopt this pattern, they have better relationships now and in the future, while the distress-maintainers have worse relationships.[39] Whereas enhancing spouses are warmer toward their partners and less hostile, distress-maintainers are angrier, use more verbal attacks, and are less responsive and supportive. Clearly, how we interpret our partner's actions influences not only the support we're willing to give but also our reactions to the support our partner already provides.

Know What to Look For: The Power of Positivity

Clearly, we need to give credit where credit is due, but support is multifaceted and isn't always easy to see.[40] For example, our partner may support us by not being critical or piling on when we're down; they might avoid asking for help because they know we're stressed out; they might encourage us to spend some time with our friends; they might give us space when we need it; or they might simply listen, despite being exhausted themselves. They might boost our confidence by telling us they love us no matter what and reminding us how great we are. It's possible we're missing all this, yet we shouldn't take it for granted. For the sake of our relationship, we should try to recognize the positive contributions our partner makes.

Here's one that's easy to miss: optimism. When we're stressed, our partner's insistence that "everything is going to be okay" can feel Pollyannaish at best, and hopelessly naïve or dismissive at worst. Although our partner's optimism may not be the support we're looking for, it may be exactly what we need. For example, even though we know better, when life gets stressful, we check out. Though the impulse to withdraw is potentially harmful, 2017 research shows that having an optimistic partner buffers against potential negative effects.[41] Because our partner assumes everything will work out, they're more understanding, caring, encouraging, and loving. As long as couples have at least one optimist, both partners enjoy higher relationship satisfaction.[42] Optimists handle rough patches better, perhaps because they recognize the positive aspects of their relationship, which help them to feel like their partner supports them. Optimists' rosy outlook and perceived support also help them have less intense disagreements and better resolution of any conflict.

Adopting an "attitude of gratitude" is good advice, too. The research on gratitude's benefits is abundant and unequivocal.[43] Being more appreciative promotes well-being, happiness, and positive emotions, and it helps us avoid complacency, burnout, and boredom. Research from 2019 shows that more grateful couples had more satisfying marriages at the start of the study and remained happier three years later.[44] Gratitude's power comes from maximizing positivity. According to the University of Michigan's Barbara Fredrickson, positive emotions are crucial because they encourage us to broaden the way we think about the world.[45] In other words, when we feel good, we consider new perspectives, explore our surroundings, acquire new information, and have greater appreciation for our life. All of which helps us grow and thrive. This "broaden and build theory of positive emotions" places a premium on highlighting our relationship's bright spots because doing so empowers us to seek new experiences, take on challenges, be more openminded, push our limits, and learn new things by ourselves and with our partner. All of which strengthens our bond as a couple, making us more resilient when confronting future challenges and enhancing our well-being.

When it comes to focusing on the positives, here's another fact you never saw coming: it's more important to receive support when life's going well than when it's going poorly. I know that seems counterintuitive, but if we look for support only when we're stressed, tired, or overwhelmed, we're potentially missing all the support we are getting when times aren't tough. However, if we step back and appreciate our partner's support during the good times, we can build up emotional capital. Instead of dwelling on the negatives, we need to share our triumphs and successes, the compliments we get, the good parts of our day, and the positive impact we make on others' lives. Not only should partners encourage each other to emphasize the good, but they should be ready to support each other when they do. Shelly Gable and colleagues at UCLA call this process "capitalization."[46] For them, the key relationship question is "Will you be there for me when things go right?" We had better hope that we can say "yes," because their data show that our partner's response to positive events is more important than their reaction to negative events. Not only does capitalization help the relationship's overall well-being and level of intimacy, but it also decreases the likelihood that the relationship ends. Clearly, the stakes are high.

What does capitalization look like? Let's imagine your partner gets a promotion at work. First, here's what not to say: "That's nice. You won't believe what happened to me today." You also want to avoid pseudo support like "Are you sure you really want more responsibility? It could be really demanding." Though a well-intentioned attempt to look after your partner's well-being, it implicitly questions their competence and potentially undermines their confidence. Instead, celebrate the win and do it in a way that conveys it's good for both of you.[47] You can do this by saying things like "That's wonderful," "We need to celebrate," "Finally, they're acknowledging how great you are," or "You have totally earned this by being so amazing at your job." These responses convey a sense of recognition, understanding, and shared joy that benefits both of you. Research from 2019 shows that when we capitalize this way, our couple identity is strengthened, allowing us to feel more like a "we" and enhancing relationship well-being.[48] When we prioritize the positives, everyone wins.

Make no mistake, we all deserve a supportive partner. However, unless we step back and look at our relationship, we may not always appreciate all the support we get. It's important to realize that support comes in many forms, including humor, being protective of the relationship, helping out in unseen ways, and not keeping a relationship scorecard. When we appreciate the full range of support we receive, we can focus on better appraising stressful situations, more carefully considering why our partner behaves in certain ways, and expressing gratitude, as well as appreciating our partner's optimism. Doing so will open our eyes and allow us to see that our partner is more supportive than we ever realized.

RELATIONSHIP RECAP

- A mature and serious partner is overrated. A goofball partner who doesn't always take life so seriously is a major asset in a relationship.

- A partner who doesn't support your ambitions or seems to sabotage your accomplishments can be a good sign; it can show that your partner is more committed than you think.
- Your partner's apparent obliviousness to everything you do for them and the relationship might feel disrespectful. But it means your partner isn't keeping score, which is an indication of a healthy relationship.
- Being overly optimistic feels naïve, but it is really helpful for your relationship.
- The best time for support isn't when you might think. When you really need support is when life is going well, not when it's going poorly.
- Ultimately, how you interpret and explain your partner's behavior matters. The best way forward is to give your partner more credit than they may deserve.

Chapter 11

"If We Break Up, I'll Be Broken"

*T*hey had been together for what felt like forever. Julie couldn't imagine life without Zach. Yet, things between them hadn't felt right for a while. She remained hopeful that the relationship would improve and was committed to making it work. It wasn't like Zach was abusive or anything, and their relationship wasn't bad all the time, just too often. Julie wanted more but also felt a bit guilty and worried that she wanted too much. She was afraid of throwing everything away.

Sometimes the best questions are simple: Was her relationship fulfilling? If she was honest, it wasn't. Before Zach, Julie had been adventurous, outgoing, and fun. Zach was a homebody. She wanted to travel; he wanted to watch TV. Julie was restless and seeking wider horizons, while Zach was perfectly content with unflinching stability. They'd been in this rut for years, and Julie didn't see a path for improvement. Zach thought everything was fine. Julie had been hoping for a miracle because she didn't want to hurt him, and she hated the idea of throwing away all the years *they had spent together. She knew that divorce would be devastating and would leave her an emotional and lonely wreck. Overwhelmed by that possibility, she continued to tough it out. That's marriage, right? It just felt like too much struggle and too little bliss. Didn't she deserve more?*

CHECKING YOUR BLIND SPOT

We started our journey with an indisputable statement: Everyone deserves a great relationship. As you've seen, in many ways, your relationship is likely stronger than you thought it was, and you've learned strategies to make it even stronger. Your confidence and appreciation for the relationship should be at an all-time high. What if they aren't?

Uh-oh

When I teach my college course on intimate relationships or give talks about love, I have a unique vantage point. From the front of the room, I get to see everyone's face and witness their reactions in real time. When a particular study's finding affirms that they're in a great relationship or suggests an optimistic sign for the future, I see looks of confident self-satisfaction and even slight smiles. However, when I share data that reflect poorly on their relationship, I see what I call the "uh-oh face." It isn't a good sign that my partner and I never fight? Uh-oh. Constantly sacrificing my own needs isn't helping my relationship? Uh-oh. I shouldn't expect my partner to change? Uh-oh. Wanting too much support from my partner might backfire? Uh-oh.

True, every relationship has its share of uh-oh moments, making it hard to know for sure what those slivers of doubt mean. Is our gut telling us something is wrong or are we over-reacting? What makes it even trickier is that our experiences are rarely entirely positive or entirely negative. There's a lot of ambiguity. The world's best relationship has its share of bad days, just as the most mismatched, dysfunctional couple has their heartfelt moments. If we want to find reasons to stay committed, we can find them. If we want to find reasons to leave, we can find those as well. Love is complicated and diffi-cult to decipher. No one ever said it would be simple.

Knowing what to do takes time. Our decision could lead to the biggest transition of our lives, so it's one we take seriously. Research on the decision-making process for ending a relation-ship suggests that it typically takes thirty weeks from the moment a person realizes their dissatisfaction to separation.[1] People took even more time when they had been in the rela-tionship longer, felt lonelier, and worried more about how the breakup would impact them. For those considering the end of their marriage, their deliberation period extended even further, averaging around five years.[2] That's a lot of time to spend wondering.

Staying for the Wrong Reasons

It isn't easy to walk away. There are plenty of reasons to stay, some rather mundane. Going our separate ways means we have to tell everyone, work out living arrangements, and divide up our stuff. Every decision, from how we divvy up the friends to what we're going to do with the kitchen utensils, burns with emotion. But that's the easy part. Trying to mentally come to grips with how we're never going to undo our history with our partner or get back the time we've spent sharing our lives is impossibly difficult. Caryl Rusbult, one of the true luminaries of relationship science, suggests that "investments" are anything we put into our relationship that we can't easily get back.[3] That includes time, but also resources, energy, shared experiences, and emotional bonds. Because we can't take any of these investments with us when the relationship ends, they complicate our decision-making and increase our reluctance to leave. Even when our love life isn't very lovable, it's hard to leave a partnership when we have devoted so much of ourselves to it. The result: we hold on for way too long.

Why? No one likes to waste time. It's why we all hate long lines, traffic, commercials, and meetings. Thinking that we've misspent part of our life with the wrong person is similarly painful. Rather than acknowledge that we made a bad choice, we double down to protect what we've already put in. Yet this type of doubling down is what economists call "throwing good money after bad."[4] We fall into the trap of wasting more of our resources in a misguided attempt to recoup what's already lost. But what's done is done. Realizing that we spent three years in a failed relationship stings, but being in a dreadful relationship for any longer hurts more. What happens if three years becomes thirteen years, or thirty years?

We also need to realize that this time wasn't a complete loss. Every successful life story has its share of challenges, disappointments, and failure along the way. The key is to glean life lessons from each setback. Time spent in a failed relationship wasn't a mistake but, rather, an opportunity to reflect and figure out where it went wrong, so we're better prepared for the future. As Rafiki said in *The Lion King,* "Oh yes, the past can hurt. But from the way I see it, you can either run from it, or...learn from it." Smart monkey.

What about our partner? It's impossible not to worry about hurting someone we've cared about, so we consider what's best for them and delay the breakup, especially when we believe they depend on the relationship.[5] On the one hand, we're kind to be so considerate. On the other, we may be giving ourselves too much credit for how much we influence our partner's life and overestimating how devastated our partner will be. We also aren't doing our partner any favors by enduring a relationship we no longer want, because most people want a partner to be with them only if they're "all in." If we're honest, our hesitancy isn't purely selfless, because we're worried about how we're going to cope.

Not Broken

Procrastination is human nature. We're experts at putting off undesirable tasks like doing our taxes, paying bills, leaving for work, starting a diet, and cleaning the house. It's not about poor time management but, rather, about a failure to control our emotions.[6] We'd simply prefer to feel good than bad. Ending our relationship is ripe for emotion-based procrastination because it's difficult and potentially painful, making us less than eager to begin the process.

Make no mistake, endings hurt. Whether we are the initiator or the one getting dumped, we're losing something that is a big part of our life. Our relationships define us, they build us, they sustain us, and they can damage us. My own research finds that when we lose a relationship, we lose a part of ourselves too. In describing their breakups, people say things like

"I feel lost," "I feel incomplete as a person," "I don't know who I am anymore," and "I've lost a big part of myself."[7] Clearly, breakups are even more difficult for those who are preoccupied with wanting more closeness.[8] For them, breakups lead to confusion about their own identity. When people feel they lose a part of themselves following divorce or separation, they feel lonelier, struggle more, and experience more grief.[9]

Yet, as painful as breakups can be, they're often not as painful as we anticipate they will be. Researchers at Carnegie Mellon and Northwestern asked people in happy relationships to imagine the future and answer this question: "If your relationship were to end, how would you feel about it?"[10] When their happy relationships ended, the researchers asked, "Now that you broke up, how bad is it?" It turned out breaking up simply wasn't as awful as they had thought it would be.

That's important because if our anticipated anguish gets blown out of proportion, it can scare us into complacency. We'll stay together not because we want to but because we're scared of the pain we think the end will bring. One of our key concerns is that we'll be lonely without our partner. While that is possible, we shouldn't underestimate how solitary we may feel within our relationship. According to 2018 research, despite being married, many people were lonely, especially those with critical and demanding spouses.[11] Part of the reason we worry about being alone is that when we lose our partner, their support goes with them. It's true that when our partner is essential to our pursuit of important goals, losing that relationship can hurt.[12] But if they aren't the driving force, breaking up doesn't hold us back, and it can help. Even if we feel like our partner is the "wind beneath our wings," research shows that we don't completely lose sight of important goals upon breakup.

Excessive worry about being alone may be the result of FOBS, or fear of being single. Research out of the University of Toronto shows that worrying about being single makes it harder to let go of a partner.[13] Even when people are unhappy, those who don't feel comfortable being on their own are willing to linger in a substandard relationship. And many don't believe that leaving will make them any happier,[14] but research shows that leaving bad, controlling, or abusive relationships increased happiness, more so than people ever thought it would. When it comes to how a breakup may impact us, we make potentially life-altering miscalculations simply because of flawed assumptions.

Decision Time

Whether our relationship is awful, good, or great, we don't like endings. Even if our relationship hasn't been everything that we hoped it would be, it's been part of us. That's hard to leave behind. But if we've given it our best shot and haven't seen improvement, it may be time to put it out of its misery. As Maya Angelou said, "I did then what I knew how to do. Now that I know better, I do better."

Make no mistake, breaking up feels an awful lot like quitting. Quitting sounds bad, so rather than give up, we stick it out and remain resolute in the face of adversity, a quality that Angela Duckworth at the University of Pennsylvania refers to as grit.[15] Studies find that grit helps in many areas of life, so it's easy to assume that grit can help turn around failing relationships. Except it doesn't. In fact, research from the University of Southern California and Northeastern University reveals that relationship grit can lead to worse outcomes.[16]

Sometimes we need to know when to call it quits, especially when persevering is costly. To see grit's influence on decision-making, researchers gave people money and took them to a casino.[17] Okay, not a real casino, but a roulette game they set up in their research lab. Before anyone took their first spin, they gave their predetermined stopping point, or how much they were willing to lose before quitting. We run into problems in life when we get caught up in the heat of the moment and fail to adhere to our a priori standards. Knowing our limits beforehand should counteract that tendency. However, participants' grit-inspired tenacity betrayed them, leading them to gamble longer and lose more money than they intended.

Imagine staring at a computer screen and pushing a single key every once in a while, for up to twenty-five minutes.[18] Sounds terrible, but in one experiment, that's all participants had to do in order to get paid. Here's the wrinkle: near the end of the task, researchers gave participants the option to quit early and still receive the full payment. Quitting seems like a no-brainer, right? However, many people stuck it out till the end, even when they didn't have to. Their stick-to-itiveness wouldn't let them bail. But why? It came down to what people thought finishing meant. When they believed that continuing with the task assessed their persistence, they stuck it out. However, when they considered it a test of their decision-making skills, they were more willing to quit.

That insight has important implications for how we think about our relationship. Should we look at it as a test of our persistence or of our ability to make the best decision? We focus more on longevity than we probably should. Each year we celebrate another anniversary, marking twelve months of perseverance, with the ultimate goal of "till death do us part." That mentality encourages us to believe that months and years inherently matter. With this in mind, we continually attempt to patch up or remain committed to troubled relationships just to keep the streak alive. Instead, we should view relationship commitment as a decision-making task where we have to do what's best for us. If that decision keeps us together, great. Longevity should be the byproduct, not the goal.

At some point, enough has to be enough and we must resist the compulsion to persist. Dan Savage, author of the relationship and sex advice column "Savage Love," gets a lot of questions from readers trying to make sense of their relationship. According to him, the best answer he can give to 80 percent of those questions is his clever and ribald acronym DTMFA (dump the motherf*cker already). He says that if he wanted to, he could suggest breakup and nothing else, because for so many people it's the best choice. Though it's probably not how we hoped things would turn out, if our relationship is coming to an end, there's probably a good reason for it. As I explain in my TEDx Talk, "Break-Ups Don't Have to Leave You Broken," "Great relationships seldom fail but bad ones do, as they should."

HOW TO SEE YOUR RELATIONSHIP MORE CLEARLY

What's next? Well, according to Norman Schwarzkopf, "the truth of the matter is that you always know the right thing to do. The hard part is doing it." While doubts may have lingered for a while, deciding to end the relationship is a big step. The key to moving forward is to handle this new challenge as thoughtfully as possible.

Set Yourself Up for Success

We all want a soft landing and will be tempted to make that happen by easing into the breakup slowly. A hint here, a brief insinuation there, a short talk, all leading to the complete break. Fight that urge. Research shows that those who gradually wind things down have more confusing breakups and end up feeling more hurt, angry, and lonely.[19] In other words, we need to be decisive and rip off the Band-Aid. It's going to sting, but ultimately that's better than allowing the relationship to suffer on life support. Besides, the longer we postpone the inevitable, the longer we have to wait to find the great relationship we deserve.

What's the best way to tell our partner it's over? Options like sending a text, enlisting a friend to tell them, leaving a letter on the bed, or ghosting them completely are easy but

---

Bonus Blind Spot:
No Looking Back

Sure, a clean break is best, but with today's technology it's a lot harder to walk away without looking back. Social media makes it easier than ever to keep tabs on our former partner by checking status updates and scanning through their pictures. Checking up could help ease the loss by providing closure or satisfying our curiosity. It could also make things worse. Research on more than 450 Facebook users explored the potential consequences of checking a former relationship partner's page.[20] Those who did more Facebook profile surveillance (i.e., "Face-

---

book stalking") had a harder time adjusting after their breakup. They experienced more negative feelings, continued sexual desire, distress, nagging feelings of love, and less personal growth.

Now, it may be that creeping on past partners' Facebook pages is just too over-the-top. Instead of stalking, we could be more up front and simply remain Facebook friends. This approach led to better outcomes, allowing people to avoid the negative feelings, lingering love, and residual sexual desire. However, they still missed out on personal growth, which could have helped their recovery by allowing them to move on with their life and experience new things. When we're bored or want to kill time, it seems harmless to pull up a former partner's profile to see what they're up to. This research makes it clear that we're better off walking away and not looking back.

bad. Our partner deserves better. Researchers reviewed forty-seven potential ways to leave a lover and narrowed them down to the most compassionate.[21] There are many passive strategies, like avoiding the partner, being unpleasant to them, or making the partner want to break up. However, if we care about letting our partner down as easily as possible, the best strategy is to "find a time when we can talk face to face about my desire to break up." Okay, but what should we say? It's best to be honest, explain why we want to leave, make it clear we don't regret the time we spent together, and emphasize the positives we experienced while in the relationship.

But be careful. Wanting to soften the blow can entice us to make some well-intentioned but ultimately bad decisions like trying to stay friends afterward. Sixty percent of people aspire to maintain friendship after a breakup.[22] When it's done for practical reasons (e.g., partners had the same friend group or they're co-parenting), it largely works out. However, holding on to friendship due to persistent feelings toward the partner is a recipe for disaster, leading to heartbreak, depression, jealousy, and difficulty finding a new partner. Even if our reasons are pragmatic, our partner's may not be, which will only complicate recovery.

When things get hard, it's natural to have second thoughts and think about getting back together. Stifle that impulse; we generally want to get back together to recapture lost love, but the data suggest we'll wind up with lower satisfaction, along with greater uncertainty and communication problems.[23] The more often we try to make it work after breaking up, the worse these issues get. Research in 2019 showed that in this case, grit helped people stick to their decision rather than flip-flop and end up back together.[24]

Better Off Broken Up

No matter how we may attempt to make them simpler, break-ups aren't easy. But they're better for us than we often realize. We tend to think of our reactions to important events as uniformly positive (e.g., getting married) or negative (e.g., breaking up). But life's more nuanced. Consider how you felt when you graduated high school or started a new job. Each was likely a mixture of good and bad. Happy to be moving on, sad about good times you'll miss, as well as apprehensive and excited about the next stage of life. Transitions are complicated. Breakups are no exception, but the problem is, we've ignored the positives for far too long.

As a graduate student, I'd generate research ideas by reflecting on my own experiences. When it came to breakups, amid a few bad ones were some that were liberating and, in retrospect, the best thing that could have happened. Yet study after study on relationship dissolution reported negative outcome after negative outcome: broken hearts, despair, rejection, loneliness, and sadness. Initially, I was discouraged, but then it hit me: those studies found negative outcomes because that was all they were looking for.

I took a different approach by simply asking, "How were you affected by the breakup of your relationship?"[25] Notice that I didn't ask how upset or devastated participants were, just their general experience. While lots of the responses contained negative experiences, many people also mentioned positive outcomes, such as:

"I have become a better person because of it."
"I feel liberated."
"I'm going out and enjoying life."
"I realized I was my own person."
"I'm involving myself in different activities."
"I'm trying to learn more about myself."
"I'm doing things I could not have done with my ex."
"I feel like I can be myself."

Around the same time, Ty Tashiro and Patricia Frazier from the University of Minnesota found that when prompted, participants reported an average of five ways their breakup would benefit their future relationships.[26] Benefits included becoming a better communicator, learning relationship skills, realizing the importance of friends' opinions, and knowing what they really wanted from relationships.

Obviously, it's unrealistic to expect that every breakup will be immediately beneficial. When our relationship seems to be going well, a split is devastating. But what if the relationship isn't going well? Ending a relationship that isn't helping us become a better person should be good. I tested this idea with 150 people who had broken up a serious long-term relationship in the previous three months.[27] Although this group should have been especially sad, those who ended an unfulfilling relationship experienced addition by subtraction, resulting in more positive emotions such as feeling confident, empowered, free, hopeful, strong, wise, satisfied, relieved, and happy. Not only that; they had more personal growth and didn't lose their sense of self. In fact, when asked to characterize the breakup's overall impact on them, 41.3 percent considered it positive, 25.7 percent neutral, and only 33 percent negative. In other words, only one out of three felt their breakup was negative.

When it comes to divorce, though it is one of life's most difficult experiences, it also has positives. When compared to others who were married, those who had been divorced were more curious, open-minded, open, outgoing, and energetic.[28] Similarly, following separation, people become more agreeable and, after divorce, more conscientious.[29] For many, the end of their relationship does not mean unavoidable despair. Even the very best breakups aren't pain-free, but amid the pain are plenty of positives. The lesson is simple: when your relationship doesn't help you become a better person, ending it does.

Building a Better Breakup

Post-breakup recovery takes work. Research helps us find the best strategies, and David Sbarra and his students at the University of Arizona do a lot of innovative research. In one study about relationship loss, participants came to the lab to answer questions about coping with the split over a nine-week period.[30] One group had it easy and came to the lab only at the beginning and end of the study, while the other group reported to the lab twice as often to complete more in-depth activities. These included a four-minute exercise where they stated whatever came to mind about the breakup and how they felt about it. Though the more intense sessions could have caused more grief, they actually helped participants feel clearer about who they were, more confident about themselves, and less distressed and lonely. By considering their breakup-related feelings more deeply, participants had the opportunity to better understand their experiences, which clarified how they viewed themselves. The take-home is that critically evaluating our former relationships and ourselves facilitates our recovery.

Too often we take the easy way out and try to avoid confronting painful experiences. That's a losing strategy because it only makes us think about them more.[31] Don't believe me? Right now, whatever you do, don't think about your first love. You did, didn't you? The more we try to put our former partner out of our mind, the more they pop right back in. My own research shows that denial and mental disengagement make us feel worse by increasing negative emotions and not feeling like ourselves anymore.[32] However, when people accept the situation and look for the good in it, they have a much better recovery.

After a breakup, it's easy to wonder, "How could any good

come of this?" I wanted to see if writing about positive aspects of a breakup could help people cope with their loss.[33] Here are the exact instructions: "Write about your deepest thoughts and positive feelings about the relationship that ended. The important thing is that you dig down into your deepest positive emotions and explore them in your writing." Doing that for twenty minutes a day over three days led to increased positive emotions such as feeling content, strong, thankful, relieved, wise, and satisfied. To take it to the next level, you can write about your experience as a "redemptive narrative" that crafts a story featuring the "silver lining" amid the negativity and reveals how positives can arise from bad situations.[34] Journal entries with redemptive themes such as "I am really sad that we broke up, but maybe it's for the best" and "I am better off without somebody who doesn't treat me right" produced less suffering following a breakup.

Now, a word of caution. Not every type of reflection is helpful. For example, when people who had recently separated wrote about their experience by attempting to create a coherent, organized, and meaningful story, it was counterproductive.[35] That's because deeper meaning can be elusive, especially for those of us who ruminate and think intensely about issues. Sure, we want to know "why" and hope that our misery will at least yield some sort of profound revelation, but sometimes things just happen and we're better off focusing elsewhere.

Like, for instance, on ourselves. Breakups force us to hit the reset button and give us a rare opportunity for guilt-free self-focus. We should take advantage of that by resurrecting or reemphasizing parts of ourselves that we ignored or neglected during the relationship and do things the relationship held us back from, a process I call "rediscovery of the self."[36] Doing this allows us to experience more positive emotions, a greater sense of self, and strong personal growth after a breakup.

Though many of us will naturally seek rediscovery, I was curious about the potential benefits for people of getting a

---

How Do You Measure Up?
Rediscovery of the Self

When a relationship ends, it shakes our sense of self. Remembering who we are outside of our former relationship can help recovery. To gauge progress since the relationship ended, I created a measure of rediscovery of the self. Here are a few items:

1. I have done the things I once enjoyed that I could not do while I was in my relationship.
   Not at All 1 2 3 4 5 6 7 A Great Deal
2. I have focused more on my needs that were neglected while with my partner.
   Not at All 1 2 3 4 5 6 7 A Great Deal
3. I have become reacquainted with the person I was before the relationship.
   Not at All 1 2 3 4 5 6 7 A Great Deal
4. I have rediscovered who I am.
   Not at All 1 2 3 4 5 6 7 A Great Deal

Higher scores indicate that you've made more progress in rediscovering the person you were prior to your relationship. If your score isn't as high as you'd like, use the items as a guide to figure out where you need to focus.

---

little push along their rediscovery journey. I recruited people who had recently broken up and randomly assigned them to do one of two types of activities over two weeks. One group did routine enjoyable activities, like hanging out with friends or going to the gym, to the movies, or out to eat. The other group focused on rediscovery of the self. For example, if they always loved the beach but didn't go because their partner hated sand, a trip to the beach would allow them to resurrect an aspect of themselves that had been dormant.

Logically, both routine and rediscovery activities should help recovery. Routine activities should help because they prevent us from sitting at home alone eating pints of ice cream and binge-watching Netflix, and rediscovery allows us to get reacquainted with who we are. While both kinds of activities were helpful, rediscovery activities led to less of a loss of self, fewer negative emotions, and less loneliness. Participants in the rediscovery group also reported more positive outcomes, such as more positive emotions, self-acceptance, purpose in life, and overall well-being.

Remember, "Great relationships seldom fail but bad ones do, as they should." Whether we like it or not, relationships that end were broken in some way. But that doesn't mean we'll be broken forever. The Japanese have an art form, *kintsugi*, in which an artist repairs broken pottery using tree sap mixed with precious metals like gold, platinum, and silver. The result is even more beautiful than the original. But it's not just an art form; it's a philosophy that treats damage as an opportunity for improvement rather than a problem to conceal. This is exactly the opportunity we have when a relationship comes to an end, to mend the cracks and emerge better than ever.

Relationships are important. Time is short. Mistakes are

costly. Relationships should be the best part of your life. I hope you have found one that builds and sustains you. If you haven't, keep looking, because you have to ask yourself: what is one hour, one day, one week, one month, or one lifetime of your happiness and fulfillment worth?

RELATIONSHIP RECAP

- Being gritty and persistent in relationships isn't always helpful and can lead to worse outcomes.
- We're bad at predicting the future and greatly overestimate how bad we'll feel after a breakup.
- Perseverance often pays off, except when it keeps you in your relationship well past its expiration date.
- Great relationships seldom fail but bad ones do, as they should.
- When your relationship doesn't help you become a better person, ending it does.
- Being on your own is far better for you than being in an unfulfilling relationship.

Afterword

Our relationships build us, define us, sustain us, and can break us. I hope this book has helped you move closer to finding the great relationship you deserve. In that pursuit, here are a few final points to keep in mind:

1. Remember that science isn't prescriptive. That is, research can't pinpoint exactly what any one person should do or guarantee the fate of a single individual's relationship. Rather, relationship science is informative and offers new perspectives that can help you put the odds in your favor. Are self-expanding novel, interesting, challenging, and exciting (NICE) activities guaranteed to save your relationship? No, but performing those self-expanding activities does increase the chances that your relationship will improve. Medical research works the same way. We know that smoking increases the risk of breathing-related illnesses like lung cancer, yet not every smoker experiences these issues. Still, we use what science has learned about smoking to inform our decisions. We also rely

on scientists to continually learn more. That's why this book should be the start of a conversation, the first step in using science to better understand your relationship. Keep reading, keep asking questions, and keep learning. As you seek further insights, be sure to weigh evidence-based scientific sources more heavily than anecdotes or personal opinions.

2. Speaking of science, I'm really proud of the number of studies (especially newer studies) I was able to incorporate into the book (there are more than 350 references) and still make it accessible. Of course, for every study I included, there are dozens more I wasn't able to include. Picking the "right" studies is a judgment call, but one that I made based on how applicable the research was to everyday life. Every study was published in a reputable source subjected to peer review. It's science. But science acknowledges its imperfection. In light of that, it's wise to be skeptical, but full-blown skepticism of every study finding that doesn't match our experience isn't the solution. The answer to science we disagree with isn't personal experience or opinion. It's more science. If there are findings or conclusions you found objectionable, contribute to the scientific process. Participate in research, take a relationship course, go to graduate school to study relationships, or contribute money to support relationship science. Check out the International Association for Relationship Research (www.iarr.org) and look for ways to get involved. If we wait for perfection, we'll wait forever. Our knowledge is incomplete; our discoveries continue; the learning goes on.

3. Don't twist what you've read to justify staying in a bad relationship. This book's goal is to provide better information to

allow readers to make more informed decisions. The notion that your relationship is stronger than you think is only meant to encourage those in decent relationships to find ways to make their relationship better. The message isn't that it's okay to fight all the time, avoid closeness, ignore your partner, not have sex, or not love your partner. Relationships should be founded in mutual love, respect, and friendship between partners who are equals, free of any form of physical or verbal abuse. If that doesn't describe your situation, it's important to see the relationship for what it is and avoid engaging in any sort of mental gymnastics that may encourage you to accept your partner's unacceptable behaviors or tolerate a less-than-stellar relationship. Once again, everyone deserves a great relationship.

When you're ninety-five years old and you think back on your life, you're not going to think: "I wish I'd owned a better phone," "I wish I'd spent more time on the Internet," or "I wish I'd spent more time at work." You're going to think: "I wish I'd spent more time with the people I loved."

The key is finding and growing the relationships that are worthy of your time.

Acknowledgments

First and foremost, I want to thank you, the reader. Your relationship is one of the most cherished parts of your life, so I appreciate you letting this book into such an important part of your world. I hope the time you spent pondering your relationship's past, present, and future has been insightful.

Before every semester, I engage in the same ritual. I read Mitch Albom's *Tuesdays with Morrie* as a reminder of what's truly important in life and to keep things in perspective. Having read the book well over thirty times, I've internalized many of Morrie Schwartz's life lessons, including the importance of gratitude.

Have you ever had a teacher, an undergraduate advisor, a graduate mentor, a departmental colleague, a research collaborator, a department chair, a dean, a provost, a university president, an agent, an editor, a student, a research assistant, a coach, a friend, a family, a parent, a sibling, a wife, or a daughter, even a Labrador retriever, who believed in you and helped you realize your potential? I've been fortunate enough to have every one of these in my life to support, challenge, change, and encourage me. Without them and those relationships, this book would not have been possible. Make no mistake, I could not have done it alone.

It would take several pages to name everyone who has helped me along the way, but here are a few: First, my wife, Colleen. Thank you for being the most kindhearted person I have ever known. You have taught me more about love than all the research studies in the world. To my daughter, Avery, keep on being my superstar.

Thank you to my superagent, Heather Jackson, for believing in me and this project. Your patience and support for a first-time author will never be forgotten. I am also grateful for my editor, Tracy Behar, who made every sentence better by asking insightful questions, helping me clarify my thoughts, and getting me back on track when I became too technical. Your expertise has made me not only a better writer, but a better teacher of writing as well. I thank you, and my future students thank you. I'm also grateful to everyone at Little, Brown for helping bring this book to life, but especially Ian Straus, Jayne Yaffe Kemp, Lucy Kim, Jess Chun, and Jules Horbachevsky. I'm also grateful to Eileen Chetti for her copy-editing expertise.

I'd also like to thank my mom and dad (who was a fantastic baseball coach); my in-laws, John and Erma; my teaching mentor, Dr. Susan Luek; my research mentor, Dr. Art Aron; and my friends Brett, Jenna, Roosh, Kristen, Jason, Anthony, and Bruce, as well as my academic colleagues, whom I also count as good friends: Brent, Kevin, Ben, Tim, Dave, Natalie, Lisa, Christine, and Lindsay. I'd also like to thank my fellow relationship scientists who dedicate their careers to the research

I shared in this book. Similarly, I'd like to thank all the research participants who volunteered for those studies. Because thousands of people are willing to give us a glimpse into their relationships, we all learn and benefit from their experience.

Finally, I'd like to thank my students. Though you are too numerous to name, every single one of you has made me a better teacher and person.

References

Introduction

1. S. Lebowitz, "10 things everyone wants to know about their relationship, according to Google," *Business Insider,* December 13, 2017, https://www.businessinsider.com/most-popular-google-searches-on-relationships-2017-12.
2. D. Brooks and G. Collins, "Advice for high school graduates," *New York Times,* June 10, 2009, https://opinionator.blogs.nytimes.com/2009/06/10/advice-for-high-school-graduates/.
3. R. Weissbourd et al., "The talk: How adults can promote young people's healthy relationships and prevent misogyny and sexual harassment," Making Caring Common Project, Harvard Graduate School of Education, 2017, https://static1.squarespace.com/static/5b7c56e255b02c683659fe43/t/5bd51a0324a69425bd079b59/1540692500558/mcc_the_talk_final.pdf.
4. J. Holt-Lunstad et al., "Loneliness and social isolation as risk factors for mortality: A meta-analytic review," *Perspectives on Psychological Science* 10, no. 2 (2015): 227–237.
5. V. Murthy, "Work and the loneliness epidemic," *Harvard Business Review,* September 2017, https://hbr.org/cover-story/2017/09/work-and-the-loneliness-epidemic.

6. W. J. Chopik and E. O'Brien, "Happy you, healthy me? Having a happy partner is independently associated with better health in oneself," *Health Psychology* 36, no. 1 (2017): 21–30.

7. E. J. Boothby et al., "The world looks better together: How close others enhance our visual experiences," *Personal Relationships* 24 (2017): 694–714.

8. S. Schnall et al., "Social support and the perception of geographical slant," *Journal of Experimental Social Psychology* 44, no. 5 (2008): 1246–1255.

9. G. Gigerenzer and R. Garcia-Retamero, "Cassandra's regret: The psychology of not wanting to know," *Psychological Review* 124, no. 2 (2017): 179–196.

10. Relationship Decisions website, accessed June 3, 2020, http://relationshipdecisions.org.

11. S. Joel, G. MacDonald, and E. Page-Gould, "Wanting to stay and wanting to go: Unpacking the content and structure of relationship stay/leave decision processes," *Social Psychological and Personality Science* 9, no. 6 (2018): 631–644.

Chapter 1

1. T. K. MacDonald and M. Ross, "Assessing the accuracy of predictions about dating relationships: How and why do lovers' predictions differ from those made by observers?" *Personality and Social Psychology Bulletin* 25, no. 11 (1999): 1417–1429.

2. J. S. Lerner et al., "Emotion and decision making," *Annual Review of Psychology* 66 (2015): 799–823.

3. S. Vazire and E. N. Carlson, "Self-knowledge of personality: Do people know themselves?" *Social and Personality Psychology Compass* 4, no. 8 (2010): 605–620.

4. M. Csikszentmihalyi and T. J. Figurski, "Self-awareness and aversive experience in everyday life," *Journal of Personality* 50, no. 1 (1982): 15–28.

5. US Bureau of Labor Statistics, US Department of Labor, "American time use survey," last modified December 20, 2016, https://www.bls.gov/tus/charts/leisure.htm.

6. T. D. Wilson et al., "Just think: The challenges of the disengaged mind," *Science* 345, no. 6192 (2014): 75–77.

7. L. K. Son and N. Kornell, "The virtues of ignorance," *Behavioural Processes* 83, no. 2 (2010): 207–212.

8. D. A. Moore and P. J. Healy, "The trouble with overconfidence," *Psychological Review* 115, no. 2 (2008): 502–517.

9. D. Dunning et al., "The overconfidence effect in social prediction," *Journal of Personality and Social Psychology* 58, no. 4 (1990): 568–581.

10. J. Kruger and D. Dunning, "Unskilled and unaware of it: How difficulties in recognizing one's own incompetence lead to inflated self-assessments," *Journal of Personality and Social Psychology* 77, no. 6 (1999): 1121–1134.

11. R. J. Eidelson, "Affiliative rewards and restrictive costs in developing relationships," *British Journal of Social Psychology* 20, no. 3 (1981): 197–204.

12. J. A. Lavner, B. R. Karney, and T. N. Bradbury, "Relationship problems over the early years of marriage: Stability or change?" *Journal of Family Psychology* 28 (2014): 979–985.

13. T. L. Huston et al., "The connubial crucible: Newlywed years as predictors of marital delight, distress, and divorce," *Journal of Personality and Social Psychology* 80 (2001): 237–252.

14. H. C. Williamson et al., "Are problems that contribute to divorce present at the start of marriage, or do they emerge over time?" *Journal of Social and Personal Relationships* 33, no. 8 (2016): 1120–1134.

15. P. Rozin and E. B. Royzman, "Negativity bias, negativity dominance, and contagion," *Personality and Social Psychology Review* 5, no. 4 (2001): 296–320.

16. D. E. Levari et al., "Prevalence-induced concept change in human judgment," *Science* 360, no. 6396 (2018): 1465–1467.

Chapter 2

1. S. Sprecher and S. Metts, "Development of the 'Romantic Beliefs Scale' and examination of the effects of gender and gender-role orientation," *Journal of Social and Personal Relationships* 6, no. 4 (1989): 387–411.

2. M. A. Harrison and J. C. Shortall, "Women and men in love: Who really feels it and says it first?" *Journal of Social Psychology* 151, no. 6 (2011): 727–736.

3. Sprecher and Metts, "Development of the 'Romantic Beliefs Scale.'" If you're interested, you can find the full Romantic Beliefs Scale here: Pearson Education website, accessed June 3, 2020, http://wps.ablongman.com/ab_mcl_activities_1/57/14645/3749274.cw/index.html.

4. D. Joel et al., "Sex beyond the genitalia: The human brain mosaic," *Proceedings of the National Academy of Sciences of the United States of America* 112, no. 50 (2015): 15468–15473.

5. J. S. Hyde, "The gender similarities hypothesis," *American Psychologist* 60, no. 6 (2005): 581–592.

6. J. S. Hyde, "Gender similarities and differences," *Annual Review of Psychology* 65 (2014): 373–398.

7. E. Zell, Z. Krizan, and S. R. Teeter, "Evaluating gender similarities and differences using metasynthesis," *American Psychologist* 70, no. 1 (2015): 10–20.

8. P. B. Perrin et al., "Aligning Mars and Venus: The social construction and instability of gender differences in romantic relationships," *Sex Roles* 64, nos. 9–10 (2011): 613–628.

9. J. L. Petersen and J. S. Hyde, "A meta-analytic review of research on gender differences in sexuality, 1993–2007," *Psychological Bulletin* 136, no. 1 (2010): 21–38.

10. B. J. Carothers and H. T. Reis, "Men and women are from Earth: Examining the latent structure of gender," *Journal of Personality and Social Psychology* 104, no. 2 (2013): 385–407.

11. Hyde, "Gender similarities and differences"; Petersen and Hyde, "Meta-analytic review of research on gender."

12. C. A. Seavey, P. A. Katz, and S. R. Zalk, "Baby X: The effect of gender labels on adult responses to infants," *Sex Roles: A Journal of Research* 1, no. 2 (1975): 103–109; L. S. Sidorowicz and G. S. Lunney, "Baby X revisited," *Sex Roles: A Journal of Research* 6, no. 1 (1980): 67–73.

13. M. Stern and K. H. Karraker, "Sex stereotyping of infants: A review of gender labeling studies," *Sex Roles: A Journal of Research* 20, nos. 9–10 (1989): 501–522.

14. R. Nickerson, "Confirmation bias: A ubiquitous phenomenon in many guises," *Review of General Psychology* 2, no. 2 (1998): 175–220.

15. J. Gray, *Men Are from Mars, Women Are from Venus: A Practical Guide for Improving Communication and Getting What You Want in Your Relationships* (New York: HarperCollins, 1992).

16. J. M. Gottman et al., "Predicting marital happiness and stability from newlywed interactions," *Journal of Marriage and Family Therapy* 60 (1998): 5–22.

17. J. A. Hall and M. Canterberry, "Sexism and assertive courtship strategies," *Sex Roles* 65, nos. 11–12 (2011): 840–853.

18. S. T. Fiske and S. E. Taylor, *Social Cognition,* 2nd ed. (New York: McGraw-Hill, 1991).

19. J. A. Simpson and S. W. Gangestad, "Individual differences in sociosexuality: Evidence for convergent and discriminant validity," *Journal of Personality and Social Psychology* 60, no. 6 (1991): 870–883.

20. L. Penke and J. B. Asendorpf, "Beyond global sociosexual orientations: A more differentiated look at sociosexuality and its effects on courtship and romantic relationships," *Journal of Personality and Social Psychology* 95 (2008): 1113–1135.

21. You can find the full sociosexuality scale here: Lars Penke website, accessed June 3, 2020, http://www.larspenke.eu/research /soi-r.html.

22. D. A. Weiser et al., "Swiping right: Sociosexuality, intentions to engage in infidelity, and infidelity experiences on Tinder," *Personality and Individual Differences* 133 (2018): 29–33.

23. Petersen and Hyde, "Meta-analytic review of research on gender."

24. P. M. Todd et al., "Different cognitive processes underlie human mate choices and mate preferences," *Proceedings of the National Academy of Sciences of the United States of America* 104, no. 38 (2007): 15011–15016.

25. E. J. Finkel and P. W. Eastwick, "Arbitrary social norms influence sex differences in romantic selectivity," *Psychological Science* 20, no. 10 (2009): 1290–1295.

26. S. Sprecher, M. Schmeeckle, and D. Felmlee, "The principle of least interest: Inequality in emotional involvement in romantic relationships," *Journal of Family Issues* 27, no. 9 (2006): 1255–1280.

27. J. A. Hall and M. S. Mast, "Are women always more interpersonally sensitive than men? Impact of goals and content domain," *Personality and Social Psychology Bulletin* 34, no. 1 (2008): 144–155.

Chapter 3

1. G. L. Flett, P. L. Hewitt, and S. S. Sherry, "Deep, dark, and dysfunctional: The destructiveness of interpersonal perfectionism," in *The Dark Side of Personality: Science and Practice in Social, Personality, and Clinical Psychology,* ed. V. Zeigler-Hill and D. K. Marcus (Washington, DC: American Psychological Association, 2016), 211–229.

2. R. W. Hill, M. C. Zrull, and S. Turlington, "Perfectionism and interpersonal problems," *Journal of Personality Assessment* 69, no. 1 (1997): 81–103.

3. A. Hoffmann, J. Stoeber, and J. Musch, "Multidimensional perfectionism and assortative mating: A perfect date?" *Personality and Individual Differences* 86 (2015): 94–100.

4. A. Bruk, S. G. Scholl, and H. Bless, "Beautiful mess effect: Self–other differences in evaluation of showing vulnerability," *Journal of Personality and Social Psychology* 115, no. 2 (2018): 192–205.

5. S. W. S. Lee and N. Schwarz, "Framing love: When it hurts to think we were made for each other," *Journal of Experimental Social Psychology* 54 (2014): 61–67.

6. A. M. Grant and B. Schwartz, "Too much of a good thing: The challenge and opportunity of the inverted U," *Perspectives on Psychological Science* 6, no. 1 (2011): 61–76.

7. L. F. Emery et al., "Do we look happy? Perceptions of romantic relationship quality on Facebook," *Personal Relationships* 22, no. 1 (2015): 1–7.

8. L. F. Emery et al., "Can you tell that I'm in a relationship? Attachment and relationship visibility on Facebook," *Personality and Social Psychology Bulletin* 40, no. 11 (2014): 1466–1479.

9. J. Naftulin, "Michelle Obama reveals she and Barack have gone to marriage counseling: 'We get help with our marriage when we need it,'" *Insider,* November 12, 2018, https://www.insider.com /michelle-obama-barack-obama-marriage-counseling-2018-11.

10. A. M. Parker, W. B. de Bruin, and B. Fischhoff, "Maximizers versus satisficers: Decision-making styles, competence, and outcomes," *Judgment and Decision Making* 2, no. 6 (2007): 342–350.

11. B. Schwartz et al., "Maximizing versus satisficing: Happiness is a matter of choice," *Journal of Personality and Social Psychology* 83 (2002): 1178–1197.

12. R. L. Shiner, "Maximizers, satisficers, and their satisfaction with and preferences for reversible versus irreversible decisions," *Social Psychological and Personality Science* 6, no. 8 (2015): 896–903.

13. C. R. Knee, "Implicit theories of relationships: Assessment and prediction of romantic relationship initiation, coping, and longevity," *Journal of Personality and Social Psychology* 74, no. 2 (1998): 360–370.

14. E. T. Higgins, "Self-discrepancy: A theory relating self and affect," *Psychological Review* 94, no. 3 (1987): 319–340.

15. S. A. Vannier and L. F. O'Sullivan, "Great expectations: Examining unmet romantic expectations and dating relationship outcomes using an investment model framework," *Journal of Social and Personal Relationships* 35, no. 8 (2018): 1045–1066.

16. C. M. Thompson and A. L. Vangelisti, "What happens when the standard for openness goes unmet in romantic relationships? Analyses of stress, coping, and relational consequences," *Journal of Social and Personal Relationships* 33, no. 3 (2016): 320–343.

17. C. R. Knee et al., "Implicit theories of relationships: Who cares if romantic partners are less than ideal?" *Personality and Social Psychology Bulletin* 27, no. 7 (2001): 808–819.

18. R. D. Heino, N. B. Ellison, and J. L. Gibbs, "Relationshopping: Investigating the market metaphor in online dating," *Journal of Social and Personal Relationships* 27, no. 4 (2010): 427–447.

19. Schwartz et al., "Maximizing versus satisficing."

20. To get a more detailed picture, complete the full scale that researchers use in their studies. See Happysmarts Project website, accessed June 3, 2020, https://www.happysmarts.com/scale/maximizer-satisfier-scale/.

21. M. J. Hornsey et al., "How much is enough in a perfect world? Cultural variation in ideal levels of happiness, pleasure, freedom, health, self-esteem, longevity, and intelligence," *Psychological Science* 29, no. 9 (2018): 1393–1404.

22. Knee, "Implicit theories of relationships: Assessment and prediction."

23. D. J. Weigel, C. B. Lalasz, and D. A. Weiser, "Maintaining relationships: The role of implicit relationship theories and partner fit," *Communication Reports* 29, no. 1 (2016): 23–34.

24. R. A. Cobb et al., "Implicit theories of relationships and close relationship violence: Does believing your relationship can grow relate to lower perpetration of violence?" *Personality and Social Psychology Bulletin* 39, no. 3 (2013): 279–290.

25. K. L. Carswell and E. J. Finkel, "Can you get the magic back? The moderating effect of passion decay beliefs on relationship commitment," *Journal of Personality and Social Psychology* 115, no. 6 (2018): 1002–1033.

26. E. Aronson and J. Mills, "The effect of severity of initiation on liking for a group," *Journal of Abnormal and Social Psychology* 59 (1959): 177–181.

27. L. Festinger, *Cognitive Dissonance* (Stanford, CA: Stanford University Press, 1957).

28. K. Shafer, T. M. Jensen, and J. H. Larson, "An actor-partner model of relationship effort and marital quality," *Family Relations: An Interdisciplinary Journal of Applied Family Studies* 63, no. 5 (2014): 654–666.

29. L. Campbell et al., "Trust, variability in relationship evaluations, and relationship processes," *Journal of Personality and Social Psychology* 99, no. 1 (2010): 14–31.

30. S. W. Whitton and M. A. Whisman, "Relationship satisfaction instability and depression," *Journal of Family Psychology* 24 (2010): 791–794.

31. X. B. Arriaga, "The ups and downs of dating: Fluctuations in satisfaction in newly formed romantic relationships," *Journal of Personality and Social Psychology* 80, no. 5 (2001): 754–765.

32. C. J. Totenhagen et al., "The calm after the storm: Relationship length as associated with couples' daily variability," *Journal of Social and Personal Relationships* 33, no. 6 (2016): 768–791.

33. B. G. Ogolsky, C. A. Surra, and J. K. Monk, "Pathways of commitment to wed: The development and dissolution of romantic relationships," *Journal of Marriage and Family* 78, no. 2 (2016): 293–310.

Chapter 4

1. I. Aharon et al., "Beautiful faces have variable reward value: fMRI and behavioral evidence," *Neuron* 32 (2001): 537–551.

2. J. K. McNulty, L. A. Neff, and B. R. Karney, "Beyond initial attraction: physical attractiveness in newlywed marriage," *Journal of Family Psychology* 22 (2008): 135–143.

3. C. Ma-Kellams, M. C. Wang, and H. Cardiel, "Attractiveness and relationship longevity: Beauty is not what it is cracked up to be," *Personal Relationships* 24, no. 1 (2017): 146–161.

4. D. H. Felmlee, "Fatal attractions: Affection and disaffection in intimate relationships," *Journal of Social and Personal Relationships* 12, no. 2 (1995): 295–311.

5. L. R. Ramsey, J. A. Marotta, and T. Hoyt, "Sexualized, objectified, but not satisfied: Enjoying sexualization relates to lower relationship satisfaction through perceived partner-objectification," *Journal of Social and Personal Relationships* 34, no. 2 (2017): 258–278.

6. K. Dion, E. Berscheid, and E. Walster, "What is beautiful is good," *Journal of Personality and Social Psychology* 24, no. 3 (1972): 285–290.

7. A. Feingold, "Good-looking people are not what we think," *Psychological Bulletin* 111, no. 2 (1992): 304–341.

8. E. J. Lemay, M. S. Clark, and A. Greenberg, "What is beautiful is good because what is beautiful is desired: Physical attractiveness stereotyping as projection of interpersonal goals," *Personality and Social Psychology Bulletin* 36, no. 3 (2010): 339–353.

9. E. E. Bruch and M. E. J. Newman, "Aspirational pursuit of mates in online dating markets," *Science Advances* 4, no. 8 (2018), eaap9815.

10. V. Swami et al., "A dark side of positive illusions? Associations between the love-is-blind bias and the experience of jealousy," *Personality and Individual Differences* 53, no. 6 (2012): 796–800.

11. J. R. Oltmanns, P. M. Markey, and J. E. French, "Dissimilarity in physical attractiveness within romantic dyads and mate retention behaviors," *Journal of Social and Personal Relationships* 34, no. 4 (2017): 565–577.

12. M. A. Fugère, A. J. Cousins, and S. MacLaren, "(Mis)matching in physical attractiveness and women's resistance to mate guarding," *Personality and Individual Differences* 87 (2015): 190–195.

13. T. Reynolds and A. L. Meltzer, "Adopting a dyadic perspective to better understand the association between physical attractiveness and dieting motivations and behaviors," *Body Image* 22 (2017): 48–52.

14. M. A. Fugère et al., "The importance of physical attractiveness to the mate choices of women and their mothers," *Evolutionary Psychological Science* 3 (2017): 243–252.

15. Felmlee, "Fatal attractions."

16. P. K. Jonason, M. Lyons, and A. Blanchard, "Birds of a bad feather flock together: The dark triad and mate choice," *Personality and Individual Differences* 78 (2015): 34–38.

17. P. K. Jonason and G. D. Webster, "The dirty dozen: A concise measure of the dark triad," *Psychological Assessment* 22 (2010): 420–432. If you're interested in the full scale, you can try it here: Open Psychometrics Project, accessed June 3, 2020, https:// openpsychometrics.org/tests/SD3/.

18. W. K. Campbell and S. M. Campbell, "On the self-regulatory dynamics created by the particular benefits and costs of narcissism: A contextual reinforcement model and examination of leadership," *Self and Identity* 8 (2009): 214–232.

19. S. N. Wurst et al., "Narcissism and romantic relationships: The differential impact of narcissistic admiration and rivalry," *Journal of Personality and Social Psychology* 112, no. 2 (2017): 280–306.

20. D. N. Jones and D. A. Weiser, "Differential infidelity patterns among the Dark Triad," *Personality and Individual Differences* 57 (2014): 20–24.

21. G. Brewer et al., "Dark triad traits, infidelity and romantic revenge," *Personality and Individual Differences* 83 (2015): 122–127.

22. S. I. Rick, D. A. Small, and E. J. Finkel, "Fatal (fiscal) attraction: Spendthrifts and tightwads in marriage," *Journal of Marketing Research* 48, no. 2 (2011): 228–237.

23. S. M. Kalick and T. E. Hamilton, "The matching hypothesis reexamined," *Journal of Personality and Social Psychology* 51, no. 4 (1986): 673–682.

24. Fugère et al., "(Mis)matching in physical attractiveness."

25. A. Feingold, "Matching for attractiveness in romantic partners and same-sex friends: A meta-analysis and theoretical critique," *Psychological Bulletin* 104, no. 2 (1988): 226–235.

26. McNulty et al., "Beyond initial attraction."

27. A. L. Meltzer et al., "Sex differences in the implications of partner physical attractiveness for the trajectory of marital satisfaction," *Journal of Personality and Social Psychology* 106, no. 3 (2014): 418–428.

28. A. L. Meltzer et al., "Marriages are more satisfying when wives are thinner than their husbands," *Social Psychological and Personality Science* 2 (2011): 416–424.

29. L. L. Hunt, P. W. Eastwick, and E. J. Finkel, "Leveling the playing field: Acquaintance length predicts reduced assortative mating on attractiveness," *Psychological Science* 26 (2015): 1046–1053.

30. G. J. Lewandowski, A. Aron, and J. Gee, "Personality goes a long way: The malleability of opposite-sex physical attractiveness," *Personal Relationships* 14, no. 4 (2007): 571–585.

31. V. Swami et al., "More than just skin deep? Personality information influences men's ratings of the attractiveness of women's body sizes," *Journal of Social Psychology* 150, no. 6 (2010): 628–647.

32. M. D. Botwin, D. M. Buss, and T. K. Shackelford, "Personality and mate preferences: Five factors in mate selection and marital satisfaction," *Journal of Personality* 65, no. 1 (1997): 107–136.

33. R. M. Montoya, R. S. Horton, and J. Kirchner, "Is actual similarity necessary for attraction? A meta-analysis of actual and

perceived similarity," *Journal of Social and Personal Relationships* 25, no. 6 (2008): 889–922.

34. E. C. Klohnen and S. Luo, "Interpersonal attraction and personality: What is attractive—self similarity, ideal similarity, complementarity or attachment security?" *Journal of Personality and Social Psychology* 85, no. 4 (2003): 709–722.

35. S. L. Murray, J. G. Holmes, and D. W. Griffin, "The self-fulfilling nature of positive illusions in romantic relationships: Love is not blind, but prescient," *Journal of Personality and Social Psychology* 71, no. 6 (1996): 1155–1180.

36. D. H. Barelds and P. Dijkstra, "Positive illusions about a partner's physical attractiveness and relationship quality," *Personal Relationships* 16, no. 2 (2009): 263–283.

37. D. P. H. Barelds and P. Dijkstra, "Positive illusions about a partner's personality and relationship quality," *Journal of Research in Personality* 45, no. 1 (2011): 37–43.

38. P. J. E. Miller, S. Niehuis, and T. L. Huston, "Positive illusions in marital relationships: A 13-year longitudinal study," *Personality and Social Psychology Bulletin* 32, no. 12 (2006): 1579–1594.

39. D. Carnegie, *How to Win Friends and Influence People* (New York: Simon and Schuster, 1936).

Chapter 5

1. K. Driesmans, L. Vandenbosch, and S. Eggermont, "True love lasts forever: The influence of a popular teenage movie on Belgian girls' romantic beliefs," *Journal of Children and Media* 10, no. 3 (2016): 304–320.

2. A. Aron et al., "Reward, motivation, and emotion systems associated with early-stage intense romantic love," *Journal of Neurophysiology* 94, no. 1 (2005): 327–337; A. Bartels and S. Zeki, "The neural basis of romantic love," *Neuroreport: For Rapid Communication of Neuroscience Research* 11, no. 17 (2000): 3829–3834.

3. E. Emanuele et al., "Raised plasma nerve growth factor levels associated with early-stage romantic love," *Psychoneuroendocrinology* 20 (2005): 1–7.

4. P. C. Regan, "Love, companionate and passionate," in *Encyclopedia of Human Relationships,* ed. H. T. Reis and S. Sprecher (Thousand Oaks, CA: Sage Publications, 2009), 1007–1011.

5. E. Hatfield and S. Sprecher, "Measuring passionate love in intimate relationships," *Journal of Adolescence* 9, no. 4 (1986): 383–410.

6. Regan, "Love, companionate and passionate."

7. D. G. Blanchflower and A. J. Oswald, "Money, sex and happiness: An empirical study," *Scandinavian Journal of Economics* 106 (2004): 393–415.

8. J. M. Twenge, R. A. Sherman, and B. E. Wells, "Declines in sexual frequency among American adults, 1989–2014," *Archives of Sexual Behavior* 46 (2017): 2389–2401.

9. L. Smith LeBeau and J. T. Buckingham, "Relationship social comparison tendencies, insecurity, and perceived relationship quality," *Journal of Social and Personal Relationships* 25 (2008): 71–86.

10. A. L. Meltzer et al., "Quantifying the sexual afterglow: The lingering benefits of sex and their implications for pair-bonded relationships," *Psychological Science* 28, no. 5 (2017): 587–598.

11. E. A. Schoenfeld et al., "Does sex really matter? Examining the connections between spouses' nonsexual behaviors, sexual frequency, sexual satisfaction, and marital satisfaction," *Archives of Sexual Behavior* 46, no. 2 (2017): 489–501.

12. J. K. McNulty, C. A. Wenner, and T. D. Fisher, "Longitudinal associations among relationship satisfaction, sexual satisfaction, and frequency of sex in early marriage," *Archives of Sexual Behavior* 45, no. 1 (2016): 85–97.

13. E. A. Schoenfeld, C. A. Bredow, and T. L. Huston, "Do men and women show love differently in marriage?" *Personality and Social Psychology Bulletin* 38 (2012): 1396–1409.

14. Schoenfeld et al., "Does sex really matter?"; McNulty et al., "Longitudinal associations among relationship satisfaction."

15. G. Loewenstein et al., "Does increased sexual frequency enhance happiness?" *Journal of Economic Behavior and Organization* 116 (2015): 206–218.

16. D. A. Donnelly and E. O. Burgess, "The decision to remain in an involuntarily celibate relationship," *Journal of Marriage and Family* 70, no. 2 (2008): 519–535.

17. A. Muise, U. Schimmack, and E. A. Impett, "Sexual frequency predicts greater well-being, but more is not always better," *Social Psychological and Personality Science* 7, no. 4 (2016): 295–302.

18. Sexual Health and Relationships Lab, accessed June 3, 2020, http://www.amymuise.com.

19. J. A. Maxwell et al., "How implicit theories of sexuality shape sexual and relationship well-being," *Journal of Personality and Social Psychology* 112, no. 2 (2017): 238–279.

20. B. J. Gillespie, "Correlates of sex frequency and sexual satisfaction among partnered older adults," *Journal of Sex and Marital Therapy* 43, no. 5 (2017): 403–423.

21. S. J. Matthews et al., "The battle against bedroom boredom: Development and validation of a brief measure of sexual novelty in relationships," *Canadian Journal of Human Sexuality* 27, no. 3 (2018): 277–287.

22. Schoenfeld et al., "Does sex really matter?"

23. A. Ben-Ari and Y. Lavee, "Dyadic closeness in marriage: From the inside story to a conceptual model," *Journal of Social and Personal Relationships* 24, no. 5 (2007): 627–644.

24. S. Sprecher and S. Metts, "Development of the 'Romantic Beliefs Scale' and examination of the effects of gender and gender-role orientation," *Journal of Social and Personal Relationships* 6, no. 4 (1989): 387–411.

25. F. Zsok et al., "What kind of love is love at first sight? An empirical investigation," *Personal Relationships* 24, no. 4 (2017): 869–885.

26. K. M. Welker et al., "Effects of self-disclosure and responsiveness between couples on passionate love within couples," *Personal Relationships* 21, no. 4 (2014): 692–708.

27. N. K. Grote and I. H. Frieze, "The measurement of friendship-based love in intimate relationships," *Personal Relationships* 1, no. 3 (1994): 275–300.

28. G. W. Lewandowski Jr., "Why you should date your best friend," The Conversation, February 11, 2017, https://theconversation .com/why-you-should-date-your-best-friend-72784.

29. V. L. Sheets, "Passion for life: Self-expansion and passionate love across the life span," *Journal of Social and Personal Relationships* 31, no. 7 (2014): 958–974; M. L. Hecht, P. J. Marston, and L. K. Larkey, "Love ways and relationship quality in heterosexual relationships," *Journal of Social and Personal Relationships* 11, no. 1 (1994): 25–43.

30. Grote and Frieze, "The measurement of friendship-based love."

31. J. Lauer and R. Lauer, "Marriages made to last," *Psychology Today* 85 (1985): 22–26.

32. S. Sprecher and P. C. Regan, "Passionate and companionate love in courting and young married couples," *Sociological Inquiry* 62 (1998): 163–185.

33. L. E. VanderDrift, J. E. Wilson, and C. R. Agnew, "On the benefits of valuing being friends for nonmarital romantic partners," *Journal of Social and Personal Relationships* 30, no. 1 (2013): 115–131.

Chapter 6

1. A. Aron, M. Paris, and E. N. Aron, "Falling in love: Prospective studies of self-concept change," *Journal of Personality and Social Psychology* 69, no. 6 (1995): 1102–1112.

2. B. A. Mattingly, G. W. Lewandowski Jr., and K. P. McIntyre, "You make me a better/worse person: A two-dimensional model

of relationship self-change," *Personal Relationships* 21 (2014): 176–190.

3. K. P. McIntyre, B. A. Mattingly, and G. W. Lewandowski Jr., "When 'we' changes 'me': The two-dimensional model of relational self-change and relationship outcomes," *Journal of Social and Personal Relationships* 32 (2015): 857–878.

4. E. B. Slotter and L. Kolarova, "Making sure you see the real me: The role of self-esteem in spontaneous self-expansion," *Social Psychological and Personality Science* (2019).

5. L. J. Human et al., "Is change bad? Personality change is associated with poorer psychological health and greater metabolic syndrome in midlife," *Journal of Personality* 81, no. 3 (2013): 249–260.

6. S. N. Hira and N. C. Overall, "Improving intimate relationships: Targeting the partner versus changing the self," *Journal of Social and Personal Relationships* 28, no. 5 (2011): 610–633.

7. S. D. Jayamaha, C. Antonellis, and N. C. Overall, "Attachment insecurity and inducing guilt to produce desired change in romantic partners," *Personal Relationships* 23, no. 2 (2016): 311–338.

8. N. C. Overall et al., "Attachment anxiety and reactions to relationship threat: The benefits and costs of inducing guilt in romantic partners," *Journal of Personality and Social Psychology* 106 (2014): 235–256.

9. Y. Kanat-Maymon, Y. Argaman, and G. Roth, "The association between conditional regard and relationship quality: A daily diary study," *Personal Relationships* 24, no. 1 (2017): 27–35.

10. J. S. Gore and S. E. Cross, "Defining and measuring self-concept change," *Psychological Studies* 56, no. 1 (2011): 135–141; E. B. Slotter and W. L. Gardner, "How needing you changes me: The influence of attachment anxiety on self-concept malleability in romantic relationships," *Self and Identity* 11, no. 3 (2012): 386–408.

11. P. R. Pietromonaco and L. A. Beck, "Attachment processes in adult romantic relationships," in *APA Handbook of Personality and Social Psychology,* vol. 3, *Interpersonal Relations,* ed. M. Mikulincer et al. (Washington, DC: American Psychological Association, 2015), 33–64.

12. R. Cuperman, R. L. Robinson, and W. Ickes, "On the malleability of self-image in individuals with a weak sense of self," *Self and Identity* 13, no. 1 (2014): 1–23.

13. G. W. Lewandowski Jr., N. Nardone, and A. J. Raines, "The role of self-concept clarity in relationship quality," *Self and Identity* 9, no. 4 (2010): 416–433.

14. M. Parise et al., "Self-concept clarity and relationship satisfaction at the dyadic level," *Personal Relationships* (2019).

15. J. D. Campbell et al., "Self-concept clarity: Measurement, personality correlates, and cultural boundaries," *Journal of Personality and Social Psychology* 70, no. 1 (1996): 141–156.

16. B. W. Roberts and W. F. DelVecchio, "The rank-order consistency of personality traits from childhood to old age: A quantitative review of longitudinal studies," *Psychological Bulletin* 126, no. 1 (2000): 3–25.

17. J. S. Reiff, H. E. Hershfield, and J. Quoidbach, "Identity over time: Perceived similarity between selves predicts well-being 10 years later," *Social Psychological and Personality Science* (2019).

18. E. J. Finkel, *The All or Nothing Marriage: How the Best Marriages Work* (New York: Dutton, 2017).

19. N. W. Hudson and B. W. Roberts, "Goals to change personality traits: Concurrent links between personality traits, daily behavior, and goals to change oneself," *Journal of Research in Personality* 53 (2014): 68–83.

20. L. F. Emery et al., " 'You've changed': Low self-concept clarity predicts lack of support for partner change," *Personality and Social Psychology Bulletin* 44, no. 3 (2018): 318–331.

21. N. C. Overall, G. J. O. Fletcher, and J. A. Simpson, "Helping each other grow: Romantic partner support, self-improvement,

and relationship quality," *Personality and Social Psychology Bulletin* 36 (2010): 1496–1513.

22. N. Parker, "The angel in the marble," Medium.com, July 8, 2013, https://medium.com/@nilsaparker/the-angel-in-the-marble -f7aa43f333dc.

23. S. M. Drigotas et al., "Close partner as sculptor of the ideal self: Behavioral affirmation and the Michelangelo phenomenon," *Journal of Personality and Social Psychology* 77, no. 2 (1999): 293–323.

24. S. M. Drigotas, "The Michelangelo phenomenon and personal well-being," *Journal of Personality* 70, no. 1 (2002): 59–77.

25. J. H. Buhler et al., "Does Michelangelo care about age? An adult life-span perspective on the Michelangelo phenomenon," *Journal of Social and Personal Relationships* 36 (2018): 1392–1412.

26. N. W. Hudson and R. C. Fraley, "Volitional personality trait change: Can people choose to change their personality traits?" *Journal of Personality and Social Psychology* 109, no. 3 (2015): 490–507.

27. A. Cloutier and J. Peetz, "People, they are a changin': The links between anticipating change and romantic relationship quality," *Journal of Social and Personal Relationships* 34 (2017): 676–698.

28. V. Young, M. Curran, and C. Totenhagen, "A daily diary study: Working to change the relationship and relational uncertainty in understanding positive relationship quality," *Journal of Social and Personal Relationships* 30, no. 1 (2013): 132–148.

29. E. Hatfield, "Equity theory and research: An overview," in *Small Groups and Social Interaction,* vol. 2., ed. H. H. Blumberg et al. (Chichester, England: Wiley, 1983), 401–412.

30. J. Traupmann et al., "Measuring equity in intimate relations," *Applied Psychological Measurement* 5 (1981): 467–480.

31. A. DeMaris, "The 20-year trajectory of marital quality in enduring marriages: Does equity matter?" *Journal of Social and Personal Relationships* 27, no. 4 (2010): 449–471.

32. D. Bellani, G. E. Andersen, and L. Pessin, "When equity matters for marital stability: Comparing German and U.S. couples," *Journal of Personal and Social Relationships* 35 (2018): 1273–1298.

33. J. Quittschalle and P. Y. Herzberg, "Males benefit twice—The influence of equity on affective and physical attraction in couples," *Personal Relationships* 24, no. 3 (2017): 513–533.

34. M. Ross and F. Sicoly, "Egocentric biases in availability and attribution," *Journal of Personality and Social Psychology* 37, no. 3 (1979): 322–336.

35. D. Schneider, "Market earnings and household work: New tests of gender performance theory," *Journal of Marriage and Family* 73 (2011): 845–860.

36. University of Michigan, "Exactly how much housework does a husband create?" *ScienceDaily,* April 8, 2008, www.sciencedaily.com/releases/2008/04/080403191009.htm.

37. Z. Ravanera, R. Beaujot, and J. Liu, "Models of earning and caring: Determinants of the division of work," *Canadian Review of Sociology* 46, no. 4 (2009): 319–337.

38. J. H. van Hooff, "Rationalising inequality: Heterosexual couples' explanations and justifications for the division of housework along traditionally gendered lines," *Journal of Gender Studies* 20, no. 1 (2011): 19–30.

39. T. Leopold, "Diverging trends in satisfaction with housework: Declines in women, increases in men," *Journal of Marriage and Family* (2018).

Chapter 7

1. P. A. M. Van Lange et al., "Willingness to sacrifice in close relationships," *Journal of Personality and Social Psychology* 72 (1997): 1373–1395.

2. E. A. Impett, S. L. Gable, and L. A. Peplau, "Giving up and giving in: The costs and benefits of daily sacrifice in intimate

relationships," *Journal of Personality and Social Psychology* 89 (2005): 327–344.

3. E. Impett, A. Muise, and C. Harasymchuk, "Giving in the bedroom: The costs and benefits of responding to a partner's sexual needs in daily life," *Journal of Social and Personal Relationships* 36 (2019): 2455–2473.

4. C. J. Totenhagen et al., "Good days, bad days: Do sacrifices improve relationship quality?" *Journal of Social and Personal Relationships* 30, no. 7 (2013): 881–900.

5. M. L. Visserman et al., "Me or us? Self-control promotes a healthy balance between personal and relationship concerns," *Social Psychological and Personality Science* 8 (2017): 55–65.

6. E. A. Impett et al., "Suppression sours sacrifice: Emotional and relational costs of suppressing emotions in romantic relationships," *Personality and Social Psychology Bulletin* 38, no. 6 (2012): 707–720.

7. Impett et al., "Giving up and giving in."

8. D. C. Jack and D. Dill, "The Silencing the Self Scale: Schemas of intimacy associated with depression in women," *Psychology of Women Quarterly* 16, no. 1 (1992): 97–106.

9. M. S. Harper and D. P. Welsh, "Keeping quiet: Self-silencing and its association with relational and individual functioning among adolescent romantic couples," *Journal of Social and Personal Relationships* 24, no. 1 (2007): 99–116.

10. V. E. Whiffen, M. L. Foot, and J. M. Thompson, "Self-silencing mediates the link between marital conflict and depression," *Journal of Social and Personal Relationships* 24, no. 6 (2007): 993–1006.

11. B. A. Mattingly, K. P. McIntyre, and G. W. Lewandowski Jr., eds., *Interpersonal Relationships and Self-Concept Change* (Cham, Switzerland: Springer Publishers, 2020).

12. A. Aron et al., "The self-expansion model of motivation and cognition in close relationships," in *The Oxford Handbook of*

Close Relationships, ed. J. A. Simpson and L. Campbell (New York: Oxford University Press, 2013), 90–115.

13. A. Muise et al., "Broadening your horizons: Self-expanding activities promote desire and satisfaction in established romantic relationships," *Journal of Personality and Social Psychology* 116, no. 2 (2019): 237–258.

14. L. E. VanderDrift, G. W. Lewandowski Jr., and C. R. Agnew, "Reduced self-expansion in current romance and interest in relationship alternatives," *Journal of Social and Personal Relationships* 28 (2011): 356–373.

15. G. W. Lewandowski Jr. and R. A. Ackerman, "Something's missing: Need fulfillment and self-expansion as predictors of susceptibility to infidelity," *Journal of Social Psychology* 146 (2006): 389–403.

16. B. A. Mattingly et al., "Implicit theories of relationships and self-expansion: Implications for relationship functioning," *Journal of Social and Personal Relationships* 36 (2018): 1579–1599.

17. S. Sinek, "What's the difference between fulfillment and happiness?" LinkedIn, September 2, 2017, accessed May 30, 2019, https://www.linkedin.com/pulse/whats-difference -between-fulfillment-happiness-simon-sinek/.

18. R. F. Baumeister et al., "Some key differences between a happy life and a meaningful life," *Journal of Positive Psychology* 8, no. 6 (2013): 505–516.

19. S. Dubner, "The cobra effect," *Freakonomics,* episode 96, October 11, 2012, http://freakonomics.com/podcast/the-cobra-effect-a -new-freakonomics-radio-podcast/.

20. B. Q. Ford et al., "The psychological health benefits of accepting negative emotions and thoughts: Laboratory, diary, and longitudinal evidence," *Journal of Personality and Social Psychology* 115, no. 6 (2018): 1075–1092.

21. J. R. Ferrari and D. M. Tice, "Procrastination as a self-handicap for men and women: A task-avoidance strategy in a laboratory setting," *Journal of Research in Personality* 34, no. 1 (2000): 73–83.

22. K. R. Von Culin, E. Tsukayama, and A. L. Duckworth, "Unpacking grit: Motivational correlates of perseverance and passion for long-term goals," *Journal of Positive Psychology* 9, no. 4 (2014): 306–312.

23. L. F. Emery, C. Walsh, and E. B. Slotter, "Knowing who you are and adding to it: Reduced self-concept clarity predicts reduced self-expansion," *Social Psychological and Personality Science* 6, no. 3 (2015): 259–266.

24. F. Righetti and E. Impett, "Sacrifice in close relationships: Motives, emotions, and relationship outcomes," *Social and Personality Psychology Compass* 11, no. 10 (2017).

25. H. C. Fivecoat et al., "Partner support for individual self-expansion opportunities: Effects on relationship satisfaction in long-term couples," *Journal of Social and Personal Relationships* 32, no. 3 (2015): 368–385.

26. C. Harasymchuk et al., "Spicing up the relationship? The effects of relational boredom on shared activities," *Journal of Social and Personal Relationships* 34, no. 6 (2017): 833–854.

27. A. Aron et al., "The self-expansion model of motivation and cognition in close relationships," in *The Oxford Handbook of Close Relationships,* ed. J. A. Simpson and L. Campbell (New York: Oxford University Press, 2013), 90–115.

28. C. J. Carpenter and E. L. Spottswood, "Exploring romantic relationships on social networking sites using the self-expansion model," *Computers in Human Behavior* 29, no. 4 (2013): 1531–1537.

29. A. Muise et al., "Broadening your horizons: Self-expanding activities promote desire and satisfaction in established romantic relationships," *Journal of Personality and Social Psychology* 116, no. 2 (2019): 237–258.

30. K. K. Melton, M. Larson, and M. L. Boccia, "Examining couple recreation and oxytocin via the ecology of family experiences framework," *Journal of Marriage and Family* 81 (2019): 771–782.

Chapter 8

1. D. M. Frost and C. Forrester, "Closeness discrepancies in romantic relationships: Implications for relational well-being, stability, and mental health," *Personality and Social Psychology Bulletin* 39, no. 4 (2013): 456–469.

2. C. Hazan and P. Shaver, "Romantic love conceptualized as an attachment process," *Journal of Personality and Social Psychology* 52, no. 3 (1987): 511–524.

3. P. K. Jonason et al., "Relationship dealbreakers: Traits people avoid in potential mates," *Personality and Social Psychology Bulletin* 41, no. 12 (2015): 1697–1711.

4. M. Mikulincer and P. R. Shaver, "An attachment and behavioral systems perspective on social support," *Journal of Social and Personal Relationships* 26 (2009): 7–19.

5. S. E. Stanton and L. Campbell, "Can't get you off my mind: Relationship reflection creates cognitive load for more anxiously attached individuals," *Journal of Social and Personal Relationships* 32, no. 4 (2015): 441–455.

6. A. N. Cooper et al., "Volatility in daily relationship quality: The roles of attachment and gender," *Journal of Social and Personal Relationships* 35, no. 3 (2018): 348–371.

7. C. Chang, "Ambivalent Facebook users: Anxious attachment style and goal cognition," *Journal of Social and Personal Relationships* 36 (2019): 2528–2548.

8. L. F. Emery et al., "Can you tell that I'm in a relationship? Attachment and relationship visibility on Facebook," *Personality and Social Psychology Bulletin* 40, no. 11 (2014): 1466–1479.

9. T. C. Marshall et al., "Attachment styles as predictors of Facebook-related jealousy and surveillance in romantic relationships," *Personal Relationships* 20, no. 1 (2013): 1–22.

10. C. R. Harris and R. S. Darby, "Jealousy in adulthood," in *Handbook of Jealousy: Theory, Research, and Multidisciplinary*

Approaches, ed. S. L. Hart and M. Legerstee (Hoboken, NJ: Wiley-Blackwell, 2010), 547–571.

11. R. Wegner et al., "Attachment, relationship communication style and the use of jealousy induction techniques in romantic relationships," *Personality and Individual Differences* 129 (2018): 6–11.

12. T. J. Wade and A. B. Weinstein, "Jealousy induction: Which tactics are perceived as most effective?" *Journal of Social, Evolutionary, and Cultural Psychology* 5, no. 4 (2011): 231–238.

13. A. A. Fleischmann et al., "Tickling the monster: Jealousy induction in relationships," *Journal of Social and Personal Relationships* 22, no. 1 (2005): 49–73.

14. D. M. Buss, *The Dangerous Passion: Why Jealousy Is As Necessary As Love and Sex* (New York: Free Press, 2000).

15. C. Dandurand and M. F. Lafontaine, "Jealousy and couple satisfaction: A romantic attachment perspective," *Marriage and Family Review* 50, no. 2 (2014): 154–173.

16. R. A. Elphinston et al., "Romantic jealousy and relationship satisfaction: The costs of rumination," *Western Journal of Communication* 77, no. 3 (2013): 293–304.

17. E. Berscheid, M. Snyder, and A. M. Omoto, "The Relationship Closeness Inventory: Assessing the closeness of interpersonal relationships," *Journal of Personality and Social Psychology* 57, no. 5 (1989): 792–807.

18. D. J. Mashek, A. Aron, and M. Boncimino, "Confusions of self with close others," *Personality and Social Psychology Bulletin* 29, no. 3 (2003): 382–392.

19. E. B. Slotter and W. L. Gardner, "How needing you changes me: The influence of attachment anxiety on self-concept malleability in romantic relationships," *Self and Identity* 11, no. 3 (2012): 386–408.

20. E. B. Slotter and W. L. Gardner, "The dangers of dating the 'bad boy' (or girl): When does romantic desire encourage us to take

on the negative qualities of potential partners?" *Journal of Experimental Social Psychology* 48, no. 5 (2012): 1173–1178.

21. D. J. Mashek and M. D. Sherman, "Desiring less closeness with intimate others," in *Handbook of Closeness and Intimacy,* ed. D. J. Mashek and A. P. Aron (Mahwah, NJ: Lawrence Erlbaum Associates, 2004), 343–356.

22. D. Mashek et al., "Wanting less closeness in romantic relationships," *Basic and Applied Social Psychology* 33, no. 4 (2011): 333–345.

23. S. B. Richman et al., "Reaching out by changing what's within: Social exclusion increases self-concept malleability," *Journal of Experimental Social Psychology* 57 (2015): 64–77.

24. R. F. Baumeister and M. R. Leary, "The need to belong: Desire for interpersonal attachments as a fundamental human motivation," *Psychological Bulletin* 117, no. 3 (1995): 497–529.

25. B. Le et al., "Missing a romantic partner: A prototype analysis," *Personal Relationships* 15, no. 4 (2008): 511–532.

26. B. Le et al., "Missing you maintains us: Missing a romantic partner, commitment, relationship maintenance, and physical infidelity," *Journal of Social and Personal Relationships* 28, no. 5 (2011): 653–667.

27. K. J. Bao and S. Lyubomirsky, "Making it last: Combating hedonic adaptation in romantic relationships," *Journal of Positive Psychology* 8, no. 3 (2013): 196–206.

28. L. D. Nelson and T. Meyvis, "Interrupted consumption: Disrupting adaptation to hedonic experiences," *Journal of Marketing Research* 45 (2008): 654–664.

29. L. C. Jiang and J. T. Hancock, "Absence makes the communication grow fonder: geographic separation, interpersonal media, and intimacy in dating relationships," *Journal of Communication* 63 (2013): 556–577.

30. G. Kelmer et al., "Relationship quality, commitment, and stability in long-distance relationships," *Family Process* 52, no. 2 (2013): 257–270.

31. D. J. Lindemann, "Going the distance: Individualism and interdependence in the commuter marriage," *Journal of Marriage and Family* 79, no. 5 (2017): 1419–1434.

32. L. Stafford, A. J. Merolla, and J. D. Castle, "When long-distance dating partners become geographically close," *Journal of Social and Personal Relationships* 23, no. 6 (2006): 901–919.

33. G. J. Leonardelli, C. L. Pickett, and M. B. Brewer, "Optimal distinctiveness theory: A framework for social identity, social cognition, and intergroup relations," in *Advances in Experimental Social Psychology,* vol. 43, ed. M. P. Zanna and J. M. Olson (San Diego: Academic Press, 2010), 63–113.

34. E. B. Slotter, C. W. Duffy, and W. L. Gardner, "Balancing the need to be 'me' with the need to be 'we': Applying Optimal Distinctiveness Theory to the understanding of multiple motives within romantic relationships," *Journal of Experimental Social Psychology* 52 (2014): 71–81.

35. A. Aron, E. N. Aron, and D. Smollan, "Inclusion of other in the self scale and the structure of interpersonal closeness," *Journal of Personality and Social Psychology* 63 (1992): 596–612.

36. S. Gächter, C. Starmer, and F. Tufano, "Measuring the closeness of relationships: A comprehensive evaluation of the 'Inclusion of the Other in the Self' scale," *PLOS One* 10, no. 6 (2015).

37. C. R. Agnew et al., "Cognitive interdependence: Commitment and the mental representation of close relationships," *Journal of Personality and Social Psychology* 74, no. 4 (1998): 939–954.

38. A. Aron et al., "The experimental generation of interpersonal closeness: A procedure and some preliminary findings," *Personality and Social Psychology Bulletin* 23, no. 4 (1997): 363–377.

39. R. B. Slatcher, "When Harry and Sally met Dick and Jane: Creating closeness between couples," *Personal Relationships* 17, no. 2 (2010): 279–297.

40. Y. U. Girme, N. C. Overall, and S. Faingataa, " 'Date nights' take two: The maintenance function of shared relationship activities," *Personal Relationships* 21, no. 1 (2014): 125–149.

Chapter 9

1. A. Rauer et al., "What are the marital problems of happy couples? A multimethod, two-sample investigation," *Family Process* (2019).
2. D. M. Buss, "Conflict between the sexes: Strategic interference and the evocation of anger and upset," *Journal of Personality and Social Psychology* 56, no. 5 (1989): 735–747.
3. L. A. Baxter and W. W. Wilmot, "Taboo topics in close relationships," *Journal of Social and Personal Relationships* 2, no. 3 (1985): 253–269.
4. R. J. Eidelson and N. Epstein, "Cognition and relationship maladjustment: Development of a measure of dysfunctional relationship beliefs," *Journal of Consulting and Clinical Psychology* 50 (1982): 715–720.
5. H. M. Foran and A. M. S. Slep, "Validation of a self-report measure of unrealistic relationship expectations," *Psychological Assessment* 19, no. 4 (2007): 382–396.
6. C. E. Clifford et al., "Testing the impact of sliding versus deciding in cyclical and noncyclical relationships," *Personal Relationships* 24, no. 1 (2017): 223–238.
7. L. K. Knobloch and J. A. Theiss, "Relational uncertainty and relationship talk within courtship: A longitudinal actor-partner interdependence model," *Communication Monographs* 78, no. 1 (2011): 3–26.
8. M. E. Roloff and D. H. Solomon, "Conditions under which relational commitment leads to expressing or withholding relational complaints," *International Journal of Conflict Management* 13, no. 3 (2002): 276–291.
9. L. K. Knobloch and D. H. Solomon, "Measuring the sources and content of relational uncertainty," *Communication Studies* 50, no. 4 (1999): 261–278.

10. L. K. Knobloch, "The content of relational uncertainty within marriage," *Journal of Social and Personal Relationships* 25, no. 3 (2008): 467–495.

11. A. L. McCurry, P. Schrodt, and A. M. Ledbetter, "Relational uncertainty and communication efficacy as predictors of religious conversations in romantic relationships," *Journal of Social and Personal Relationships* 29, no. 8 (2012): 1085–1108.

12. J. M. Gottman, "A theory of marital dissolution and stability," *Journal of Family Psychology* 7 (1993): 57–75.

13. A. Hooper et al., "Revisiting the basics: Understanding potential demographic differences with John Gottman's Four Horsemen and emotional flooding," *Family Journal* 25, no. 3 (2017): 224–229.

14. R. A. Ackerman et al., "The interpersonal legacy of a positive family climate in adolescence," *Psychological Science* 24, no. 3 (2013): 243–250.

15. K. Sanford, "A latent change score model of conflict resolution in couples: Are negative behaviors bad, benign, or beneficial?" *Journal of Social and Personal Relationships* 31, no. 8 (2014): 1068–1088.

16. K. S. Birditt, M. R. Nevitt, and D. M. Almeida, "Daily interpersonal coping strategies: Implications for self-reported well-being and cortisol," *Journal of Social and Personal Relationships* 32, no. 5 (2015): 687–706.

17. N. B. Nichols et al., "Two types of disengagement during couples' conflicts: Withdrawal and passive immobility," *Psychological Assessment* 27, no. 1 (2015): 203–214.

18. L. B. Luchies et al., "The doormat effect: When forgiving erodes self-respect and self-concept clarity," *Journal of Personality and Social Psychology* 98, no. 5 (2010): 734–749.

19. J. K. McNulty, "Forgiveness increases the likelihood of subsequent partner transgressions in marriage," *Journal of Family Psychology* 24, no. 6 (2010): 787–790.

20. J. K. McNulty, "The dark side of forgiveness: The tendency to forgive predicts continued psychological and physical aggression in marriage," *Personality and Social Psychology Bulletin* 37, no. 6 (2011): 770–783.

21. J. P. Caughlin and T. D. Golish, "An analysis of the association between topic avoidance and dissatisfaction: Comparing perceptual and interpersonal explanations," *Communication Monographs* 69, no. 4 (2002): 275–295.

22. Clifford et al., "Testing the impact of sliding."

23. C. M. Thompson and A. L. Vangelisti, "What happens when the standard for openness goes unmet in romantic relationships? Analyses of stress, coping, and relational consequences," *Journal of Social and Personal Relationships* 33, no. 3 (2016): 320–343.

24. J. P. Caughlin et al., "Family secrets in various family configurations: A Communication Boundary Management perspective," *Communication Studies* 51 (2000): 116–134.

25. J. F. Jensen and A. J. Rauer, "Turning inward versus outward: Relationship work in young adults and romantic functioning," *Personal Relationships* 21, no. 3 (2014): 451–467.

26. K. Cortes and A. E. Wilson, "When slights beget slights: Attachment anxiety, subjective time, and intrusion of the relational past in the present," *Personality and Social Psychology Bulletin* 42, no. 12 (2016): 1693–1708.

27. J. M. Gottman and N. Silver, *Why Marriages Succeed or Fail: And How You Can Make Yours Last* (New York: Simon and Schuster, 1995).

28. R. L. Weiss, "Strategic behavioral marital therapy: Toward a model for assessment and intervention," in *Advances in Family Intervention, Assessment, and Theory*, vol. 1, ed. J. P. Vincent (Greenwich, CT: JAI Press, 1980), 229–271.

29. K. Tan, A. M. Jarnecke, and S. C. South, "Impulsivity, communication, and marital satisfaction in newlywed couples," *Personal Relationships* 24, no. 2 (2017): 423–439.

30. C. R. Agnew et al., "Cognitive interdependence: Commitment and the mental representation of close relationships," *Journal of Personality and Social Psychology* 74, no. 4 (1998): 939–954.

31. E. Auger, T. D. Menzies, and J. E. Lydon, "Daily experiences and relationship well-being: The paradoxical effects of relationship identification," *Journal of Personality* 85, no. 5 (2017): 741–752.

32. S. M. Laurent and M. W. Myers, "I know you're me, but who am I? Perspective taking and seeing the other in the self," *Journal of Experimental Social Psychology* 47, no. 6 (2011): 1316–1319.

33. E. J. Finkel et al., "A brief intervention to promote conflict reappraisal preserves marital quality over time," *Psychological Science* 24, no. 8 (2013): 1595–1601.

34. R. D. Rogge et al., "Is skills training necessary for the primary prevention of marital distress and dissolution? A 3-year experimental study of three interventions," *Journal of Consulting and Clinical Psychology* 81, no. 6 (2013): 949–961.

35. C. R. Rogers, *Client-Centered Therapy: Its Current Practice, Implications and Theory* (Boston: Houghton Mifflin, 1951).

36. R. B. Venaglia and E. P. Lemay Jr., "Accurate and biased perceptions of partner's conflict behaviors shape emotional experience," *Journal of Social and Personal Relationships* 36 (2019): 3293–3312.

37. N. C. Overall and J. K. McNulty, "What type of communication during conflict is beneficial for intimate relationships?" *Current Opinion in Psychology* 13 (2017): 1–5.

38. A. M. Gordon and S. Chen, "Do you get where I'm coming from? Perceived understanding buffers against the negative impact of conflict on relationship satisfaction," *Journal of Personality and Social Psychology* 110, no. 2 (2016): 239–260.

39. Venaglia and Lemay, "Accurate and biased perceptions."

Chapter 10

1. G. Seidman, "5 essential qualities for a romantic partner," *Psychology Today,* February 25, 2017, https://www.psychologytoday.com/us/blog/close-encounters/201702/5-essential-qualities-romantic-partner.
2. J. A. Hall, "Humor in romantic relationships: A meta-analysis," *Personal Relationships* 24, no. 2 (2017): 306–322.
3. L. Campbell, R. A. Martin, and J. R. Ward, "An observational study of humor use while resolving conflict in dating couples," *Personal Relationships* 15, no. 1 (2008): 41–55.
4. A. B. Horn et al., "Positive humor in couples as interpersonal emotion regulation: A dyadic study in everyday life on the mediating role of psychological intimacy," *Journal of Social and Personal Relationships* 36, no. 8 (2019): 2376–2396.
5. L. E. Kurtz and S. B. Algoe, "Putting laughter in context: Shared laughter as behavioral indicator of relationship well-being," *Personal Relationships* 22, no. 4 (2015): 573–590.
6. G. G. Gallup Jr. et al., "Do orgasms give women feedback about mate choice?" *Evolutionary Psychology* 12, no. 5 (2014): 958–978.
7. C. M. Hui et al., "The Manhattan effect: When relationship commitment fails to promote support for partners' interests," *Journal of Personality and Social Psychology* 106, no. 4 (2014): 546–570.
8. N. Bolger, A. Zuckerman, and R. C. Kessler, "Invisible support and adjustment to stress," *Journal of Personality and Social Psychology* 79, no. 6 (2000): 953–961.
9. Z. Francis, V. Sieber, and V. Job, "You seem tired, but so am I: Willpower theories and intention to provide support in romantic relationships," *Journal of Social and Personal Relationships* 37, no. 3 (2019) 738–757.
10. M. Howland and J. A. Simpson, "Getting in under the radar: A dyadic view of invisible support," *Psychological Science* 21, no. 12 (2010): 1878–1885.

11. Y. U. Girme et al., "Does support need to be seen? Daily invisible support promotes next day relationship well-being," *Journal of Family Psychology* 32, no. 7 (2018): 882–893.

12. C. L. Gosnell and S. L. Gable, "You deplete me: Impacts of providing positive and negative event support on self-control," *Personal Relationships* 24, no. 3 (2017): 598–622.

13. N. Bolger et al., "Invisible support and adjustment to stress."

14. J. A. Williamson et al., "More social support is associated with more positive mood but excess support is associated with more negative mood," *Journal of Social and Personal Relationships* (2019).

15. Girme et al., "Does support need to be seen?"

16. P. E. Shrout, C. M. Herman, and N. Bolger, "The costs and benefits of practical and emotional support on adjustment: A daily diary study of couples experiencing acute stress," *Personal Relationships* 13, no. 1 (2006): 115–134.

17. N. Bolger and D. Amarel, "Effects of social support visibility on adjustment to stress: experimental evidence," *Journal of Personality and Social Psychology* 92 (2007): 458–475.

18. L. A. Beck and M. S. Clark, "What constitutes a healthy communal marriage and why relationship stage matters," *Journal of Family Theory and Review* 2, no. 4 (2010): 299–315.

19. V. S. Helgeson and H. L. Fritz, "A theory of unmitigated communion," *Personality and Social Psychology Review* 2, no. 3 (1998): 173–183.

20. J. L. Derrick and S. L. Murray, "Enhancing relationship perceptions by reducing felt inferiority: The role of attachment style," *Personal Relationships* 14, no. 4 (2007): 531–549.

21. S. Thai et al., "Being better than you is better for us: Attachment avoidance and social comparisons within romantic relationships," *Journal of Social and Personal Relationships* 33, no. 4 (2016): 493–514.

22. M. S. Clark and J. R. Mills, "A theory of communal (and exchange) relationships," in *Handbook of Theories of Social*

Psychology, ed. P. M. Van Lange et al. (Thousand Oaks, CA: Sage Publications, 2012), 232–250.

23. M. J. Bresnahan, H. C. Chiu, and T. R. Levine, "Self-construal as a predictor of communal and exchange orientation in Taiwan and the USA," *Asian Journal of Social Psychology* 7, no. 2 (2004): 187–203.

24. S. N. Jarvis, J. McClure, and N. Bolger, "Exploring how exchange orientation affects conflict and intimacy in the daily life of romantic couples," *Journal of Social and Personal Relationships* (2019).

25. Clark and Mills, "Theory of communal (and exchange) relationships."

26. Ibid.

27. R. T. Pinkus et al., "For better and for worse: Everyday social comparisons between romantic partners," *Journal of Personality and Social Psychology* 95, no. 5 (2008): 1180–1201.

28. J. Mills et al., "Measurement of communal strength," *Personal Relationships* 11, no. 2 (2004): 213–230.

29. L. Campbell and T. Marshall, "Anxious attachment and relationship processes: An interactionist perspective," *Journal of Personality* 79, no. 6 (2011): 917–947.

30. R. L. Brock and E. Lawrence, "Too much of a good thing: Underprovision versus overprovision of partner support," *Journal of Family Psychology* 23, no. 2 (2009): 181–192.

31. R. S. Lazarus and S. Folkman, *Stress, Appraisal, and Coping* (New York: Springer Publishing, 1984).

32. K. R. Blake et al., "Relationship quality and cognitive reappraisal moderate the effects of negative urgency on behavioral inclinations toward aggression and intimate partner violence," *Psychology of Violence* 8, no. 2 (2018): 218–228.

33. B. C. Feeney and E. P. Lemay Jr., "Surviving relationship threats: The role of emotional capital," *Personality and Social Psychology Bulletin* 38, no. 8 (2012): 1004–1017.

34. C. M. Walsh and L. A. Neff, "The importance of investing in your relationship: Emotional capital and responses to partner transgressions," *Journal of Social and Personal Relationships* (2019).

35. T. N. Bradbury and F. D. Fincham, "Attributions in marriage: Review and critique," *Psychological Bulletin* 107, no. 1 (1990): 3–33.

36. F. D. Fincham, "Attributions in close relationships: From Balkanization to integration," in *Social Cognition,* ed. M. B. Brewer and M. Hewstone (Malden, MA: Blackwell Publishing, 2004), 165–193.

37. J. N. Hook et al., "Negative internal causal attributions of a specific offense and forgiveness," *Personal Relationships* 22, no. 3 (2015): 449–459.

38. J. M. Graham and C. W. Conoley, "The role of marital attributions in the relationship between life stressors and marital quality," *Personal Relationships* 13, no. 2 (2006): 231–241.

39. J. A. Durtschi et al., "Dyadic processes in early marriage: Attributions, behavior, and marital quality," *Family Relations: An Interdisciplinary Journal of Applied Family Studies* 60, no. 4 (2011): 421–434.

40. Brock and Lawrence, "Too much of a good thing."

41. M. Parise et al., "Keeping calm when riding the rapids: Optimism and perceived partner withdrawal," *Personal Relationships* 24, no. 1 (2017): 131–145.

42. S. Srivastava et al., "Optimism in close relationships: How seeing things in a positive light makes them so," *Journal of Personality and Social Psychology* 91, no. 1 (2006): 143–153.

43. S. Allen, "The science of gratitude," Greater Good Science Center, University of California, Berkeley, white paper prepared for the John Templeton Foundation, 2018, https://ggsc.berkeley.edu/images/uploads/GGSC-JTF_White_Paper-Gratitude-FINAL.pdf.

44. J. K. McNulty and A. Dugas, "A dyadic perspective on gratitude sheds light on both its benefits and its costs: Evidence that low gratitude acts as a 'weak link,'" *Journal of Family Psychology* 33, no. 7 (2019): 876–881.

45. B. L. Fredrickson, "The role of positive emotions in positive psychology: The broaden-and-build theory of positive emotions," *American Psychologist* 56, no. 3 (2001): 218–226.

46. S. L. Gable, G. C. Gonzaga, and A. Strachman, "Will you be there for me when things go right? Supportive responses to positive event disclosures," *Journal of Personality and Social Psychology* 91, no. 5 (2006): 904–917.

47. B. J. Peters, H. T. Reis, and S. L. Gable, "Making the good even better: A review and theoretical model of interpersonal capitalization," *Social and Personality Psychology Compass* (2018).

48. A. F. Pagani et al., "If you shared my happiness, you are part of me: Capitalization and the experience of couple identity," *Personality and Social Psychology Bulletin* (2019).

Chapter 11

1. L. Lee, "Sequences in separation: A framework for investigating endings of the personal (romantic) relationship," *Journal of Social and Personal Relationships* 1, no. 1 (1984): 49–73.

2. A. J. Stewart et al., *Separating Together: How Divorce Transforms Families* (New York: Guilford Press, 1997).

3. C. E. Rusbult, C. R. Agnew, and X. B. Arriaga, "The investment model of commitment processes," in *Handbook of Theories of Social Psychology,* vol. 2, ed. P. A. M. Van Lange, A. W. Kruglanski, and E. T. Higgins (Thousand Oaks, CA: Sage Publications, 2012), 218–231.

4. H. Garland, "Throwing good money after bad: The effect of sunk costs on the decision to escalate commitment to an ongoing

project," *Journal of Applied Psychology* 75, no. 6 (1990): 728–731.

5. S. Joel et al., "How interdependent are stay/leave decisions? On staying in the relationship for the sake of the romantic partner," *Journal of Personality and Social Psychology* 115, no. 5 (2018): 805–824.

6. D. M. Tice and E. Bratslavsky, "Giving in to feel good: The place of emotion regulation in the context of general self-control," *Psychological Inquiry* 11, no. 3 (2000): 149–159.

7. G. W. Lewandowski Jr. et al., "Losing a self-expanding relationship: Implications for the self-concept," *Personal Relationships* 13, no. 3 (2006): 317–331.

8. E. B. Slotter and W. L. Gardner, "How needing you changes me: The influence of attachment anxiety on self-concept malleability in romantic relationships," *Self and Identity* 11, no. 3 (2012): 386–408.

9. A. Manvelian et al., "With or without you? Loss of self following marital separation," *Journal of Social and Clinical Psychology* 37, no. 4 (2018): 297–324.

10. P. W. Eastwick et al., "Mispredicting distress following romantic breakup: Revealing the time course of the affective forecasting error," *Journal of Experimental Social Psychology* 44, no. 3 (2008): 800–807.

11. N. Hsieh and L. Hawkley, "Loneliness in the older adult marriage: Associations with dyadic aversion, indifference, and ambivalence," *Journal of Social and Personal Relationships* 35, no. 10 (2018): 1319–1339.

12. S. Gomillion, S. L. Murray, and V. M. Lamarche, "Losing the wind beneath your wings: The prospective influence of romantic breakup on goal progress," *Social Psychological and Personality Science* 6, no. 5 (2015): 513–520.

13. S. S. Spielmann et al., "Settling for less out of fear of being single," *Journal of Personality and Social Psychology* 105 (2013): 1049–1073.

14. X. B. Arriaga et al., "Individual well-being and relationship maintenance at odds: The unexpected perils of maintaining a relationship with an aggressive partner," *Social Psychological and Personality Science* 4, no. 6 (2013): 676–684.

15. A. Duckworth, *Grit: The Power of Passion and Perseverance* (New York: Scribner, 2016).

16. G. M. Lucas et al., "When the going gets tough: Grit predicts costly perseverance," *Journal of Research in Personality* 59 (2015): 15–22.

17. A. Larbi and C. Fons-Rosen, "Know when to fold 'em: The grit factor" (working papers, 899, Barcelona Graduate School of Economics, 2016), https://www.eui.eu/Documents/Departments Centres/Economics/Seminarsevents/Alaoui-paper.pdf.

18. T. Halkjelsvik and J. Rise, "Persistence motives in irrational decisions to complete a boring task," *Personality and Social Psychology Bulletin* 41, no. 1 (2015): 90–102.

19. Lee, "Sequences in separation."

20. T. C. Marshall, "Facebook surveillance of former romantic partners: Associations with postbreakup recovery and personal growth," *Cyberpsychology, Behavior, and Social Networking* 15, no. 10 (2012): 521–526.

21. S. Sprecher, C. Zimmerman, and E. M. Abrahams, "Choosing compassionate strategies to end a relationship: Effects of compassionate love for partner and the reason for the breakup," *Social Psychology* 41, no. 2 (2010): 66–75.

22. R. L. Griffith et al., "Staying friends with ex-romantic partners: Predictors, reasons, and outcomes," *Personal Relationships* 24, no. 3 (2017): 550–584.

23. R. M. Dailey et al., "On-again/off-again dating relationships: How are they different from other dating relationships?" *Personal Relationships* 16, no. 1 (2009): 23–47.

24. L. F. O'Sullivan et al., "Plenty of fish in the ocean: How do traits reflecting resiliency moderate adjustment after experiencing a

romantic breakup in emerging adulthood?" *Journal of Youth and Adolescence* 48, no. 5 (2019): 949–962.

25. G. W. Lewandowski Jr., "Relationship dissolution and the self-concept: The role of interpersonal closeness and self-expansion" (PhD diss., Stony Brook University, 2002).

26. T. Tashiro and P. Frazier, "'I'll never be in a relationship like that again': Personal growth following romantic relationship breakups," *Personal Relationships* 10 (2003): 113–128.

27. G. W. Lewandowski Jr. and N. Bizzoco, "Addition through subtraction: Growth following the dissolution of a low quality relationship," *Journal of Positive Psychology* 2, no. 1 (2007): 40–54.

28. P. T. Costa Jr. et al., "Personality at midlife: Stability, intrinsic maturation, and response to life events," *Assessment* 7, no. 4 (2000): 365–378.

29. J. Specht, B. Egloff, and S. C. Schmukle, "Stability and change of personality across the life course: The impact of age and major life events on mean-level and rank-order stability of the Big Five," *Journal of Personality and Social Psychology* 101, no. 4 (2011): 862–882.

30. G. M. Larson and D. A. Sbarra, "Participating in research on romantic breakups promotes emotional recovery via changes in self-concept clarity," *Social Psychological and Personality Science* 6, no. 4 (2015): 399–406.

31. D. M. Wegner, "Ironic processes of mental control," *Psychological Review* 101 (1994): 34–52.

32. Lewandowski and Bizzoco, "Addition through subtraction."

33. G. W. Lewandowski Jr., "Promoting positive emotions following relationship dissolution through writing," *Journal of Positive Psychology* 4, no. 1 (2009): 21–31.

34. E. B. Slotter and D. E. Ward, "Finding the silver lining: The relative roles of redemptive narratives and cognitive reappraisal in individuals' emotional distress after the end of a romantic

relationship," *Journal of Social and Personal Relationships* 32, no. 6 (2015): 737–756.

35. D. A. Sbarra et al., "Expressive writing can impede emotional recovery following marital separation," *Clinical Psychological Science* 1, no. 2 (2013): 120–134.

36. Lewandowski and Bizzoco, "Addition through subtraction."

Index

About the Author

GARY W. LEWANDOWSKI JR., PhD, is a husband, dad, softball coach, soccer coach, and Labrador retriever owner. In addition, he is an award-winning teacher, researcher, writer, and relationship expert. He is a professor and former chair in the Department of Psychology at Monmouth University in New Jersey. Dr. Lewandowski's research, writing, and public speaking focus on three main areas: romantic relationships, self and identity, and the scholarship of teaching and learning (SoTL). He has published more than 50 academic articles and book chapters, given more than 120 conference presentations, authored more than 150 articles for mass media outlets, co-edited the book *The Science of Relationships: Answers to Your Questions About Dating, Marriage, and Family,* and co-authored an innovative research methods textbook, *Discovering the Scientist Within: Research Methods in Psychology,* now in its second edition.

His work has been featured by the *Washington Post,* IFLScience.com, the *Daily Mail, Business Insider, Salon, The*

New Republic, Time, and *Newsweek,* and he has appeared in the *New York Times, The Atlantic,* and *VICE* and on CNN and NPR, among other media outlets. He created the popular relationship advice website ScienceofRelationships.com (now Luvze.com), authors the *Psychology of Relationships* blog at *Psychology Today,* and his TEDx Talk, "Break-ups Don't Have to Leave You Broken," has been viewed nearly 2 million times.

In recognition of his accomplishments, Dr. Lewandowski received the Emerging Researcher Award from the New Jersey Psychological Association and was inducted into the Society for Experimental Social Psychology. Dr. Lewandowski is also a nationally recognized teacher who, in addition to receiving Monmouth University's Distinguished Teacher Award, was featured in the Princeton Review's *Best 300 Professors* book, which selected the "best" from an initial list of forty-two thousand professors from across the country.

You can learn more at www.GaryLewandowski.com or follow him on Twitter (@LewandowskiPhD).